Cambridge IGCSE™ and O Level

Computer Science

Second Edition

David Watson
Helen Williams

This text has not been through the Cambridge International endorsement process. Any references or materials related to answers, grades, papers or examinations are based on the opinion of the author(s). The Cambridge International syllabus or curriculum framework, associated assessment guidance material and specimen papers should always be referred to for definitive guidance.

Every effort has been made to trace all copyright holders, but if any have been inadvertently overlooked, the Publishers will be pleased to make the necessary arrangements at the first opportunity.

Although every effort has been made to ensure that website addresses are correct at time of going to press, Hodder Education cannot be held responsible for the content of any website mentioned in this book. It is sometimes possible to find a relocated web page by typing in the address of the home page for a website in the URL window of your browser.

Hachette UK's policy is to use papers that are natural, renewable and recyclable products and made from wood grown in well-managed forests and other controlled sources. The logging and manufacturing processes are expected to conform to the environmental regulations of the country of origin.

Orders: please contact Hachette UK Distribution, Hely Hutchinson Centre, Milton Road, Didcot, Oxfordshire, OX11 7HH. Telephone: +44 (0)1235 827827. Email education@hachette.co.uk. Lines are open from 9 a.m. to 5 p.m., Monday to Friday. You can also order through our website: www.hoddereducation.com

ISBN: 978 1 3983 1848 9

© David Watson and Helen Williams 2022

First published in 2016.
This edition published in 2022 by
Hodder Education,
An Hachette UK Company
Carmelite House
50 Victoria Embankment
London EC4Y 0DZ

www.hoddereducation.co.uk

Impression number   5   4   3

Year   2026 2025 2024

All rights reserved. Apart from any use permitted under UK copyright law, no part of this publication may be reproduced or transmitted in any form or by any means, electronic or mechanical, including photocopying and recording, or held within any information storage and retrieval system, without permission in writing from the publisher or under licence from the Copyright Licensing Agency Limited. Further details of such licences (for reprographic reproduction) may be obtained from the Copyright Licensing Agency Limited, www.cla.co.uk

Cover photo © phonlamaiphoto - stock.adobe.com

Illustrations by Aptara, Inc.

Typeset in India by Aptara Inc.

Printed and bound by CPI Group (UK) Ltd, Croydon, CR0 4YY

A catalogue record for this title is available from the British Library.

Contents

Introduction ... iv

Section 1 **Computer Systems**
1. Data representation ... 1
2. Data transmission ... 15
3. Hardware ... 25
4. Software ... 49
5. The internet and its uses ... 62
6. Automated and emerging technologies ... 80

Section 2 **Algorithms, programming and logic**
7. Algorithm design and problem solving ... 98
8. Programming ... 113
9. Databases ... 133
10. Boolean logic ... 137

Practice Paper 1A Computer Systems ... 142
Practice Paper 2A Algorithms, programming and logic ... 152

Answers to exam-style questions ... 163
Answers to Practice Paper 1A ... 185
Answers to Practice Paper 2A ... 188
Index ... 196

Introduction

Welcome to the *Cambridge IGCSE™ and O Level Computer Science Study and Revision Guide Second Edition*. This book has been written to help you revise everything you need to know for your Computer Science examinations, alongside the *Cambridge IGCSE and O Level Computer Science Second Edition* Student's Book. Following the new Computer Science syllabus (first exams in June 2023), this book covers all the key content along with sample questions and answers and exam-style practice questions. Sample practice papers also appear at the end of the book and online at https://www.hoddereducation.co.uk/cambridgeextras. These practice papers, written by the authors, are slightly longer than the actual Cambridge IGCSE papers to ensure questions covering more of the syllabus can be offered. There is also an online glossary for key words that appear in red bold in this book.

How to use this book

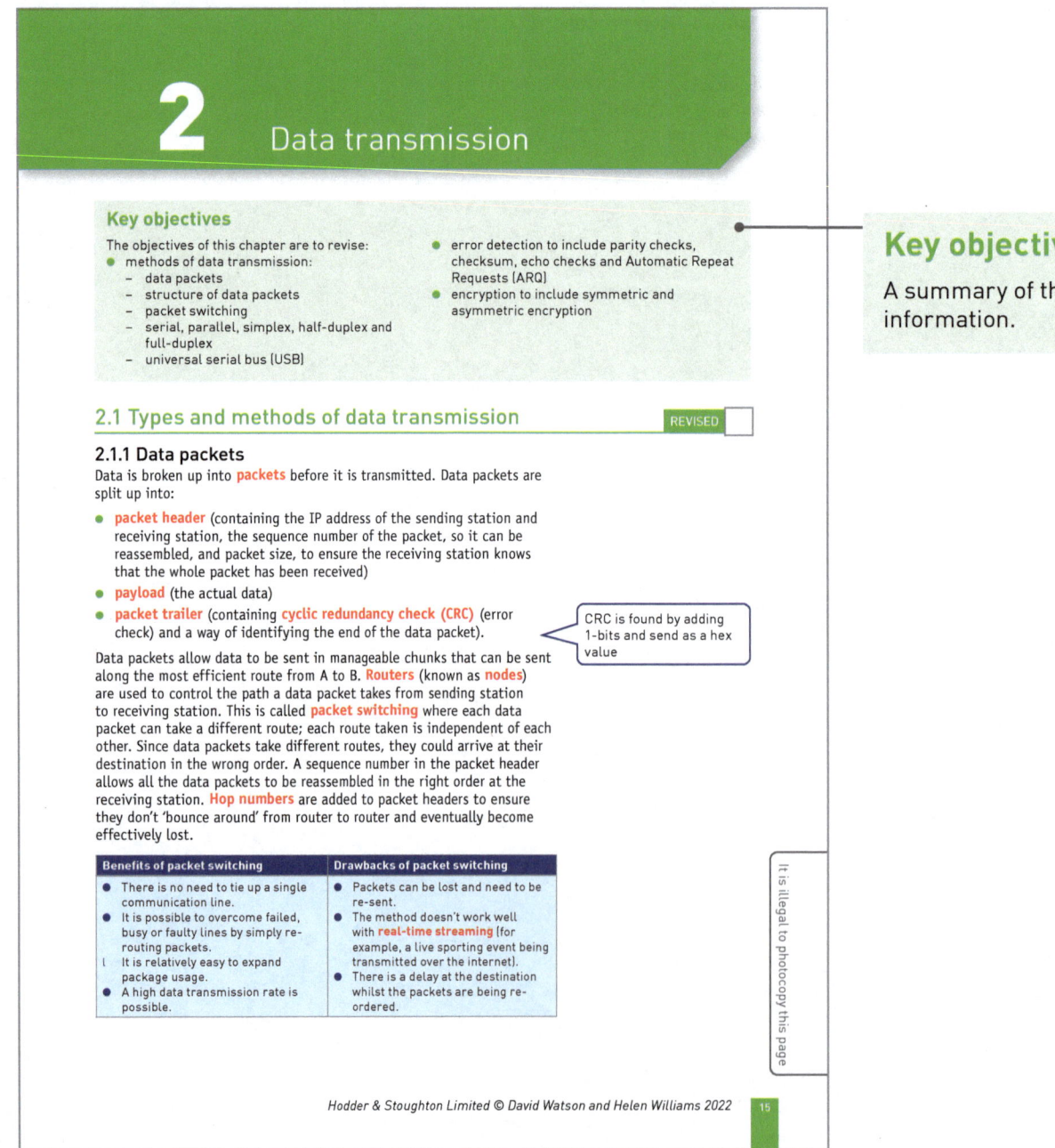

Key objectives
A summary of the main information.

Introduction

Sample question and answer

REVISED

Exam-style questions with sample student answers to show how the question can be answered. In the Theory section, high-level answers (in blue) are strong answers while low-level (in purple) answers require more revision.

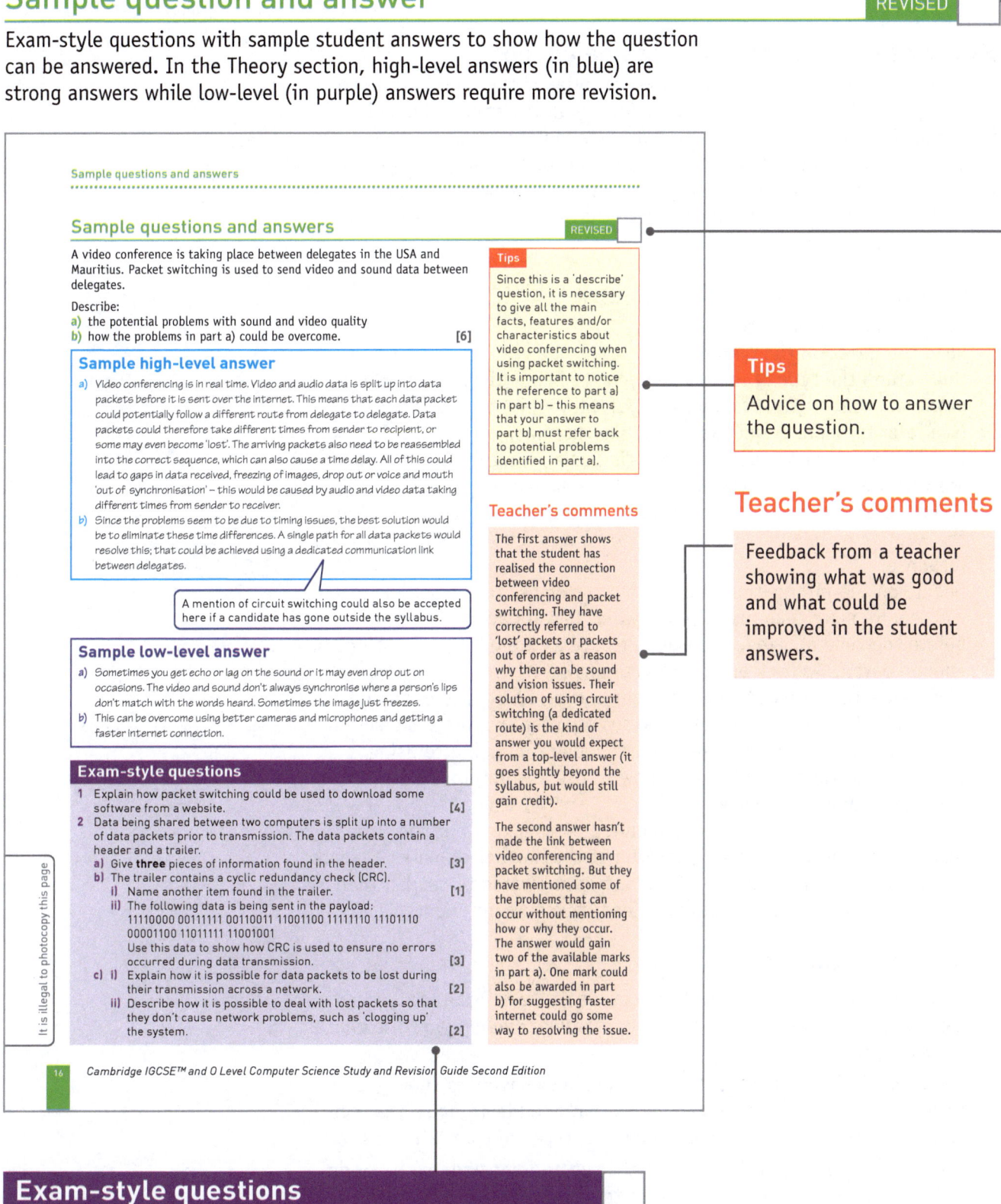

Tips

Advice on how to answer the question.

Teacher's comments

Feedback from a teacher showing what was good and what could be improved in the student answers.

Exam-style questions

Exam-style questions for you to try and see what you have learned.

Answers

Outline answers to the exam-style questions and Practice Papers 1A and 2A from page 163. Practice Paper 1B and 2B and their answers are online.

Hodder & Stoughton Limited © David Watson and Helen Williams 2022

Study tips

REVISED

Know what questions you may be asked

Find a copy of the IGCSE Computer Science syllabus that you have been studying and will take the exam for and use your revision guide and textbook. The list of topics will make an excellent checklist for your revision. If you find something that you do not understand or have not made any notes about, stop and find out about it while you remember. Anything that is mentioned in the syllabus could be used in a question.

Read and understand questions

What are you being asked to do?
1 Read the question thoroughly.
2 Understand the type of instruction you are being given: *complete*, *describe*, *explain*, *give*, *state* and *suggest* all require different actions (see later for more details about key instructions).
3 If the question makes use of a specific scenario, make sure all your answers are relevant to the scenario. For example, if the question is about website security measures taken by a bank, suggesting taking the website offline outside banking hours would not be an appropriate response.
4 Decide on the information required but remember that most answers will require more than just a single word. If you have finished well before the time allotted, you may not have answered your questions in enough detail. Go back and check your answers.
5 Always use the correct technical terms and avoid the use of trade names at all costs (no marks will be awarded for answers such as *Google*, *Word* or *Norton* for example). If you are referring to using Word, your answer should discuss how to use a word processor with no mention of any trade names.
6 Decide how much information is required by checking out the instructions given and also by looking at the number of marks allocated to the question (for example, if a question is awarded 5 marks, then your answer will need to include at least five marking points).

Know your subject

- Make sure that you understand computer science terms and that you can spell them correctly: for example, *phishing*, *pharming*, *verification*, *autonomous* and so on.
- Learn the definitions and be able to provide examples to show your understanding. There are certain items that need learning so that you can apply them, such as validation checks, types of translator and so on.
- Do not ignore items in the syllabus that you do not understand or do not have notes on. Do some research to fill all your gaps in knowledge.
- Beware of cramming facts into your brain without understanding them or being able to apply them. You need to revise but try and make it interesting rather than just reading and re-reading your notes. Remember, writing things down, rather than just reading about them, means you are more likely to recollect important facts. Always practice exam-style questions (including looking at past papers) and remember to time yourself since you do not want to run out of time when you do the actual exam.

Cambridge IGCSE™ and O Level Computer Science Study and Revision Guide Second Edition

- Do not try to learn too much at the last minute. Use the best revision technique that suits you. It is often a good idea to write out revision cards so you can do a last-minute check. For example, a binary arithmetic check card could look something like this:

> ### Binary arithmetic
> - Binary headings (128, 64, 32, 16, 8, 4, 2, 1)
> - Remember 1 + 1 = 0 carry 1; 1 + 1 + 1 = 1 carry 1, etc.
> - Two's complement uses −128 in left-most bit position
> - Shifting binary numbers left is the same as multiplying by factors of 2
> - Shifting binary numbers right is the same as dividing by factors of 2

- Questions asked will be within the syllabus boundaries. If something appears new to you, then the question will give you lots of guidance so you can call on facts that you should already know.
- Make sure that you read all of the question carefully.
- Make sure that you understand the work that you have done – if you only try to remember it, you will not be able to apply your knowledge.
- Mark allocations are there to help you decide on how to use your time sensibly, so do not spend 30 minutes on a question worth only two marks.

Help yourself

- Get a good night's sleep or take a decent lunch break before doing the exam. The most important thing that goes into the exam room is your brain and it does not function well if you have not had enough rest. Think of exam preparation in the same way as preparation for taking part in a sporting event.
- Stay calm. Everyone gets nervous in some way, so work out how best to relax yourself before starting the exam.
- Read the whole paper through first and do not write anything at this stage. This will help you gather your thoughts and get some idea of how much effort each question is going to need. Remember, you do not have to answer questions in numerical order. Answer those questions first that you are confident about. This will boost your confidence and will help when you come to the more challenging questions.
- Remember to read each question thoroughly before answering it. Highlight or underline key words in the question so you do not lose marks needlessly by missing out something important (for example, you may have to give an answer in GiB and you give your answer in KiB which could lose you marks – this could be avoided by highlighting the word 'GiB').
- Use clear English and good handwriting.
- Do not use correction fluid and cross out unwanted work neatly. If you have written the answer on a different page, remember to show very clearly where your answer can now be found.
- Once finished, if you have any time left, go back and check your answers. You may have missed something out which could make a difference.
- Attempt to answer all questions. Leaving blank spaces is not a good idea. You just might get credit by writing down something which you think could be relevant.

Hodder & Stoughton Limited © David Watson and Helen Williams 2022

Introduction

Command words

The use of certain words in questions gives you a strong clue about how to answer them. The following table gives a list of common key words used, their meaning and a sample question.

Key word	Meaning	Example
Calculate	Work out from given facts, figures or information.	Calculate the size of the file needed to store 1200 photos which are each 12 MiB in size.
Compare	Identify/comment on similarities and/or differences.	Compare the features of random access memory (RAM) and read-only memory (ROM).
Define	Give precise meaning.	Define what is meant by the term packet switching.
Demonstrate	Show how or give an example.	Demonstrate how hexadecimal is converted to binary.
Describe	State the points of a topic/give characteristics and main features.	Describe how piezoelectric technology is used by an inkjet printer to produce a hard copy of a photograph.
Evaluate	Judge or calculate the quality, importance, amount or value of something.	Evaluate the importance of using robotics in medicine.
Explain	Set out purposes or reasons; make the relationships between things evident; provide why and/or how and support with relevant evidence.	Explain why packet switching may not be a good way of transmitting real time data.
Give	Produce an answer from a given source or from memory.	Give a reason why hexadecimal notation is used.
Identify	Name/select/recognise.	Identify the type of memory used by a computer to store the start-up routines.
Outline	Set out the main points.	Outline the role of registers and buses in the fetch, decode, execute cycle.
Show	Provide structured evidence that leads to a given result.	Show how to convert a denary number to a hexadecimal number.
State	Express in clear terms.	State the advantages of using USB-C connectivity rather than using USB-A connectivity.
Suggest	Apply knowledge and understanding to situations where there are a range of valid responses in order to make proposals/put forward considerations.	Suggest how data entry for a name could be verified and validated.

Assessment

REVISED

The information in this section is taken from the Cambridge IGCSE and O Level Computer Science syllabuses (0478/0984/2210) for examination from 2023. You should always refer to the appropriate syllabus document for the year of examination to confirm the details and for more information. The syllabus document is available on the Cambridge International website at: www.cambridgeinternational.org

There are two examination papers:

	Paper 1 Computer systems	Paper 2 Algorithms, programming and logic
Duration	1 hour 45 minutes	1 hour 45 minutes
Marks	75 marks	75 marks
Percentage of overall marks	50%	50%
Syllabus topics examined	1–6	7–10

Cambridge IGCSE™ and O Level Computer Science Study and Revision Guide Second Edition

1 Data representation

Key objectives

The objectives of this chapter are to revise:
- number systems
- the binary, denary and hexadecimal number systems
- conversion of numbers between all three number systems
- use of the hexadecimal (hex) number system
- binary addition
- overflow error
- logical shifts
- two's complement format for negative and positive binary numbers
- text, sound and images
- ASCII and Unicode character sets
- representation of sound in a computer
- sampling rate and sample resolution
- image representation, including resolution and colour depth
- data storage and file compression
- calculation of file sizes
- the need for data (file) compression
- lossy and lossless compression

1.1 Number systems

REVISED

1.1.1 Binary represents data

No matter how complex the system, the basic building block in all computers is the binary number system. This system is chosen because it consists of 1s and 0s only which correspond to ON and OFF states in the computer system.

1.1.2 Binary, denary and hexadecimal number systems

The binary system

The **binary number system** is based on the number 2; it can only use the two values 0 and 1 (these are referred to as **bits**). The binary heading values are 2^0, 2^1, 2^2, 2^3 and so on.

> The maximum size of a binary number you will see in the exam is 16 bits

If an 8-bit system is being used the headings are: 128 (2^7), 64 (2^6), 32 (2^5), 16 (2^4), 8 (2^3), 4 (2^2), 2 (2^1) and 1 (2^0). A typical binary number, based on this system, would be 0 1 1 1 1 0 0 1.

The denary system is a base 10 number system with column headings: 10^0 (1), 10^1 (10), 10^2 (100), 10^3 (1000) and so on.

Converting from binary to denary

To convert from binary to denary, simply add together all the heading values where a 1-value appears.

For example:

0 1 1 1 1 0 0 1 = 64 + 32 + 16 + 8 + 1 (= 121)

0 1 1 1 1 0 0 0 1 0 1 1 = 1024 + 512 + 256 + 128 + 8 + 2 + 1 (= 1931)

... and so on.

1.1 Number systems

Converting from denary to binary

To convert from positive denary to binary, it is necessary to carry out successive divisions by 2 until a zero value results. The remainders are read from bottom to top to give the binary value:

For example, to convert 142 to binary:

2	142	
2	71	remainder: 0
2	35	remainder: 1
2	17	remainder: 1
2	8	remainder: 1
2	4	remainder: 0
2	2	remainder: 0
2	1	remainder: 0
	0	remainder: 1

read the remainder from bottom to top to get the binary number:
1 0 0 0 1 1 1 0

(Note: if the answer is, for example, 111011 and 8-bits are used to represent numbers, then just infill with zeros to give: 00111011.)

The hexadecimal system

The **hexadecimal number system** is based on the number 16. The 16 digits are represented by the numbers 0 to 9 and the letters A to F (representing 10 to 15). The hexadecimal headings are 16^0, 16^1, 16^2, 16^3, and so on. A typical hexadecimal number would be 1F3A.

Converting from binary to hexadecimal and hexadecimal to binary

To convert a binary number to a hexadecimal number, it is first necessary to split the binary number into 4-bit groups starting from the right-hand side. If the final (left-most group) doesn't contain four binary digits, then infill by zeros is done. Each 4-bit group is then assigned a hexadecimal digit. For example:

1011 1111 0000 1001 becomes (11) (15) (0) (9) that is, BF09

1 0011 1110 0111 must first be rewritten as **000**1 0011 1110 0111 which becomes (1) (3) (14) (7) that is 13E7

To convert from hexadecimal to binary, it is necessary to write the 4-bit binary code for each hexadecimal digit. For example:

45A becomes 0100 0101 1010

E48D becomes 1110 0100 1000 1101

Converting from hexadecimal to denary and from denary to hexadecimal

To convert a hexadecimal number to denary, it is necessary to multiply each hexadecimal digit by its heading value and then add them together. For example,

1FD = (1 × 256) + (15 × 16) + (12 × 1) = 508

4EB5 = (4 × 4096) + (14 × 256) + (11 × 16) + (5 × 1) = 20 149

To convert from denary to hexadecimal, it is necessary to carry out successive divisions by 16 until zero value results. The remainders are read from bottom to top to give the hexadecimal value. For example, to convert 2004 to hexadecimal:

16	2004	
16	125	remainder: 4
16	7	remainder: 13
	0	remainder: 7

read the remainder from bottom to top to get the hexadecimal number: 7D4 (D = 13)

1.1.3 Uses of the hexadecimal system

The hexadecimal number system is often used by computer programmers and designers because it is easier to deal with, for example AF01, than the binary equivalent of 1010111100000001. Some of the main uses of the hexadecimal system are listed here.

- **Error codes** refer to memory locations where the error occurs; they are automatically generated by the computer.
- A **Media Access Control (MAC) address** identifies a device on a network (via the NIC). The MAC address is in the format NN-NN-NN-DD-DD-DD (first six digits are the manufacturer code and the last six digits are the serial number of the device).
- An **Internet Protocol (IP) address** is given to a device when it joins a network; there are two types – IPv4 (32-bit code) and IPv6 (uses 128-bit code).
- **Hypertext mark-up language (HTML) colour codes**; the colour of each pixel on screen is made up of a combination of red, green and blue; the amount of each colour is represented by a hex code. For example, # FF 00 00 is pure red, # FF 80 00 is a shade of orange, # B1 89 04 is a tan colour.

1.1.4 Addition of binary numbers

Binary addition involves a carry and a sum for each of the 2 or 3 bits being added:

binary digit			operation	carry	sum
0	0	0	0 + 0 + 0	0	0
0	0	1	0 + 0 + 1	0	1
0	1	0	0 + 1 + 0	0	1
0	1	1	0 + 1 + 1	1	0
1	0	0	1 + 0 + 0	0	1
1	0	1	1 + 0 + 1	1	0
1	1	0	1 + 1 + 0	1	0
1	1	1	1 + 1 + 1	1	1

For example:

Add 00100111 + 01001010

We will set this out showing carry and sum values:

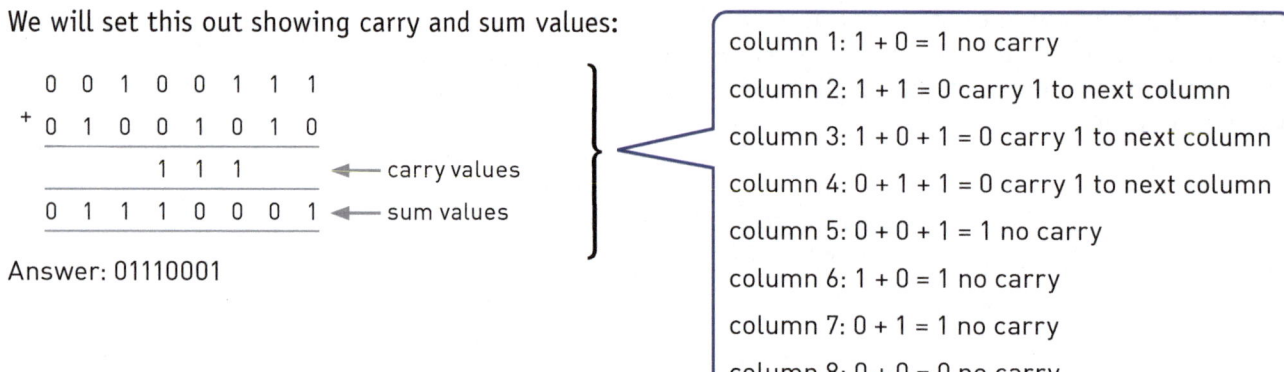

Answer: 01110001

column 1: 1 + 0 = 1 no carry
column 2: 1 + 1 = 0 carry 1 to next column
column 3: 1 + 0 + 1 = 0 carry 1 to next column
column 4: 0 + 1 + 1 = 0 carry 1 to next column
column 5: 0 + 0 + 1 = 1 no carry
column 6: 1 + 0 = 1 no carry
column 7: 0 + 1 = 1 no carry
column 8: 0 + 0 = 0 no carry

Overflow

Overflow occurs if the result of a calculation is too large for the allocated word size (for example a word size of 8 bits can represent a maximum value of 255).

For example:

Add 0 1 1 0 1 1 1 0 and 1 1 0 1 1 1 1 0 (using an 8-bit word size)

```
            0 1 1 0 1 1 1 0
         +  1 1 0 1 1 1 1 0
         ──────────────────
        1)    1 1 1 1 1      ← carry values
ninth bit → 1) 0 1 0 0 1 1 0 0  ← sum values
```

This addition has generated a ninth bit. The 8 bits of the answer 0 1 0 0 1 1 0 0 give the denary value (64 + 8 + 4) of 76 which is clearly incorrect (the denary value of the addition is 110 + 222 = 332).

The generation of a ninth bit is a clear indication that the sum has exceeded the maximum value possible for 8 bits; that is, 255 ($2^8 - 1$). This is known as an **overflow error** and is an indication that a number is too big to be stored in the computer using, in this case, an 8-bit register.

This shows that the greater the number of bits which can be used to represent a number then the larger the number that can be stored. For example, a 16-bit register would allow a maximum value of $2^{16} - 1$ (= 65 535) to be stored, a 32-bit register would allow a maximum value of $2^{32} - 1$ (= 4 294 967 295), and so on.

1.1.5 Logical binary shifts

Logical shifts involve shifting (moving) bits to the left (multiplying by 2 for each shift) or the right (dividing by 2 for each shift). If shifting to the left or right results in a loss of 1-bits, then this would result in an error.

When shifting a binary number, any gaps created by the shift operation can be filled by zeros. For example, the denary number 54 is 00110110 in binary. If we put this into an 8-bit register:

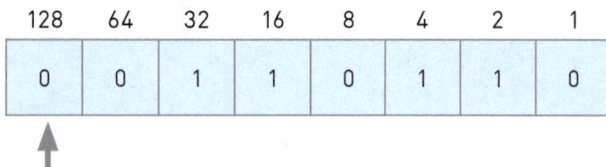

The left-most bit is often referred to as the **most significant bit**

If we now shift the bits in this register two places to the left:

128	64	32	16	8	4	2	1
1	1	0	1	1	0	0	0

Note how the two right-most bit positions are now filled with 0s

The value of the binary bits is now $54 \times 2^2 = 216$.

Suppose we now shift the original number one place to the right:

128	64	32	16	8	4	2	1
0	0	0	1	1	0	1	1

Note how the left-most bit position is now filled with a 0

The value of the binary bits is now $54 \div 2^1 = 27$.

Suppose we now shift the original binary number four places to the left:

128	64	32	16	8	4	2	1
0	1	1	0	0	0	0	0

This should give $54 \times 2^4 = 864$, but actually gives 96 which is clearly incorrect. Since two of the 1-bits were lost following a logical shift, an error would be generated. Similarly, if we shift the original binary number four places to the right:

128	64	32	16	8	4	2	1
0	0	0	0	0	0	1	1

Again, an error would be generated since the result of the right shift should be $54 \div 2^4 = 3.375$, but actually results in the value 3.

1.1.6 Two's complement (binary numbers)

To allow for the possibility of representing negative integers we make use of **two's complement** notation. For example:

−128	64	32	16	8	4	2	1
1	1	1	0	0	1	1	0
0	1	1	0	0	1	1	0

This represents a negative number:
−128 + 64 + 32 + 4 + 2 = −26

We can still store positive values. For example, this represents 64 + 32 + 4 + 2 = 102

Converting denary numbers into binary in two's complement format, involves placing 1-bits in the appropriate position remembering that the right-most bit now represents −128.

1.1 Number systems

To convert negative denary numbers into binary in two's complement format can be done in two ways.

Consider the number +67 in 8-bit (two's complement) binary format:

−128	64	32	16	8	4	2	1
0	1	0	0	0	0	1	1

One method of finding the binary equivalent to −67 is to simply put 1-bits in their correct places:

−128	64	32	16	8	4	2	1
1	0	1	1	1	1	0	1

−128 + 32 + 16 + 8 + 4 + 1 = −67

Looking at the two binary numbers above, this gives us another possible way of finding the binary representation of a negative denary number:

first, write the positive binary value, such as 67	0	1	0	0	0	0	1	1
then invert each binary value	1	0	1	1	1	1	0	0
then add 1 to that number								1
this gives us the binary for −67	1	0	1	1	1	1	0	1

Sample questions and answers

REVISED

a) Write the denary number 44 as an 8-bit binary number.
b) Carry out a logical shift two places left on your binary number found in part a). Comment on your answer.
c) Carry out a logical shift two places right on your binary number found in part a). Comment on your answer.
d) Write the denary number 220 as an 8-bit binary number. Add this binary number to your binary number found in part a). Comment on your answer.
e) Write −44 as an 8-bit binary number using two's complement format. [9]

> **Tips**
>
> When a comment about your answer is required, explain whether the result you get is what you would have expected; then give a reason why it is (or is not) as expected. Where a mathematical sequence of operations is needed (as in parts d) and e)), it is imperative that you show all your working so that some marks can still be gained even if your answer is incorrect. Throughout questions of this type, keep your work logical and thorough so that the examiner can easily follow your logic.
>
> To reduce the possibility of errors, it is a good idea to write your 8-bit binary number in register/word format:
>
> | 128 | 64 | 32 | 16 | 8 | 4 | 2 | 1 |
> |---|---|---|---|---|---|---|---|
> | | | | | | | | |

1 Data representation

Sample high-level answer

a)

128	64	32	16	8	4	2	1
0	0	1	0	1	1	0	0

b)

128	64	32	16	8	4	2	1
1	0	1	1	0	0	0	0

This is equivalent to 128 + 32 + 16 = 176. Shifting two places left should give the result 44 × 2^2 = 176, which means the actual result is the same as the expected result.

c)

128	64	32	16	8	4	2	1
0	0	0	0	1	0	1	1

This is equivalent to 8 + 2 + 1 = 11. Shifting two places right should give the result 44 ÷ 2^2 = 11, which means the actual result is the same as the expected result.

d)

128	64	32	16	8	4	2	1
1	1	0	1	1	1	0	0

This is the 8-bit binary representation of 220. Adding this to the original binary number from part (a): 0 0 1 0 1 1 0 0 results in the answer:

	128	64	32	16	8	4	2	1
1	0	0	0	0	1	0	0	0

A ninth bit is generated following this binary addition

The expected result for this addition (220 + 44) is 264. However, the value 8 is generated. This is clearly incorrect and is due to the fact that the result of the sum exceeds the maximum value which can be represented by an 8-bit word (that is, 255). An **overflow error** has occurred.

e)

44:	0	0	1	0	1	1	0	0
inverted:	1	1	0	1	0	0	1	1
add 1:								1
result:	1	1	0	1	0	1	0	0

(−128 + 64 + 16 + 4 = −44)

Teacher's comments

The first student has given a very well-explained answer and they have used the 8-bit word format; this greatly helps in parts b), c) and e) of this question.

1.1 Number systems

Sample low-level answer

a)
2	44	
2	22	remainder: 0
2	11	remainder: 0
2	5	remainder: 1
2	2	remainder: 1
2	1	remainder: 0
	0	remainder: 1

Gives the answer: 0 0 1 1 0 1

b) 0 0 1 1 0 1 becomes 1 1 0 1

c) 0 0 1 1 0 1 becomes 0 0 0 0 1 1 0 1

d)
220	2	
110	2	remainder: 0
55	2	remainder: 0
27	2	remainder: 1
13	2	remainder: 1
6	2	remainder: 1
3	2	remainder: 0
1	2	remainder: 1
0		remainder: 1

Gives the answer: 0 0 1 1 1 0 1 1

e) – 0 0 1 1 0 1

Teacher's comments

The second student has used the correct conversion method in parts a) and d), but they have written the binary numbers in the wrong order and the answer to part a) is not in 8-bit format. Answer b) is incorrect since they haven't added extra zeros (they could have gained a follow-through mark from part a) if they added the extra two zeros). Part c) would gain a follow through mark since this time the additional zeros were added. Part e) is completely wrong. Probably two or three marks maximum out of 9.

Exam-style questions

1. a) i) Convert the 16-bit binary number 1100 0000 1101 1110 to hexadecimal.
   ii) Convert the hexadecimal number 2 A 9 F to a 16-bit binary number. [3]
   b) i) Convert the hexadecimal number 3 F C to a denary number.
   ii) Convert the denary number 2 8 1 6 to a hexadecimal number. [3]

2. a) Convert the following denary numbers into 8-bit binary numbers:
   i) 95
   ii) 30
   iii) 205 [3]
   b) i) Carry out the binary addition of parts a)i) and a)ii).
   ii) Carry out the binary addition of parts a)i) and a)iii). Comment on your answer. [3]

3. Describe three uses of the hexadecimal number system. [6]

4. Convert the denary number 75 into an 8-bit binary number using the two's complement format. [3]

5. a) i) Convert the denary number 116 into a binary 8-bit number.
   ii) Carry out a logical shift two places to the right on the binary number obtained in part a)i).
   iii) Carry out a logical shift three places to the left on the binary number obtained in part a)i). Comment on your answer. [5]
   b) i) Write the hexadecimal numbers 3 C and 4 4 as 8-bit binary numbers.
   ii) Add the two binary numbers found in part b)i).
   iii) Carry out a logical shift six places to the right on your answer to part b)ii). Comment on your answer. [5]

Cambridge IGCSE™ and O Level Computer Science Study and Revision Guide Second Edition

1.2 Text, sound and images

REVISED

1.2.1 Text

All keyboard characters (including control codes) are represented in a computer using 7-bit American Standard Code for Information Interchange (**ASCII code**) or 8-bit Extended ASCII code **character set**. For example, each ASCII value is found in a stored table when a key is pressed on the keyboard. The main drawback of the ASCII code system is it can't be used to represent non-Western languages, such as Chinese or Japanese characters. One way round this is to use **Unicode**, which can support up to 4 bytes per character (that is, up to 32 bits per character).

1.2.2 Sound

Sound is analogue data. To store sound in a computer, it is necessary to convert the analogue data into a digital format. The digital data can then be played back through a loudspeaker once it has been converted back to electrical signals (see Chapter 3 for more details).

To convert sound to digital, the sound waves must be sampled at regular time intervals. The amplitude (loudness) of the sound uses a number of bits to represent the range (for example, 0 to 15 bits). The greater the number of bits used to represent the amplitude, the greater the accuracy of the sampled sound. The number of bits per sample is called the **sampling resolution**; the **sampling rate** is the number of sound samples taken per second. Look at these two diagrams to show the difference.

In the first diagram, only 8 bits (0 to 7) are used to represent the amplitude, whereas 16 bits are used in the second diagram. This means the second diagram allows 16 distinct values to represent amplitude, whereas the first diagram only has eight values to represent the same amplitude range.

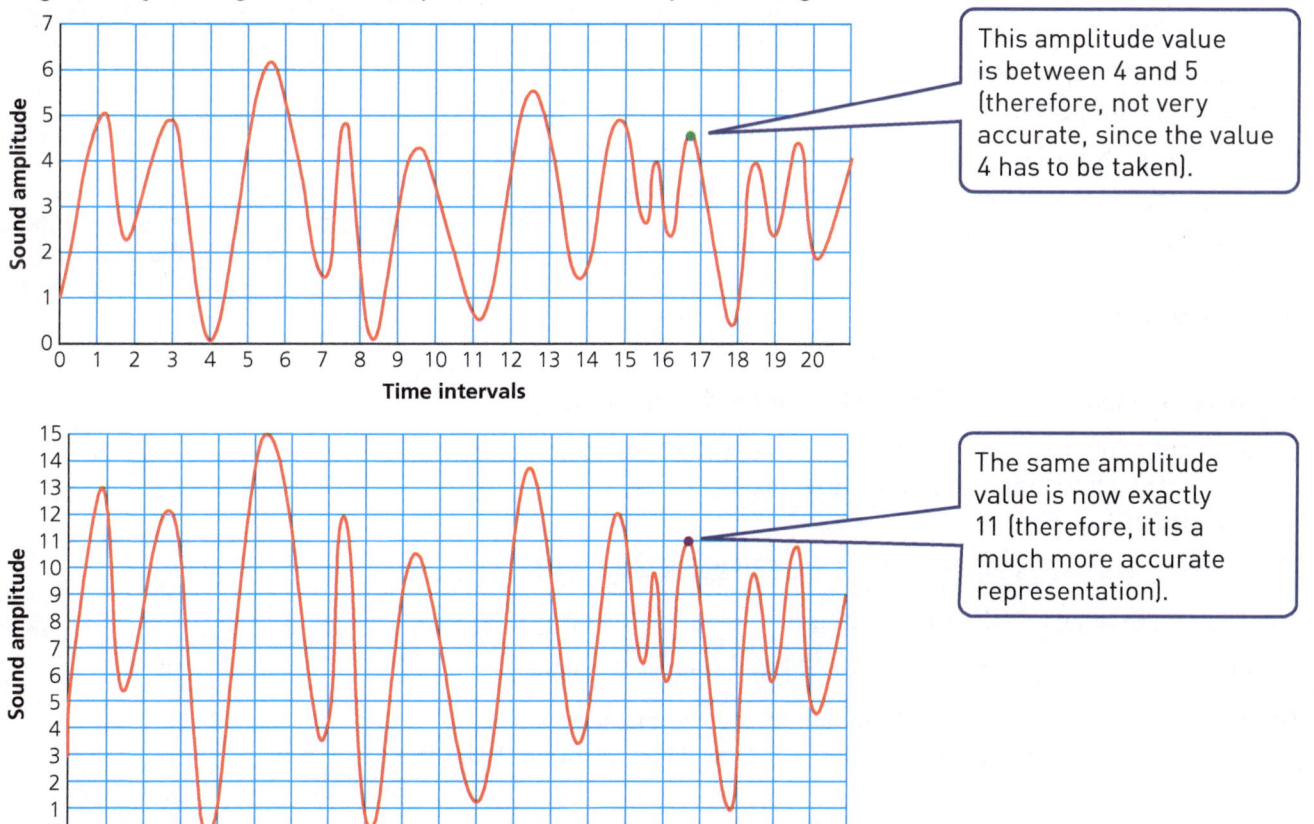

This amplitude value is between 4 and 5 (therefore, not very accurate, since the value 4 has to be taken).

The same amplitude value is now exactly 11 (therefore, it is a much more accurate representation).

1.2.3 Representation of (bitmap) images

Bitmap images are made up of **pixels** (picture elements). An image is made up of a two-dimensional matrix of pixels. Each pixel can be represented as a binary number, so bitmap images are stored as a series of binary numbers, so that:

- a black and white image only requires 1 bit per pixel (1 = white, 0 = black)
- if each pixel is represented by 2 bits, there are 2^2 (= 4) possible values (00, 01, 10 and 11) – therefore, four colours could be represented or four shades of grey
- if each pixel is represented by 3 bits, there are 2^3 (= 8) possible values – therefore, eight colours could be represented or eight shades of grey; and so on.

The number of bits to represent each possible colour is called the **colour depth**. **Image resolution** refers to the number of pixels that make up an image, for example 4096 × 3072 (= 12 582 912) pixels could be used to make up an image. Each pixel will be represented by a number of bits (for example, a colour depth of 32 bits).

> **Tip**
> As colour depth and/or resolution increase, the quality of the image will improve; but this also causes an increase in file size which impacts on the storage/memory requirements.

1.3 Data storage and file compression

REVISED

1.3.1 Measurement of data storage

Recall that a **bit** refers to each binary digit and is the smallest unit; four bits make up a nibble (an old unit) and eight bits make up a byte. Memory size and storage size are both measured in terms of bytes

Data storage and memory is measured in terms of bytes:

- 1 KiB (kibibyte) = 2^{10} bytes
- 1 MiB (mebibyte) = 2^{20} bytes
- 1 GiB (gibibyte) = 2^{30} bytes
- 1 TiB (tebibyte) = 2^{40} bytes
- 1 PiB (pebibyte) = 2^{50} bytes
- 1 EiB (exbibyte) = 2^{60} bytes

> **Tip**
> Remember that answers must be given in the units specified by the question.

1.3.2 Calculation of file size

The file size of an image is calculated by:

image resolution (number of pixels) × colour depth (in bits)

For example, a photograph is taken by a camera that uses a colour depth of 32 bits; the photograph is 1024 × 1080 pixels in size. We can work out the file size as follows:

1024 × 1080 × 32 = 35 389 440 bits ≡ 4 423 680 bytes ≡ 4.22 MiB

The file size of a sound file is calculated by:

sample rate (in Hz) × sample resolution (bits) × length of sample (secs)

For example, an audio file which is 60 minutes in length uses a sample rate of 44 100 and a sample resolution of 16 bits. We can work out the file size as follows:

44 100 × 16 × (60 × 60) = 2 540 160 000 bits ≡ 317 520 000 bytes ≡ 302.8 MiB

1 Data representation

1.3.3 Data compression
Files are often **compressed** to save storage used, reduce streaming and downloading/uploading times, reduce the **bandwidth** requirements and reduce costs (for example, if storing files using cloud storage).

1.3.4 Lossy and lossless file compression
Two common types of (file) compression are **lossy** and **lossless**.

Lossy	Lossless
• File compression algorithms eliminate unnecessary data. • The original file cannot be reconstructed once it has been compressed. • The files are smaller than those produced by lossless algorithms. • Examples include MPEG and **JPEG**.	• Data from the original uncompressed file can be reconstructed following compression. • No data is lost following the application of the lossless algorithms. • Most common example is RLE.

Lossy file compression
Examples of lossy file compression include the following.

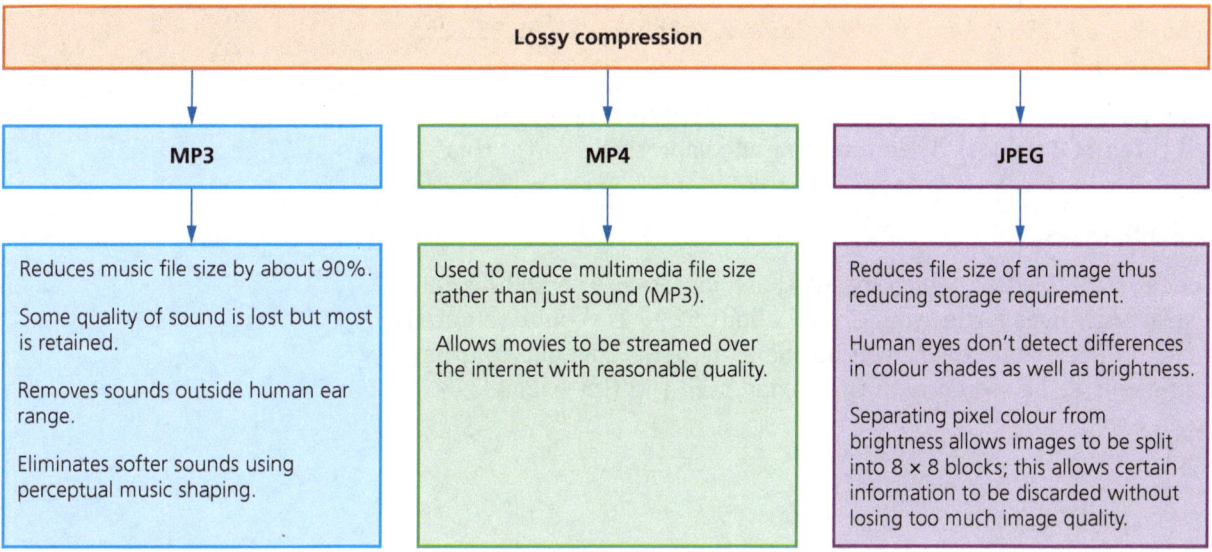

Lossless file compression
Run length encoding (RLE) is an example of lossless compression. It works by:

- reducing the size of a string of adjacent, identical data items
- the repeating unit is encoded into two values:
  - first value represents number of identical data items
  - second value represents code (such as ASCII) of data item.

Using RLE on text data
For example aaaaaaa/bbbbbbbbbb/c/d/c/d/c/d/eeeeeeee becomes:

255 08 97 // 255 10 98 // 99 /100 /99 /100 /99 /100 // 255 08 101

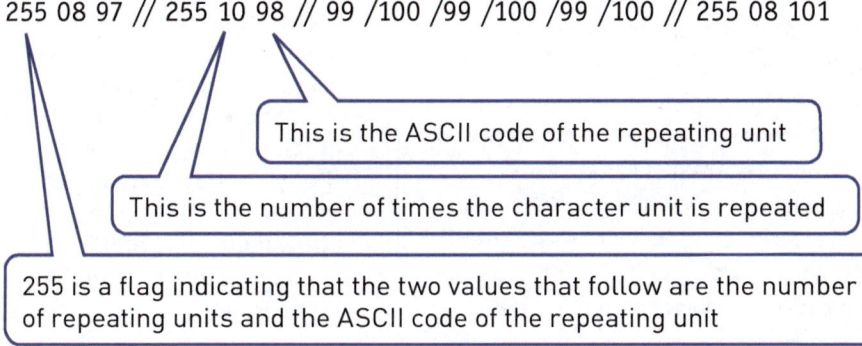

1.3 Data storage and file compression

Using RLE with images

This example shows how the file size of a colour image can be reduced using RLE.

The figure below shows an object in four colours. Each colour is made up of red, green and blue (RGB) according to the code on the right.

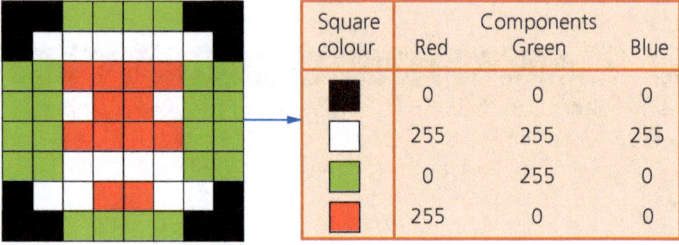

Square colour	Components		
	Red	Green	Blue
	0	0	0
	255	255	255
	0	255	0
	255	0	0

This produces the following data:

2 0 0 0 4 0 255 0 3 0 0 0 6 255 255 255 1 0 0 0 2 0 255 0 4 255 0 0 4 0 255 0 1 255 255 255 2 255 0 0 1 255 255 255 4 0 255 0 4 255 0 0 4 0 255 0 4 255 255 255 2 0 255 0 1 0 0 0 2 255 255 255 2 255 0 0 2 255 255 255 3 0 0 0 4 0 255 0 2 0 0 0

The original image (8 × 8 square) would need three bytes per square (to include all three RGB values). Therefore, the uncompressed file for this image is:

8 × 8 × 3 = 192 bytes.

The RLE code has 92 values, which means the compressed file will be 92 bytes in size. This gives a file reduction of about 52%. It should be noted that the file reductions in reality will not be as large as this due to other data which needs to be stored with the compressed file (for example, a file header).

Sample questions and answers

REVISED

a) i) Explain the two terms **lossy** and **lossless** file compression. [2]
   ii) Give **two** advantages of compressing files and data. [2]
   iii) Give **one** drawback of using lossy file compression and **one** drawback of using lossless file compression. [2]
b) A camera detector has an array of 2048 by 3072 pixels and uses a colour depth of 32 bits. The camera has a 64 GiB memory capacity. Calculate how many typical images could be stored on the camera. [3]

Tips

Since the first part is an 'explain' question, it is necessary to give a detailed explanation of the two terms mentioned in the question. Parts a) ii) and a)iii) just require a brief description since you are asked to give examples. Do not elaborate too much here since it will simply waste time without any gain in marks. Part b) is a calculation, so it is vital that you show **every** step in your calculation to show your logic and gain credit if your final answer is incorrect.

Sample high-level answer

a) i) With lossy file compression, the file compression algorithms eliminate all unnecessary data and the original file can no longer be reconstructed; some data is irretrievably lost. The resultant files are much smaller than the original files. Examples include MPEG and JPEG.
With lossless file compression, data from the original uncompressed file can be reconstructed following application of the lossless compression algorithms. No data is lost following the application of the lossless compression algorithms. A typical example is run length encoding (RLE).
   ii) Two advantages include: reduction in storage space used to store the files, faster download/upload of files across networks since they are much smaller. It is less expensive to store the files if cloud storage is used.

12 Cambridge IGCSE™ and O Level Computer Science Study and Revision Guide Second Edition

iii) One drawback of lossy file compression is that data is permanently lost so that the original file cannot be reconstructed. One drawback of lossless file compression is that the compressed files are still larger than those created from lossy compression.

b) number of bits = 2048 × 3072 × 32 = 201 326 592 bits
divide by 8 to convert to bytes = 25 165 824 bytes
camera memory size in bytes = 64 × 1024 × 1024 × 1024 = 68 719 476 736
number of images = (68 719 476 736) ÷ (25 165 824) = 2730 images

Sample low-level answer

a) i) lossy means data is lost permanently when a file is compressed whereas lossless doesn't lose any of the data for ever.
ii) uses up less space and it is faster and easier to send files over the internet
iii) lossy – lose data
lossless – more complicated compression algorithm

b) 2048 × 3072 pixels = 6 291 456 bytes
Number of images = (6 292 456) ÷ 64 = 98 304 images stored.

Teacher's comments

The first answer is a comprehensive description of lossy and lossless data compression and would probably gain full marks. The calculation shows all of the steps, which is a good exam technique – if you make any errors in your calculation, by showing all steps, you could still gain a good mark even if your final answer is incorrect.

The second answer would probably gain one mark for the reference to lossy files losing data permanently in contrast to lossless. It would also gain one mark for a)ii) for reference to transfer of files over the internet. However, the statement 'uses up less space' won't get any marks – it needs to refer to storage space or memory space (the word 'space' on its own is worth 0 marks). The first answer to part a) iii) is just a repeat of a) i) and the second answer isn't necessarily true. The calculation in part b) is a mess but they would probably gain a mark for the calculation of number of bits; but the rest of their answer is confused or simply incorrect.

Exam-style questions

6 The following diagram shows the sampling of a sound source:

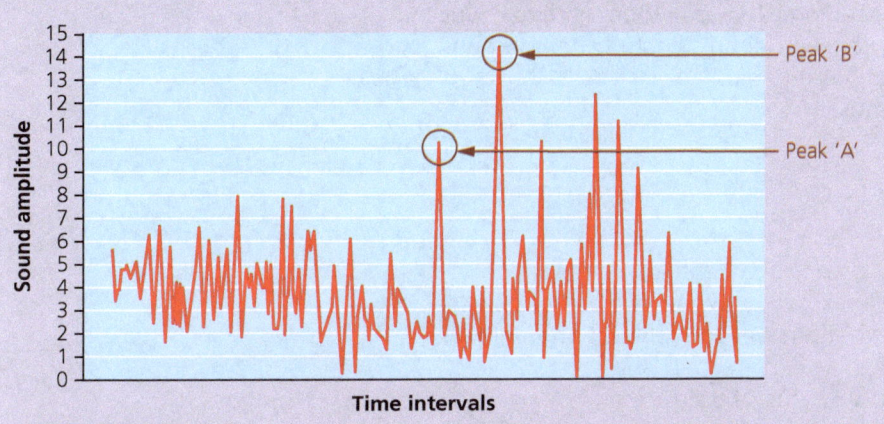

a) What type of data is natural sound? [1]
b) The sound resolution being used is 16 bits. Write down the binary values of
   i) peak 'A' and peak 'B';
   ii) peak 'B' has two potential values; describe how this problem could be resolved. [3]
c) Explain what is meant by:
   i) sampling resolution
   ii) sampling rate. [2]
d) A sound source is being sampled at 20 000 samples per second. The sampling resolution used is 32 bits.
   i) Give **one** advantage of using 32 bits rather than 8 bits.
   ii) Give **one** disadvantage of using 32 bits rather than 8 bits.
   iii) Estimate the file size if a 30 second sound sample was being recorded.
   Give your answer in MiB. [4]

Hodder & Stoughton Limited © David Watson and Helen Williams 2022

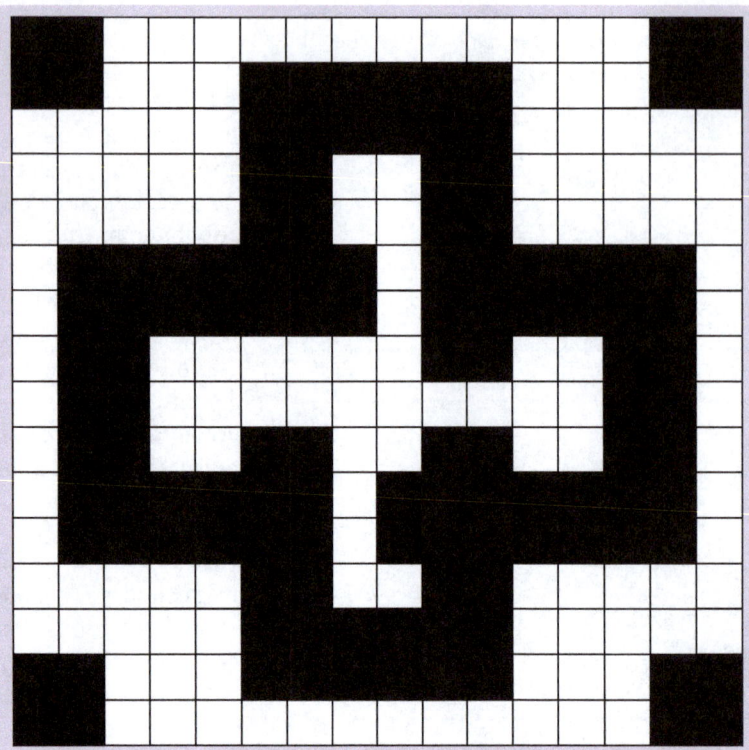

7 An ancient Roman mosaic was being scanned by archaeologists and the pattern saved on a computer. Each black tile has the binary value 0 and each white tile has the binary value 1.
   a) What is the file size of the raw data? [1]
   b) Describe how run length encoding (RLE) could be used to reduce the size of the raw file. Your answer should include calculations to show how the file size could be reduced. [6]

8 Explain the following four terms:
   a) MP3 file
   b) JPEG file
   c) 1 Tebibyte
   d) pixel [8]

9 A student gave the following answers in an end-of-term test on computer science. In each case, explain why the student's answers were incorrect. Also suggest what answer the student should have given in each case.
   a) 1 MiB is equivalent to 1 000 000 bytes of data.
   b) A file which undergoes a lossy compression algorithm can be restored to its original file whenever required.
   c) RLE works effectively on any run of repeating units.
   d) ASCII code is a subset of Unicode.
   e) To play back a sound file stored on a computer through a set of external speakers requires the use of an analogue to digital converter (ADC). [10]

10 When zooming in to an image (that is, increasing its size on screen), it may become pixelated.
   a) What is meant by the term **pixelated**? [2]
   b) Explain why an image can become pixelated. [2]
   c) Colour images are made up of red, green and blue elements. Each of the three colour elements can be represented by 256 bit combinations (from 0 to 255, where 0 = colour not present and 255 = maximum colour element present).
      i) What is the hexadecimal equivalent of 255?
      ii) Describe how it is possible to represent millions of different colours using red, green and blue elements. (You may assume, for example, that pure red is represented by # FF 00 00). [4]

2 Data transmission

> **Key objectives**
>
> The objectives of this chapter are to revise:
> - methods of data transmission:
>   - data packets
>   - structure of data packets
>   - packet switching
>   - serial, parallel, simplex, half-duplex and full-duplex
>   - universal serial bus (USB)
> - error detection to include parity checks, checksum, echo checks and Automatic Repeat Requests (ARQ)
> - encryption to include symmetric and asymmetric encryption

2.1 Types and methods of data transmission

REVISED

2.1.1 Data packets

Data is broken up into **packets** before it is transmitted. Data packets are split up into:

- **packet header** (containing the IP address of the sending station and receiving station, the sequence number of the packet, so it can be reassembled, and packet size, to ensure the receiving station knows that the whole packet has been received)
- **payload** (the actual data)
- **packet trailer** (containing **cyclic redundancy check (CRC)** (error check) and a way of identifying the end of the data packet).

> CRC is found by adding 1-bits and send as a hex value

Data packets allow data to be sent in manageable chunks that can be sent along the most efficient route from A to B. **Routers** (known as **nodes**) are used to control the path a data packet takes from sending station to receiving station. This is called **packet switching** where each data packet can take a different route; each route taken is independent of each other. Since data packets take different routes, they could arrive at their destination in the wrong order. A sequence number in the packet header allows all the data packets to be reassembled in the right order at the receiving station. **Hop numbers** are added to packet headers to ensure they don't 'bounce around' from router to router and eventually become effectively lost.

Benefits of packet switching	Drawbacks of packet switching
- There is no need to tie up a single communication line. - It is possible to overcome failed, busy or faulty lines by simply re-routing packets. - It is relatively easy to expand package usage. - A high data transmission rate is possible.	- Packets can be lost and need to be re-sent. - The method doesn't work well with **real-time streaming** (for example, a live sporting event being transmitted over the internet). - There is a delay at the destination whilst the packets are being re-ordered.

2.1 Types and methods of data transmission

Sample questions and answers

REVISED

A video conference is taking place between delegates in the USA and Mauritius. Packet switching is used to send video and sound data between delegates.

Describe:
a) the potential problems with sound and video quality
b) how the problems in part a) could be overcome. **[6]**

Sample high-level answer

a) Video conferencing is in real time. Video and audio data is split up into data packets before it is sent over the internet. This means that each data packet could potentially follow a different route from delegate to delegate. Data packets could therefore take different times from sender to recipient, or some may even become 'lost'. The arriving packets also need to be reassembled into the correct sequence, which can also cause a time delay. All of this could lead to gaps in data received, freezing of images, drop out or voice and mouth 'out of synchronisation' – this would be caused by audio and video data taking different times from sender to receiver.

b) Since the problems seem to be due to timing issues, the best solution would be to eliminate these time differences. A single path for all data packets would resolve this; that could be achieved using a dedicated communication link between delegates.

> A mention of circuit switching could also be accepted here if a candidate has gone outside the syllabus.

Sample low-level answer

a) Sometimes you get echo or lag on the sound or it may even drop out on occasions. The video and sound don't always synchronise where a person's lips don't match with the words heard. Sometimes the image just freezes.

b) This can be overcome using better cameras and microphones and getting a faster internet connection.

Exam-style questions

1. Explain how packet switching could be used to download some software from a website. **[4]**
2. Data being shared between two computers is split up into a number of data packets prior to transmission. The data packets contain a header and a trailer.
   a) Give **three** pieces of information found in the header. **[3]**
   b) The trailer contains a cyclic redundancy check (CRC).
      i) Name another item found in the trailer. **[1]**
      ii) The following data is being sent in the payload:
      11110000 00111111 00110011 11001100 11111110 11101110 00001100 11011111 11001001
      Use this data to show how CRC is used to ensure no errors occurred during data transmission. **[3]**
   c) i) Explain how it is possible for data packets to be lost during their transmission across a network. **[2]**
      ii) Describe how it is possible to deal with lost packets so that they don't cause network problems, such as 'clogging up' the system. **[2]**

Tips

Since this is a 'describe' question, it is necessary to give all the main facts, features and/or characteristics about video conferencing when using packet switching. It is important to notice the reference to part a) in part b) – this means that your answer to part b) must refer back to potential problems identified in part a).

Teacher's comments

The first answer shows that the student has realised the connection between video conferencing and packet switching. They have correctly referred to 'lost' packets or packets out of order as a reason why there can be sound and vision issues. Their solution of using circuit switching (a dedicated route) is the kind of answer you would expect from a top-level answer (it goes slightly beyond the syllabus, but would still gain credit).

The second answer hasn't made the link between video conferencing and packet switching. But they have mentioned some of the problems that can occur without mentioning how or why they occur. The answer would gain two of the available marks in part a). One mark could also be awarded in part b) for suggesting faster internet could go some way to resolving the issue.

Cambridge IGCSE™ and O Level Computer Science Study and Revision Guide Second Edition

2.1.2 Data transmission

The modes of data transmission are:

- **simplex**: data can be sent in one direction only (for example, sending data to a printer)
- **half-duplex**: data can be sent in both directions, but not at the same time (for example, using a walkie-talkie to send and receive messages)
- **full-duplex**: data can be sent in both directions at the same time (for example, when using a broadband internet connection).

Serial and parallel data transmission

- **Serial data transmission**: data is sent one bit at a time down a single wire/channel (for example, using a USB connection).
- **Parallel data transmission**: several bits of data are sent down several wires/channels at the same time – each wire/channel transmits each bit (for example, transmitting data using the internal circuits of a computer).

> Take care, do not use the word 'cable' instead of wire.

It is important to remember that serial transmission and parallel transmission can use serial, half-duplex or full-duplex as a method of data transmission.

The table below shows the comparison between serial and parallel data transmission.

Features of serial transmission	Features of parallel transmission
<ul><li>Less risk of external interference than with parallel.</li><li>More reliable transmission over longer distances.</li><li>Transmitted bits won't have the risk of being skewed.</li><li>Used if the amount of data being sent is relatively small, since transmission rate is slower than parallel.</li><li>Used to send data over long distances.</li><li>Less expensive than parallel due to fewer hardware requirements.</li></ul>	<ul><li>Faster rate of data transmission than serial, which makes it the preferred method where speed is important (such as internal connections in a computer).</li><li>Works well over shorter distances.</li><li>Due to several wires/channels being used, data can become **skewed** over long distances (no longer synchronised).</li><li>Easier to program input/output operations when parallel used.</li><li>Preferred method when sending large amounts of data.</li><li>The most appropriate transmission method if data is time-sensitive.</li><li>Requires more hardware, making it more expensive to implement than serial ports.</li></ul>

2.1.3 Universal serial bus

The **universal serial bus (USB-A)** is a form of serial data transmission. It is the industry standard. When a USB is used to connect a device to a computer:

- the computer automatically detects the device
- the device is automatically recognised and the appropriate device driver is loaded.

The following table considers the benefits and drawbacks of the USB system.

USB benefits	USB drawbacks
<ul><li>Devices plugged into the computer are automatically detected and device drivers are automatically loaded up.</li><li>Connections can only fit one way preventing incorrect connections being made.</li><li>Has become an industry standard.</li><li>Can support different data transmission rates.</li><li>No need for external power source since cable supplies +5V power.</li><li>USB protocol notifies the transmitter to re-transmit data if any errors are detected.</li><li>Relatively easy to add more USB ports if necessary by using USB hubs.</li><li>Backward compatible.</li></ul>	<ul><li>Standard USB only supports a maximum cable length of 5 m; beyond that, USB hubs are needed to extend the cable length.</li><li>Even though USB is backward compatible, very early USB standards (V1) may not always be supported by the latest computers.</li><li>Even the latest version 3 (V3) and version 4 (V4) USB-C systems have a data transfer rate which is slow compared with, for example, Ethernet connections.</li></ul>

2.1 Types and methods of data transmission

USB-C is the latest type of USB connector, which uses a totally symmetrical 24-pin USB connection, so it will fit into a USB port either way round since there is no up or down orientation. USB-C is actually USB 3.1 but has been named USB-C to distinguish it from the old format which was known as USB-A.

The main advantages (compared to existing USB-A) of the USB-C connector are:

- it is much smaller and thinner which suits the current trend in making devices much thinner
- it offers 100 watt (20 volt) power connectivity which means full-sized devices can now be charged
- it can carry data at 10 Gigabits per second (10 Gbps); this means it can now support 4K video delivery
- the USB-C connection is backward compatible (to USB 2.0 and 3.0) provided a suitable adaptor is used.

Sample question and answer

REVISED

Compare the USB-A and USB-C types of connection. [4]

Sample high-level answer

Both types of connector are backward compatible and have become the industry standard. Since USB cables also supply power, there is no need for an external power supply. It is easy to add additional USB-A and USB-C ports by using a USB hub.

The USB-A connector can only fit one way round, whereas the USB-C connector is non-orientated. Data transfer rate using USB-C is considerably faster than for USB-A. Although both types of connector supply power, the USB-C allows 20 V power connectivity which means it can be used to charge much larger devices.

> **Tip**
>
> Since this is a 'compare' question, it is necessary to consider all the similarities and all the differences between the two types of connector.

Sample low-level answer

USB-C is the newer type of USB connection. It is used by some devices like mobile phones and laptops. Its advantage is the cable works any way round since both ends are the same. Data access is much faster than with USB-A.

Teacher's comments

The first answer contains four distinct points citing the similarities and differences between USB-A and USB-C. This gives the answer a good balance.

The second answer is much briefer even though four points were made.
- The first point, although true, is not worth a mark.
- The second point is true, but it is not a comparison as asked for in the question.
- The answer confused a symmetrical connection that allows the USB-C to fit into a device any way round with having the same connector on both ends of the cable – which is incorrect.
- Data access isn't faster, but data transfer is faster.

Overall, no marks were gained even though four points were made.

2 Data transmission

Exam-style questions

3 Explain what is meant by the following **four** terms:
   a) Data skewing
   b) USB-C connection
   c) Parallel data transmission
   d) Half-duplex data transmission [8]

4 Four statements about data transmission are shown in the following table. Tick (✓) the appropriate columns to indicate the method and direction of data transmission being described by each statement. [4]

Statement	Transmission method		Direction of data transmission		
	Serial	Parallel	Simplex	Half-duplex	Full-duplex
Data is being sent in both directions, one bit at a time along a single wire, but not at the same time.					
16 bits of data are being sent along 16 individual channels in both directions simultaneously.					
Data is being sent 8 bits at a time down eight wires in one direction only.					
Data is being sent one bit at a time down a single wire; the transmission occurs in both directions simultaneously.					

2.2 Methods of error detection

REVISED

2.2.1 The need to check for errors

When data is transferred there is always a risk that the data may be corrupted, lost or even gained. Errors can occur during data transmission due to:

- electrical interference – can corrupt data
- packet switching – can lead to data being lost or out of synchronisation
- skewing of data – bits arrive at their destination no longer synchronised.

The next section considers methods used to check for errors following data transmission.

2.2.2 Parity checks, checksum and echo checks

Parity checks

A **parity check** is a method used to check whether data has been changed or corrupted following data transmission. Parity can be even (even number of 1-bits) or odd (odd number of 1-bits). The left-most bit is reserved for a **parity bit**.

If two bits have been changed (for example, 11110000 changed to 00111100) the parity may stay the same and wouldn't be picked up by a parity check. In such cases, another error detection method, such as a checksum, needs to be carried out.

Parity blocks can be used to determine exactly which bit has been corrupted or changed following data transmission.

2.2 Methods of error detection

Worked example

In this example, nine bytes of data have been transmitted. Another byte, known as the parity byte, has also been sent (this byte consists entirely of the parity bits produced by the vertical parity check and also indicates the end of the block of data).

Even parity is being used. The table shows how the data arrived at the receiving end. And each row and column needs to be checked to see if they still show even parity.

	Parity bit	Bit 2	Bit 3	Bit 4	Bit 5	Bit 6	Bit 7	Bit 8
Byte 1	1	1	1	1	0	1	1	0
Byte 2	1	0	0	1	0	1	0	1
Byte 3	0	1	1	1	1	1	1	0
Byte 4	1	0	0	0	0	0	1	0
Byte 5	0	1	1	0	1	0	0	1
Byte 6	1	0	0	0	1	0	0	0
Byte 7	1	0	1	0	1	1	1	1
Byte 8	0	0	0	1	1	0	1	0
Byte 9	0	0	0	1	0	0	1	0
Parity byte	1	1	0	1	0	0	0	1

The table shows:
- byte 8 (row 8) now has incorrect parity (there are three 1-bits)
- bit 5 (column 5) also now has incorrect parity (there are five 1-bits).

First, the table shows that an error has occurred following data transmission (there has been a change in parity in one of the bytes).

Second, at the intersection of row 8 and column 5, the position of the incorrect bit value (which caused the error) can be found. The 1-bit at this intersection should be a 0-bit; this means that byte 8 should have been:

0	0	0	1	0	0	1	0

which would also correct column five, giving an even vertical parity (now has four 1-bits).

Checksum

A **checksum** is another method used to check if data has been changed/corrupted following data transmission. The checksum is calculated by the sending computer, from the block of data using an agreed algorithm. The data is then sent as a block along with the checksum. The checksum is re-calculated by the receiving computer using the same algorithm used by the sending computer. Any differences in the checksum indicates an error.

Echo check

An **echo check** requires data to be sent back to the sending computer where it is compared with the data originally sent. Any errors and the data is re-sent. This is not a very reliable method; if the two sets of data are different, it is not known whether the error occurred when sending the data originally or if the error occurred when sending the data back for checking.

2.2.3 Check digits

Check digits are used to identify any errors following data entry. A check digit is a value calculated by many methods, such as ISBN-13 or modulo-11. The generated digit is added to the end (on the right-hand side) of the number. Barcodes are used on products in supermarkets; check digits are used to ensure the barcode is read correctly.

> Refer to Cambridge IGCSE and O Level Computer Science Second edition pages 60–62 for examples on check digit calculations using ISBN-13 and Modulo-11.

Check digits can detect:

- incorrect digits entered
- transposition errors
- omitted or extra digits in the number
- phonetic errors (for example, 13 (thirteen) instead of 30 (thirty)).

2.2.4 Automatic Repeat Requests

An **Automatic Repeat Request (ARQ)** is a way to check data following data transmission. It is often used by mobile phone networks to guarantee data integrity.

ARQs uses positive and negative **acknowledgements** and **timeout**. The receiving device receives an error detection code as part of the data transmission (this is typically a cyclic redundancy check). This is used to detect whether the received data contains any transmission errors. If no error is detected, a positive acknowledgement is sent back to the sending device.

However, if an error is detected, the receiving device now sends a negative acknowledgement to the sending device and requests re-transmission of the data. A timeout is used by the sending device by waiting a pre-determined amount of time. If no acknowledgement of any type has been received by the sending device within this time limit, it automatically re-sends the data until a positive acknowledgement is received or until a pre-determined number of re-transmissions has taken place.

Sample questions and answers

REVISED

a) Explain how Automatic Repeat Request (ARQ) can be used to detect errors following data transmission. [3]
b) Explain why echo check is not a very reliable method for detecting errors. [2]

Sample high-level answer

a) The receiving device receives an error detection code as part of the data transmission (usually a cyclic redundancy check). This is used to detect whether the received data contains any transmission errors. If no error is detected, a positive acknowledgement is sent back to the sending device. If an error is detected, the receiving device now sends a negative acknowledgement to the sending device and requests re-transmission of the data. A timeout is used by the sending device by waiting a pre-determined amount of time. If no acknowledgement of any type has been received by the sending device within this time limit, it automatically re-sends the data until a positive acknowledgement is received, or until a pre-determined number of re-transmissions have taken place.

b) The problem with echo check is it is unclear where the error occurred. Did it occur during the original transmission from sender to receiver, or did it occur when the receiver sent the data back to the sender? Because of this, it is not a very reliable method of detecting where an error might have occurred.

> **Tip**
> Since this is an 'explain' question, it is necessary to give all the facts to support the claims in the question. In part a), you have to give supporting information which explains how ARQ can be used to detect errors. In part b), you need to give facts which show that echo checking is not very reliable.

2.2 Methods of error detection

Sample low-level answer

a) ARQs use acknowledgement and timeout; when an error is detected, a negative acknowledgement is sent and if no error, a positive acknowledgement is sent. If no acknowledgement is received, timeout is employed.

b) Echo checks can generate an error when doing the actual check. It is therefore not a reliable error detection method.

Teacher's comments

The first student gave an answer that exceeded what was asked for. The first half of the paragraph in part a) contained three valid points and the maximum mark would have been gained already. The rest of the paragraph contained correct information but will have used up valuable time when doing an exam without gaining any additional marks.

The second answer to part a) was much briefer but two marks would be gained for a mention of acknowledgement and timeout. In part b), the point made is rather weak but just valid for a mark. So, three marks out of a possible five.

Exam-style questions

5. Nine descriptions about error checking methods are given in the table below. By ticking (✓) in the appropriate column or columns, indicate whether each description refers to checksum, parity check, ARQ or CRC. It is possible more than one column, or none of the columns, can be ticked for each statement. [9]

Description	Checksum	Parity check	ARQ	CRC
An extra bit is sent with each byte of data.				
Makes use of positive and negative acknowledgement.				
Uses timeout to determine if data needs to be re-sent.				
If an error is found, a request is made to re-send the data.				
Re-calculation is made on any additional data values sent with the main data block.				
Method used to determine which bit in a data block has been altered.				
Additional value sent at the end of a block of data used to check if a data transmission error occurred.				
Number of 1-bits are counted before and after a data block has been sent.				
Value used as part of a data packet trailer to check if any data corruption has occurred.				

6. a) The following block of data was received after transmission from a remote computer. Even parity protocol was being followed by both computers. One of the transmitted bits has become changed following transmission.
   i) Locate which bit was changed and which byte was affected.
   ii) Write down the corrected byte.
   iii) Explain, under what circumstances, this method wouldn't identify which byte had become corrupted or changed? [4]

	Parity bit	Bit 2	Bit 3	Bit 4	Bit 5	Bit 6	Bit 7	Bit 8
Byte 1	0	0	1	1	1	0	0	1
Byte 2	1	0	0	1	1	1	0	0
Byte 3	0	1	0	0	1	1	1	0
Byte 4	0	0	1	1	0	0	1	1
Byte 5	1	0	0	0	1	0	0	0
Byte 6	1	1	1	0	1	1	0	1
Byte 7	0	1	1	0	0	0	0	0
Byte 8	1	1	0	0	0	1	1	1
Byte 9	0	0	1	1	1	1	0	0
Byte 10	0	1	1	1	0	1	1	1
Parity byte	0	1	0	1	0	1	0	1

b) ARQ was used as a second method to identify errors following data transmission. Explain how ARQ is used to detect errors following data transmission. [4]

2.3 Symmetric and asymmetric encryption

REVISED

2.3.1 The purpose of encryption

When data is transmitted over public networks, there is always the risk of it being intercepted. Using **encryption** and encryption keys helps solve this problem or certainly makes it more difficult for the hacker. Encryption alters the data into a form that is unreadable by anybody for whom the data is not intended. When encrypted, this last sentence becomes:

'53f0A+yO+vRytMi9MjyS+JuUsLYTVsXpJDvj7PU6K3cYkr7l9ftMV2mxMvV2Ou/OzHPVrKtRanB/5GSzrPx+3NRYzYe9h2Dktrf0cQ22Wzrnj0DnxGvPzOGVIyYezDbSi2DoxlUewt1NVTFTmCu1k2CXL6wRCxXmbznQGkaiN8c='

As you can see this is now almost unreadable without knowing the decryption key.

The original data is called **plaintext** and data which is encrypted is called **ciphertext**.

Encryption can't stop data being intercepted, but it prevents it making any sense if intercepted. The following section summarises symmetric and asymmetric encryption.

2.3.2 Symmetric and asymmetric encryption.

Symmetric encryption uses a single encryption key. The same key is used to encrypt data and to decrypt data. Modern encryption keys use 256-bit encryption (giving about 10^{77} possible combinations) which makes it hard to crack.

Asymmetric encryption uses two keys: a **public key** (known to everyone) and a **private key** (known to one user only). Matching pairs (private and public keys) are generated by an **encryption algorithm**.

Both types of key are needed to encrypt and decrypt messages. When using asymmetric encryption, matching pairs of keys are used (these two keys are mathematically linked but cannot be derived from each other).

2.3 Symmetric and asymmetric encryption

For example, if 'A' wants to send a confidential document to 'B', 'B' sends 'A' their public key who uses this to encrypt the document before sending it to 'B'. 'B' now uses their private key to decrypt the document.

Sample question and answer

REVISED

Explain why asymmetric encryption is safer than symmetric encryption when sending data over the internet. [4]

Sample high-level answer

When using symmetric encryption, it is difficult to keep the encryption key a secret (for example, it needs to be sent in an email or a text message which can be intercepted). Therefore, the issue of security is always the main drawback of symmetrical encryption, since only a single encryption key is required for both sender and recipient. With asymmetric encryption two keys called the public key and the private key are used. When two users wish to share a document, for example, they both use the same algorithm to generate their own matching pairs of keys (private and public), which they must keep stored on their computers. The matching pairs of keys are mathematically linked but can't be derived from each other. One user sends their public key which is used to encrypt the document. When this encrypted document is received, the recipient uses their own private key to decrypt it (this works because the public key and private key on the recipient's computer are a matching pair). This makes asymmetric encryption considerably safer than symmetric encryption, provided the encryption keys are at least 128 bits in length.

Sample low-level answer

Symmetric encryption uses one key which means no document is safe if this key is stolen or intercepted. Asymmetric encryption uses two keys; this makes it far more secure.

Exam-style questions

7 Ali and Daniel both work for an international company. Ali wishes to send Daniel a confidential document over the internet.
   a) Describe how Ali and Daniel would use matching pairs of keys to ensure the document is sent safely over the internet. [4]
   b) Explain what needs to happen if Daniel wants to receive documents safely from other people within the company. [3]
8 Define the following computer terms.
   a) Ciphertext
   b) Plaintext
   c) Encryption
   d) Private key
   e) Encryption algorithm [5]

Tip

Since this is an 'explain' question, it is necessary to give all the facts to support the claims in the question and give evidence as to why asymmetric encryption is safer than symmetric encryption.

Teacher's comments

The first answer is very comprehensive and worth a lot more than the four marks. The danger in writing very comprehensive answers is the time it takes, which can cause a problem in exams which are time limited.

The second answer is much briefer but gains one mark for reference to the less secure symmetric encryption. However, just writing 'asymmetric encryption uses two keys' is insufficient to gain any marks – the student needs to mention public and private keys and why this makes it a more secure system.

3 Hardware

Key objectives

The objectives of this chapter are to revise:
- computer architecture:
  - the central processing unit (CPU) microprocessor
  - Von Neumann architecture
  - arithmetic and logic unit (ALU), control unit (CU) and registers
  - system buses – control bus, address bus, data bus
  - Fetch-Decode-Execute cycle
  - cores, cache and system clock
  - instruction sets for a CPU
  - embedded systems
- input and output devices:
  - input devices: barcode scanners, QR code scanners, digital cameras, keyboards, microphones, mouse, 2D/3D scanners and touchscreens
  - output devices: actuators, light projectors, printers, 3D printers, light emitting diode (LED) and liquid crystal display (LCD) screens, speakers and sensors
- data storage:
  - primary memory (random access memory (RAM) and read-only memory (ROM))
  - secondary storage (magnetic, optical and solid state)
  - virtual memory
  - cloud storage
- network hardware:
  - network interface cards (NICs)
  - MAC addresses
  - IP addresses
  - routers

3.1 Computer architecture

REVISED

3.1.1 The central processing unit

The **central processing unit (CPU)** has the responsibility for execution and processing of all instructions and data in a computer. It consists of:

- **control unit (CU)**
- **arithmetic and logic unit (ALU)**
- **registers** and **buses**.

A microprocessor is an **integrated circuit** (microchip) – also referred to as a processor or CPU. The microprocessor contains the ALU and control unit to enable it to interpret and execute all instructions and carry out arithmetic operations. The CPU also contains the **system clock** and primary memory.

3.1.2 Von Neumann architecture

Von Neumann introduced the idea of the stored program computer, which has been the basis of many computers for a number of years. The von Neumann architecture had the following main novel features (none of which were available in computers prior to the mid-1940s).

- The concept of a central processing unit (CPU or processor).
- The processor was able to access the memory directly.
- Computer memories could store programs as well as data.
- Stored programs were made up of instructions which could be executed in sequential order.

3.1 Computer architecture

The following diagram summarises the components of a typical CPU.

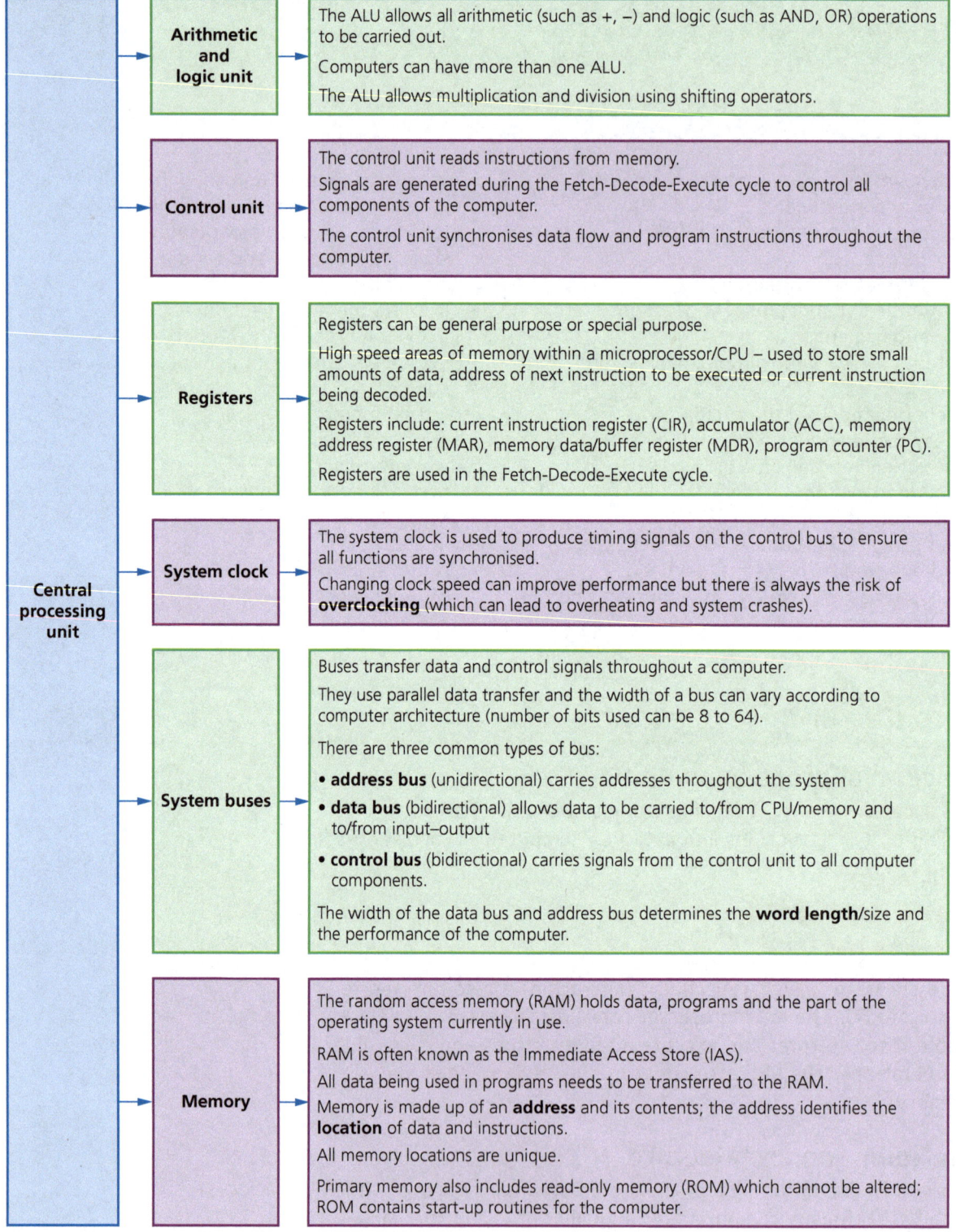

The Fetch-Decode-Execute cycle

To carry out a set of instructions, the CPU first fetches data and instructions from memory and stores them in the appropriate registers. Both the **address bus** and **data bus** are used in the process. Each instruction needs to be decoded and finally executed – this forms the **Fetch-Decode-Execute** cycle. The following diagram summarises the cycle.

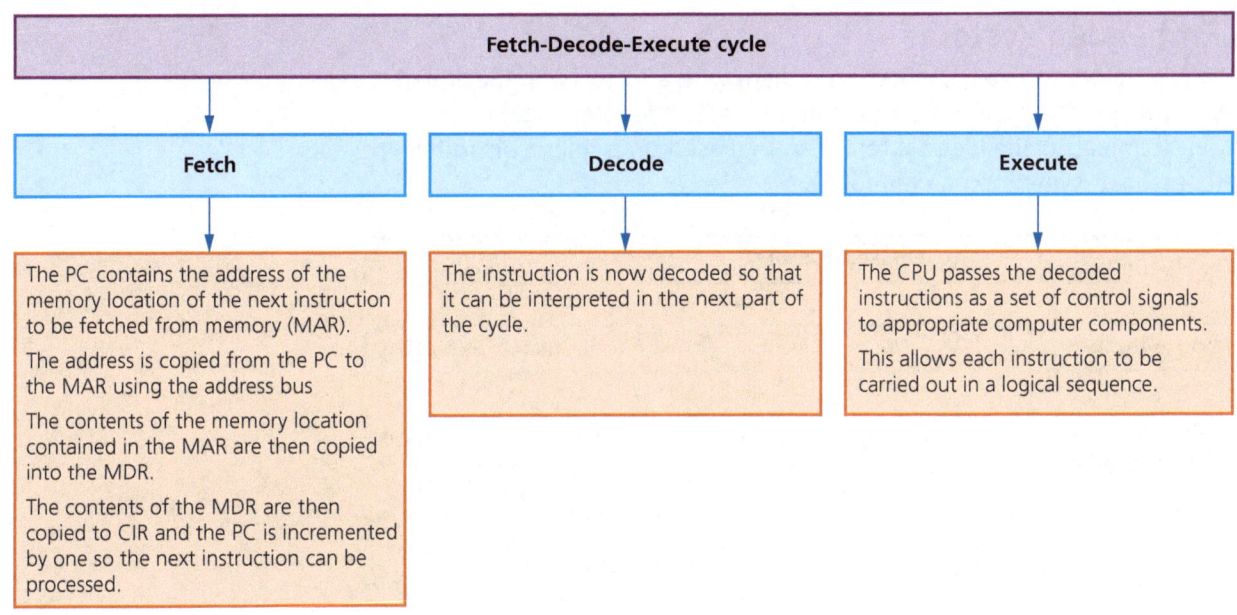

3.1.3 Cores, cache and internal clock

The system clock defines the **clock cycle** used to synchronise all computer operations. Timing signals are transmitted via the **control bus**. In general, increasing the clock speed increases the processing speed of the CPU (since it can carry out more processes per second).

The width of the address bus and data bus increases the processing speed of the CPU (for example, a bus width of 16 bits can address 2^{16} (= 65 536) memory locations, whereas a bus width of 64 bits can address 2^{64} (almost 20 000 000 000 000 000 000 memory locations).

Overclocking, caused by changing the clock speed in the **Basic Input/Output System (BIOS)**, can lead to overheating and to non-synchronised instructions which can cause the computer to crash.

Caches, which store frequently used instructions and data, can speed up CPU performance. The larger the cache memory size the better the CPU performance. Using a different number of **cores** can also improve CPU performance. One core is made up of an ALU, a CU and registers. A **quad core** processor is a microprocessor with four independently operating units (cores) that can read and execute CPU instructions. Each core communicates with the other three cores using six channels.

3.1.4 Instruction set

Instructions are a set of operations that need to be decoded in sequence; each operation is made up of an **opcode** and an **operand**.

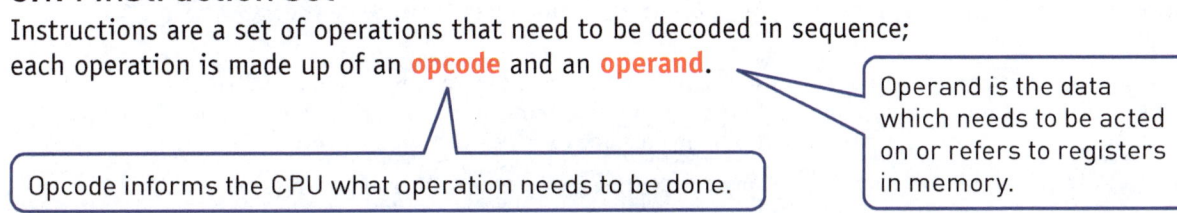

A number of allowed opcodes exist and these are referred to as the **instruction set**. The Fetch-Decode-Execute cycle controls the sequence of steps to process each instruction in sequence. Instruction sets are low level language instructions that instruct the CPU how to carry out an operation.

3.1.5 Embedded systems

An **embedded system** is a combination of hardware and software designed to carry out a specific task. Hardware can be electronic, electrical or electro-mechanical. Embedded systems can be based on a microcontroller, microprocessor or system on a chip (SoC).

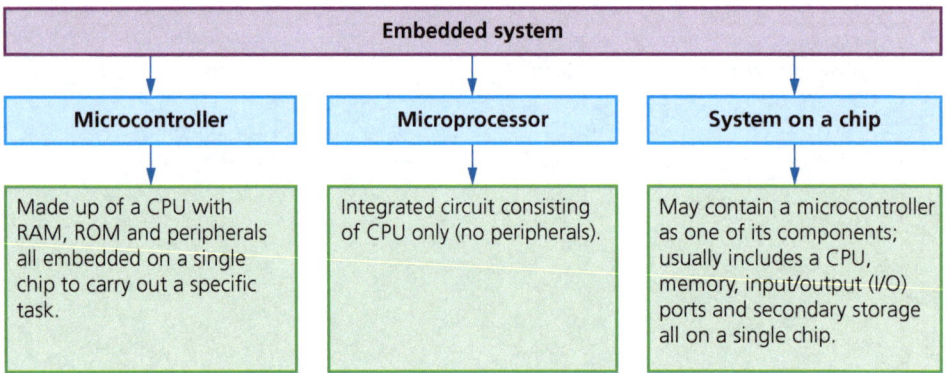

This is the general make-up of an embedded system:

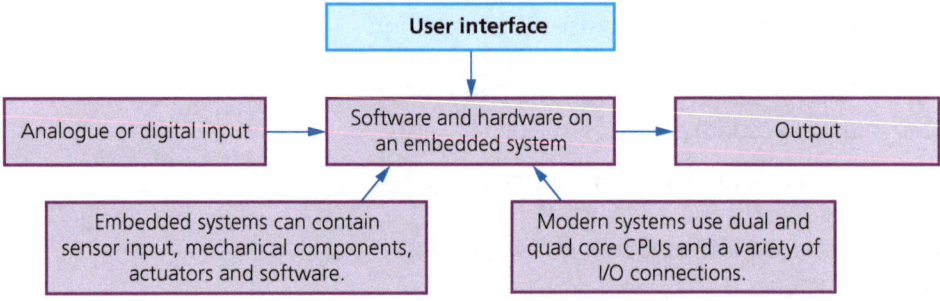

When installed either the operator inputs data manually (for example, pressing a button or turning a knob to select a temperature) or automatically (for example, reading from a sensor or from another computer system).

Embedded systems can be programmable or non-programmable. There are definite benefits and drawbacks of devices being controlled using embedded systems:

Benefits	Drawbacks
They are small in size and therefore easy to fit into devices.	It can be difficult to upgrade some devices to take advantage of new technology.
Compared to other systems, they are relatively low cost to make.	Troubleshooting faults in the device is a specialist task.
They are usually dedicated to one task making for simple interfaces and often no requirement for an operating system.	Although the interface can appear to be simple (such as a single knob) in reality it can be more confusing (for example, changing the time on a cooker clock can require several steps).
They consume very little power.	Any device that can be accessed over the internet is also open to hackers viruses and so on.
They can be controlled remotely using a mobile phone, for example.	Due to the difficulty in upgrading and fault finding, devices are often just thrown away rather than being repaired (very wasteful).
Very fast reaction to changing input (operate in real time and are feedback orientated); with mass production comes reliability.	Can lead to environmental issues created by an increase in the 'throw away' society if devices are discarded just because they have become out of date.

Examples of the use of embedded systems include:

- security systems (use sensors, such as temperature, acoustic and pressure, to monitor for intruders and sound an alarm if necessary)
- set-top box to record and play back television programmes (allow aerial, cable, satellite or Wi-Fi inputs and can be controlled remotely)
- lighting applications (to control lighting depending on time of day, whether a room is occupied and brightness of ambient light; makes use of sensors and actuators to monitor and control lighting levels)
- vending machines (monitor selection, money entered, tilting of machine and delivery of items using actuators and motors; uses sensors to detect tilting, temperature and to count money entered)
- washing machines (selection is via keypad which allows wash program to be selected)
- motor vehicles (fuel injection system, Global Positioning System (GPS) navigation, in-car entertainment, anti-lock braking system (ABS), and so on).

> Vending machines use microcontrollers to control a number of functions.

Sample questions and answers

REVISED

a) Describe the role of registers and buses in a typical computer system. [4]
b) Discuss **four** ways to improve the performance of a CPU in a computer system. [4]

Sample high-level answer

a) Registers are data holding places which form part of the CPU. They can hold an instruction, an address or data. Registers can be general or special purpose. The most common registers include:
   - current instruction register (CIR) which stores the current instruction being decoded and executed
   - accumulator (ACC) which is used when carrying out ALU calculations; it stores data temporarily during the calculations
   - memory address register (MAR) which stores the address of the memory location currently being read from or written to
   - memory data register (MDR) which stores data that has just been read from memory or data which is about to be written to memory
   - program counter (PC) which stores the address where the next instruction to be fetched can be found

   System buses are used in computers to carry out three functions:
   - address bus carries addresses throughout the computer system
   - data bus carries data to and from the CPU, memory and I/O devices (data can be an address, instruction or a numerical value)
   - control bus carries signals from the CPU to all other components to synchronize all operations

b) The performance of a CPU can be improved by the following methods:
   - increasing the size of RAM; since data is constantly moved into and out of RAM, the larger the RAM the fewer data movements there needs to be which increases operational speed
   - increasing the width of the address bus and data; this allows more memory locations to be addressed at the same time thus increasing performance of the CPU
   - increasing the clock speed; however, this needs to be met with some caution, since it can lead to overheating and potential computer crash as the number of instructions cause the CPU to overheat and for operations to become out of synchronisation
   - making the processor quad core (or even higher) allows multiple functions to be carried out simultaneously which greatly improves CPU performance

3.1 Computer architecture

> **Tips**
>
> In part a) it is necessary to consider the main features of both registers and buses in the context of a typical computer system. It is essential to state facts and expand on these facts as much as possible to ensure you give a complete description; remember four marks implies at least four facts fully explained to gain maximum credit.
>
> In part b) you are asked to discuss ways of improving CPU performance. For each example you give to enhance CPU performance, you must include a reason why it will have a positive effect or negative effect.

Sample low-level answer

a) Registers are used in computers to store data during the Fetch Decode Execute Cycle. An example of a register is the Accumulator.
   Buses allow data and instructions to be carried around the computer during processing.

b) The performance of a computer can be improved by using more RAM, changing the clock speed and using bigger buses.

Teacher's comments

The first answer has provided an almost perfect answer for both parts. The answer is a very comprehensive description of both registers and buses, but also provided examples of their use. In part b) the four improvements are expanded to show why they improve performance. A very informative answer.

The second answer shows less understanding of computer architecture. Part a) gains one mark for a mention of registers being used in the FDE cycle and also a mark for the use of buses. The answer given is too brief to gain any further credit. In part b), there is no mention of how the methods given would improve performance. The question asked for a discussion of ways to improve performance; this means it is necessary to explain why the methods mentioned would work. The answer is far too vague and needs expanding (for example, 'changing clock speed' – how would this be used; 'use bigger buses' – what exactly does that statement mean?). No marks would be gained in part b).

Exam-style questions

1 Five statements are shown on the left, and five computer terms on the right.
   By drawing lines, connect each statement to the correct computer term. [5]

Statement	Term
Ensures correct synchronisation of all computer operations	Core
Can improve the performance of the CPU by increasing its width	Overclocking
Temporary storage space that stores frequently used data and instructions	Address/data bus
Can lead to overheating and non-synchronised operations in the CPU	System clock
Part of the processing chip that does the processing work	Cache (memory)

2 Give **three** benefits and **three** drawbacks of using embedded systems in household devices. [6]

3 a) Explain what is meant by the **Fetch-Decode-Execute cycle**. [2]
   b) Describe **three** actions that take place during the Fetch-Decode-Execute cycle. [3]

3.2 Input and output devices

3.2.1 Input devices

Barcode readers

Barcodes are a series of dark and light parallel lines of varying thickness. They are a unique series of lines representing the digits 0 to 9. Barcodes are read by a scanner that uses a red laser or red light emitting diode (LED) light source. Reflected red light is read by photoelectric cells (sensors) that create a digital sequence of dark and light; for example, LDDDDLD (or 0111101 in binary).

Barcodes are used mainly on goods in a supermarket, but they can be used anywhere where an item can be scanned to identify it (for example, in a library). Barcode data is stored on a file in a products database; each barcode is used as a **key field** to uniquely identify the record which gives the data about the product – once the barcode is read, the product details (such as price) can be retrieved. They also allow for automatic stock control and sales reporting.

Advantages of using barcodes to the management

- Much easier and faster to change prices on stock items.
- Much better, more up-to-date sales information/sales trends.
- No need to price every stock item on the shelves (this reduces time and cost to the management).
- Allows for automatic stock control.
- Possible to check customer buying habits more easily by linking barcodes to, for example, customer loyalty cards.

Advantages of using barcodes to the customers

- Faster checkout queues (staff don't need to remember/look up prices of items).
- Errors in charging customers is reduced.
- The customer is given an itemised bill.
- Cost savings can be passed on to the customer.
- Better track of 'sell by dates' so food should be fresher.

QR codes

Quick response (QR) codes are another type of barcode made up of a matrix of filled-in dark squares on a light background. QR codes hold considerably more information/data than barcodes (up to 7089 digits or 4296 characters). Three large squares at the corners are used to align the QR code when it is being scanned by a camera.

QR codes can be used to advertise **products**, give automatic access to websites, store boarding passes electronically at airports and so on. QR codes are read by a camera on a smartphone or tablet using the following method.

- Camera on smartphone or tablet is pointed at the QR code.
- A stored app processes the image taken by the camera.

- The browser automatically reads the data generated by the app and decodes any web addresses embedded in the QR code.
- Any weblinks are then sent to the smartphone or tablet.

Advantages of QR codes compared to traditional barcodes
- They can hold much more information.
- There will be fewer errors; the higher capacity of the QR code allows the use of built-in error-checking systems – normal barcodes contain almost no **data redundancy** (data which is duplicated), therefore it isn't possible to guard against badly printed or damaged barcodes.
- QR codes are easier to read; they don't need expensive laser or LED scanners like barcodes – they can be read by the cameras on smartphones or tablet.
- It is easy to transmit QR codes either as text messages or images.
- It is also possible to encrypt QR codes which gives them greater protection than traditional barcodes.

Disadvantages of QR codes compared to traditional barcodes
- More than one QR format is available.
- QR codes can be used to transmit malicious codes – known as **attagging**; since there are a large number of free apps available to a user for generating QR codes, this means anyone can generate QR codes. It is therefore relatively easy to write malicious code and embed this within the QR code.

Digital cameras

Digital images taken by cameras can easily be transferred to a computer (or other device) via USB port, Bluetooth (wireless transfer) or memory card reader. Microprocessors in the camera automatically control many camera functions, such as shutter speed, focus, aperture size, flash, 'red eye' removal and so on.

Many modern cameras have tiny lenses which allow them to be used in, for example, car bumpers (as a parking aid), in drones (for aerial photos) and in endoscopes (to check the inside of pipes, for example). The image through the camera lens is captured on photodiodes (**charge couple devices** (CCD)) and converted into pixels which form an electronic matrix of the image which can be stored in memory.

Keyboards

Even with all the modern alternatives available, keyboards are still the most common data entry devices. They can be physical keyboards (connected via USB or Bluetooth) or **virtual keyboards** (for example, on a smartphone or keyboard using the **touchscreen** features).

Each character on a keyboard has an ASCII value. The computer is able to detect which key is pressed, which allows it to determine the character that was selected.

Entry of data via a keyboard is a slow process which is also prone to error and can lead to injuries such as **repetitive strain injury (RSI)**.

Microphones

Microphones have a number of applications, for example, as a sensor (to detect sound in an intruder detection system), to input text into a computer (of particular benefit to a disabled person who cannot use a keyboard) or for doing voiceovers on presentation slides and so on.

Microphones convert sound into electric currents of varying amplitude. A diaphragm in the microphone vibrates and a copper coil and cone attached to the diaphragm create an electric current as the coil vibrates back and forth. The electric current can be converted into digital data and then stored in a computer memory.

Optical mouse

A mouse is used to move an on-screen cursor which allows the user to take actions (for example, select an option from a menu). The **optical mouse** is an example of a **pointing device**. It uses tiny cameras and a red LED light source to allow the exact position of the mouse to be calculated.

Unlike a mechanical mouse, the optical mouse can work on any surface and has no moving parts to wear out. They are connected to a computer using one of the USB ports or by Bluetooth connectivity.

Advantages of an optical mouse compared to a mechanical mouse

- No moving parts therefore more reliable.
- Dirt can't get trapped in any components.
- No need for special software.

Advantages of a wired mouse (using USB) compared to a wireless mouse

- Unlike Bluetooth, wired connections have no signal loss.
- Cheaper to use (no need for batteries).
- Fewer environmental issues (for example, disposal of batteries).

Scanners

2D scanners are used, for example, to scan in documents. The information on the document is converted into an electronic format that can be stored on a computer memory.

Computers equipped with **optical character recognition (OCR)** software allow the scanned text to be converted into a **text file format**, which can then be imported into a word processor. The original text can then be manipulated as required.

2D scanners are used at airports, for example, to read passports enabling automatic border controls. The photo in the passport is scanned and then compared to an image taken by a camera at border control. Scanning faces is called facial recognition and is used in many security systems, for example, to control entry to a building or as a security device on a smartphone to prevent unauthorised use.

3D scanners scan solid objects and produce a 3D image that can then be used in **computer-aided design (CAD)** software or even sent to a 3D printer allowing the scanned object to be duplicated. 3D scanner technology uses lasers, X-rays, magnetic resonance or white light. 3D scanners are used, for example, in medical applications to build up images of parts of the human anatomy (the part of the anatomy being scanned is divided up into thin

> Scanning formats can be:
>
> PDF (portable document format)
>
> TIFF (tagged image file format) recommended for uncompressed scanned images
>
> JPEG (joint photographic experts group); standard file format if a compressed image is required.

3.2 Input and output devices

slices by the scanner producing a 3D image – this is known as tomography; it is effectively the reverse of what 3D printers do). Tomography uses X-rays to produce 3D images; magnetic resonance imaging (MRI) scanners use radio frequencies.

Touchscreens

Touchscreens are now common input devices, used at ordering stations for fast food, information kiosks at airports and on smartphones and tablets.

> All types of technology permit use of bare fingers or a special stylus.

There are three common touchscreen technologies: **capacitive**, **infrared** and **resistive**.

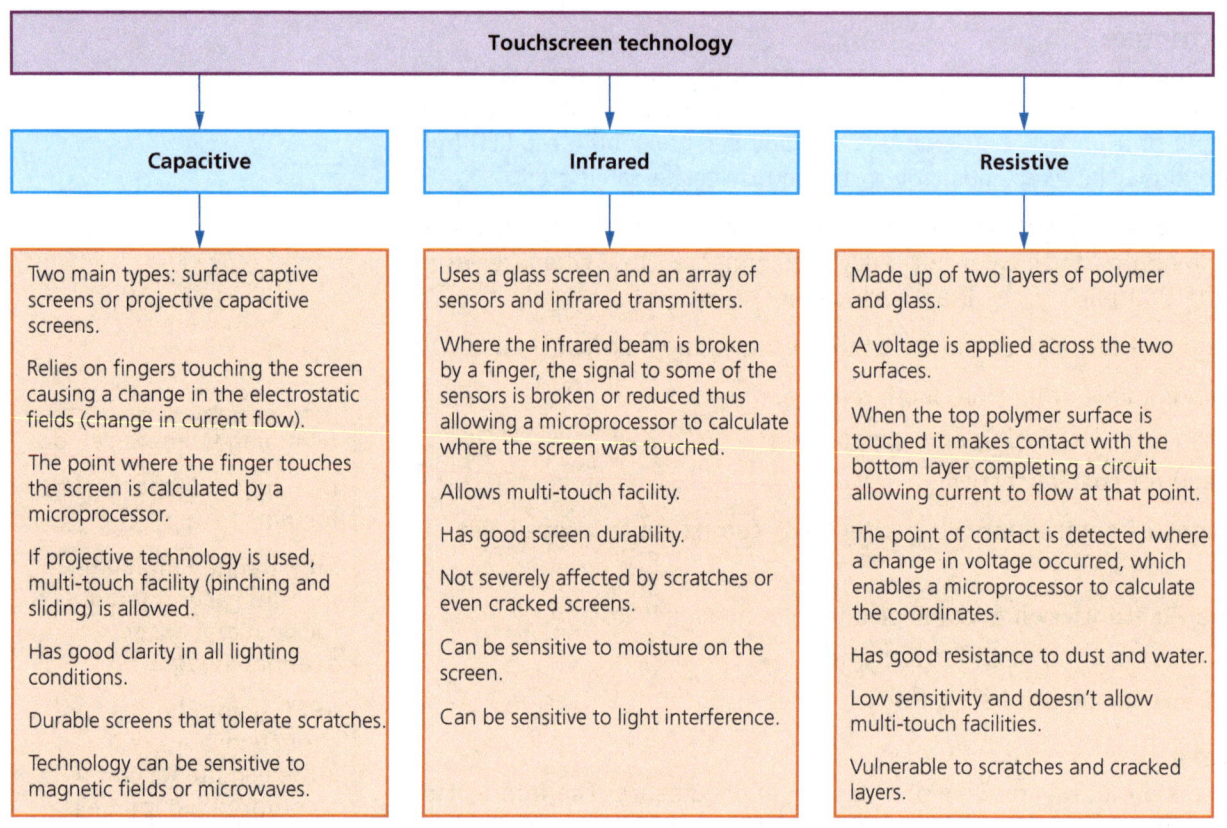

3.2.2 Output devices

Actuators

When a computer or microprocessor is used to control a process (such as a conveyer belt or a valve) it is usually necessary to use an **actuator** to start/stop the conveyor belt or open/close the value. An actuator is a mechanical or electromechanical device, such as a relay, solenoid or motor (see Section 3.2.3).

Light projectors

Light projectors are used to project computer output onto a larger screen or interactive whiteboard; the technology is quite complex since it has to convert a computer's digital output into light which can then be projected. The two most common types are digital light projectors (DLP) or liquid crystal display (LCD) projectors.

3 Hardware

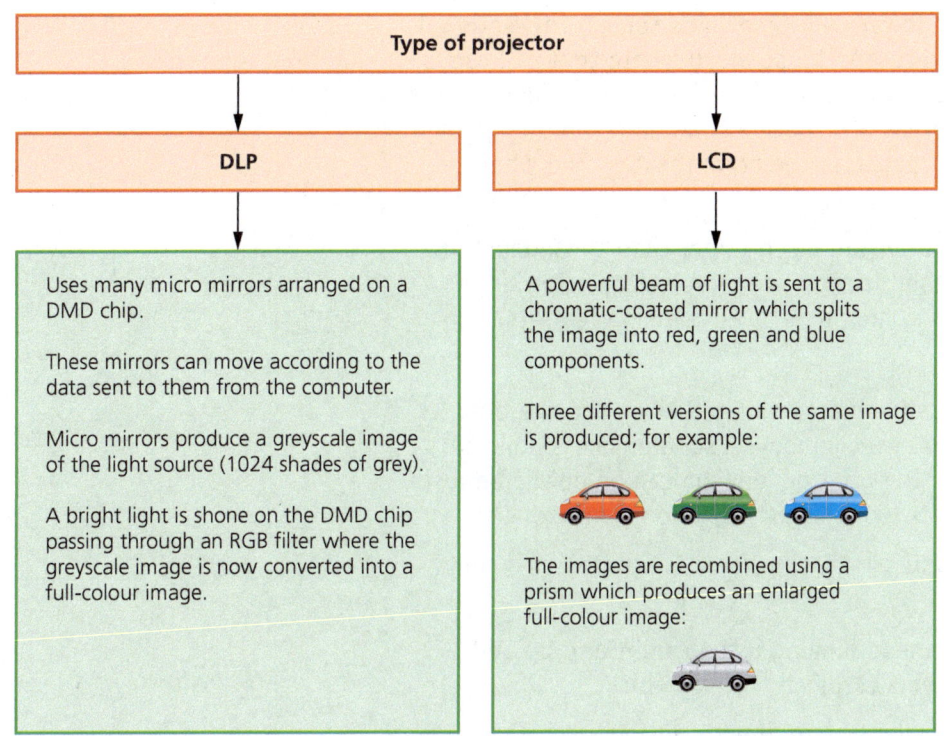

The advantages and disadvantages of the two types of projector are summarised in this table.

Advantages	Disadvantages
Digital light projector (DLP)	
Higher contrast ratios.	Image tends to suffer from 'shadows' when showing a moving image.
Higher reliability/longevity.	
Quieter running than LCD projector.	Does not have grey components in the image.
Uses a single DMD chip which equates to no issues lining up the images.	The colour definition is frequently not as good as LCD projectors (that is, the colour saturation is not as good).
Smaller and lighter than LCD projectors.	
It is better suited to dusty or smoky atmospheres than LCD projectors.	
Liquid crystal display (LCD) projector	
Gives a sharper image than DLP projectors.	Although improving, the contrast ratios are not as good as DLPs.
Has better colour saturation than DLP projectors.	Has a limited life (that is, the longevity is not as good as DLPs).
More efficient in its use of energy than DLP technology – consequently it generates less heat.	Since LCD panels are organic in nature, they tend to degrade with time (screens turn yellow and the colours are subsequently degraded over time).

Printers

There are two common types of printer: **inkjet** and **laser**.

Inkjet printers rely on spraying liquid ink droplets from a reservoir onto paper; they use either **thermal bubble** or **piezoelectric** technology to create the ink bubbles and droplets. Stepper motors move paper up a line at a time and the print head moves across the page left to right.

The inkjet ink cartridges and paper trays are only suitable for relatively small print runs (for example, a one-off photograph or a few pages of high-quality colour printing).

> Some of the latest inkjet printers now use ink reservoirs (instead of ink cartridges) which overcomes the problem of running out of ink during large print runs.

Hodder & Stoughton Limited © David Watson and Helen Williams 2022

Laser printers rely on using dry powder ink (known as toner); this solid ink is melted onto the paper using a fuser. The position where text or images is to be printed is charged negatively on a drum using a laser. Positively charged ink then sticks to the areas of negative charge on the drum which is then transferred to a sheet of paper as the drum rotates. The whole page is produced in one go.

Ink/toner cartridges and paper trays are much larger than those used in inkjet printers; consequently, laser printers are more suitable for large print runs (for example, producing hundreds of advertising leaflets).

3D printers

3D printers are used to produce solid objects that actually work; the printers are based on inkjet and laser printer technology. A solid object is built up from very thin layers of material; the printing medium can be powdered resin, powdered metal, paper or ceramics (but this list is by no means exhaustive).

3D printing is an example of additive printing (that is, an object is built up layer by layer).

Direct 3D printing uses a print head moving left to right and up and down as it builds up the thin layers (typically 0.1 mm thick).

Binder 3D printing works in a similar way to direct printing, except there are two passes of the print head for each layer; the first pass is dry powder and the second pass is a binding agent (which holds the powder layers together).

There are many uses of 3D printing: in medicine (for example, prosthetic limbs and reconstructive surgery), in aerospace to make light-weight parts, fashion and art to create one-off dresses and sculptures (and to make copies of rare paintings which are indistinguishable from the originals) and making parts for items (for example, vintage and veteran cars) which are no longer available.

LED and LCD screens

An LED screen is made up of many tiny light emitting diodes. Each LED is red, green or blue. By varying the electric current to each diode, its brightness is controlled which results in millions of different colours. LED screens are used in large outdoor advertising displays and large scoreboards at sporting events.

> Many televisions are advertised as LED when in fact they are LCD screens backlit with LEDs.

LCD screens are made up of millions of tiny liquid crystals arranged as a matrix (array) of pixels. By varying the electric field to the liquid crystals their properties change. Since LCDs do not produce any light, they need to be backlit with a light source, such as LEDs.

LEDs are used to backlight LCD screens because:

- they reach maximum brightness immediately
- they produce a very white light which gives good colour definition
- they last almost indefinitely and consume very little power.

LCD–LED screens are being replaced with **organic light emitting diodes (OLED)** screens, which generate their own light thus requiring no backlighting.

This is because OLED screens:

- allow very thin screens (2 mm or less in thickness), which means they can be formed into almost any shape
- provides brighter colours than LED backlit LCD screens
- allow for true black, unlike LCD
- consume very little power.

Speakers

Loudspeakers produce sound from varying electric currents. If sound is stored digitally on a computer, it needs to pass through a **digital to analogue converter (DAC)** first to turn the digital signals into an electric current to drive the speakers.

Speakers are made up of a paper/plastic cone, permanent magnet and a coil of wire wrapped around an iron core. Varying electric currents cause the iron core to vibrate; this is connected to the paper/plastic cone which therefore also vibrates producing sound.

3.2.3 Sensors

Sensors are input devices that read physical properties from their surroundings (for example, temperature or light). Sensors constantly send signals to a microprocessor (or computer); they usually pass through an **analogue to digital converter (ADC)** first since computers can only understand binary (digital) data.

If the computer or microprocessor is only monitoring a process, then the sensor data is compared to stored data and a warning sound or screen output is produced to alert the user. Examples include monitoring a patient's vital signs in a hospital, an intruder alarm system, and pollution levels in a river or the atmosphere.

If the computer or microprocessor is controlling a process, then the sensor data is again compared to stored/set data and action is taken if the sensor data indicates the measured parameter is out of range. Signals are then sent out to alter the process until the sensor readings are back in range again (for example, a valve may need to be open, or a heater switched off). This is called feedback. Examples of control include: automatically turn on a car's headlamps when it gets dark, controlling the temperature in a greenhouse or controlling a chemical process (for example, to maintain correct temperature, acidity (pH) or pressure).

Control data from the computer or microprocessor is often sent through a DAC first so that it can operate the actuators.

The following table summarises some common sensors.

Sensor	Description	Example applications
Temperature	Measures temperature of the surroundings by sending signals; these signals will change as the temperature changes.	• control central heating system • control/monitor chemical processes • control/monitor temperature in a greenhouse
Moisture	Measures water levels in, for example, soil (it is based on the electrical resistance of the sample being monitored).	• control/monitor moisture levels in soil • monitor moisture levels in a food processing factory
Humidity	Slightly different to moisture; measures the amount of water vapour in, for example, a sample of air (based on the fact that the conductivity of air will change depending on amount of water present).	• monitor humidity levels in a building • monitor humidity levels in a factory manufacturing microchips • monitor/control humidity levels in the air in a greenhouse
Light	Use photoelectrical cells which produce an output (in the form of an electric current) depending on the brightness of the light.	• switch street lights off or on depending on light levels • switch on car headlights automatically when it gets dark

3.2 Input and output devices

Sensor	Description	Example applications
Infrared (active)	Use an invisible beam of infrared radiation picked up by a detector; if the beam is broken, then there will be a change in the amount of infrared radiation reaching the detector (sensor).	• turn on car windscreen wipers automatically when it detects rain on the windscreen • security alarm system (intruder breaks the infrared beam)
Infrared (passive)	Measure the heat radiation given off by an object; for example the temperature of an intruder or the temperature in a fridge.	• security alarm system (detects body heat) • monitor the temperature inside an industrial freezer or chiller unit
Pressure	A transducer that generates different electric currents depending on the pressure applied.	• weigh lorries at a weigh station • measure the gas pressure in a nuclear reactor
Acoustic/sound	Basically microphones that convert detected sound into electric signals/pulses.	• pick up the noise of footsteps in a security system • detect the sound of liquids dripping at a faulty pipe joint
Gas	Most common ones are oxygen or carbon dioxide sensors; they use various methods to detect the gas being monitored and produce outputs which vary with the oxygen or carbon dioxide levels present.	• monitor pollution levels in the air at an airport • monitor oxygen and carbon dioxide levels in a greenhouse • monitor oxygen levels in a car exhaust
pH	Measure change in voltages in, for example, soil depending on how acidic the soil is.	• monitor/control acidity levels in soil • control acidity levels in a chemical process
Magnetic field	Measure changes in magnetic fields – the signal output will depend on how the magnetic field changes.	• detect magnetic field changes (for example, in mobile phones and CD players) • anti-lock braking systems in cars
Accelerometer	Measure acceleration and motion of an application, that is, the change in velocity (a piezoelectric cell is used whose output varies according the change in velocity).	• measure rapid deceleration in cars, and apply airbags in a crash • change between portrait and landscape mode in mobile phones
Proximity	Detect the presence of a nearby object.	• detect when a face is close to a mobile phone screen and switch off screen when held to the ear
Flow (rate)	Measure the flow rate of a moving liquid or gas and produce an output based on the amount of liquid or gas passing over the sensor.	• in respiratory devices and inhalers in hospitals • measure gas flows in pipes (for example, natural gas)
Level	Use ultrasonics (to detect changing levels in, for example, a tank) or capacitance/conductivity to measure static levels (for example, height of water in a river) – note level sensors can also be optical or mechanical in nature.	• monitor levels in a petrol tank in a car • in a pharmaceutical process where powder levels in tablet production need to be monitored • leak detection in refrigerant (air conditioning)

Sample questions and answers

REVISED

a) Explain the term **sensor**. [2]
b) Describe an application that uses magnetic field sensors. [3]
c) A chemical process only works correctly if the temperature is above 70 °C and the pH is below 3.5. Sensors are used as part of the control process. A heating element is used to heat the reaction if necessary and valves are opened or closed to add acid to maintain the reaction pH.
Describe how sensors, actuators and a microprocessor are used to control the conditions in this chemical process. [5]

3 Hardware

> **Tips**
>
> In part a), a simple definition is required with some expansion for the second mark. Part b) requires the description of a sensor application. You are not asked to explain how the sensor works, simply the application it refers to. Part c) is also a description. However, this time you are asked to explain the interaction between sensors, actuators and a microprocessor. If at all possible, it is worth drawing a simple diagram of the process which will help in your description.

Sample high-level answer

a) A sensor is an input device that measures physical properties from the environment.

b) An application of magnetic field sensors is in anti-lock brakes used in vehicles (ABS). When a wheel locks up, this is detected by the microprocessor (which is constantly monitoring the sensor readings). The rotational speed of each wheel is carefully controlled by applying braking force wherever necessary to prevent locking up. The driver feels a judder through the brake pedal as brakes are rapidly applied and released.

c) The following diagram of the process will help in the description that follows.

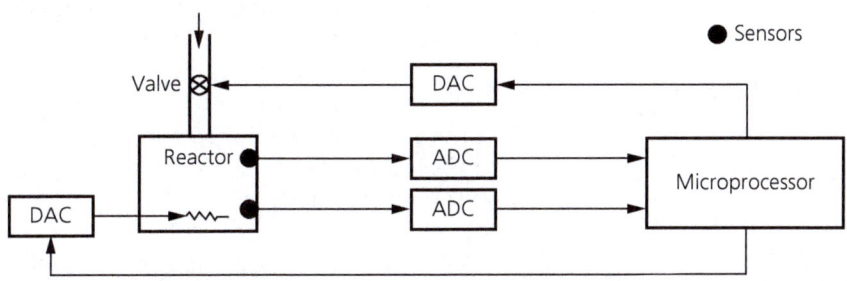

- Temperature and pH sensors constantly collect data and send it to the microprocessor (via an ADC).
- The microprocessor compares incoming data with pre-set data values stored in memory.
- If the temperature < 70 °C then a signal is sent to the heater from the microprocessor (a DAC may be needed) to switch on.
- If pH > 3.5 then the microprocessor sends a signal to open the valve (a DAC may be needed) to add acid.

Sample low-level answer

a) A sensor is an input device.

b) Magnetic sensors can measure position sensing and angular sensing; for these reasons, these sensors are used in mobile phones and gaming controllers. When used in these devices they can estimate the orientation of the device (for example, control of a screen character in a game by rotating or twisting the controller).

c) The system uses temperature and pH sensors. When the temperature or pH changes, the sensors send signals to the microprocessor. The sensors control the actuators which are used to switch on a heater or open a valve to add acid.

Teacher's comments

The first set of answers is very clear and concise for all three parts. The use of a diagram of the control system is particularly helpful in the explanation of how sensors, actuators and a microprocessor interact. In part b), the candidate has given a 'what' (ABS), a 'why' (to detect when wheels lock up) and a 'how' (applies brake force and alleviates brake force as necessary).

The second answer is a very brief answer for part a), but gains a mark for input device. Part b) is interesting as it is a very good example of the use of magnetic sensors (mobile phones and gaming controllers). The description is short but clear including a 'what' (used in gaming controller), a 'why' (to measure orientation of the device) and 'how' (by measuring twisting and rotational movement). Full marks would be gained. Part c) was not well answered. One mark for naming sensors and the data is sent to a microprocessor. But there is the very common error of stating sensors only send data when they detect a change in conditions – this is incorrect, since sensors constantly send data to the microprocessor. They also incorrectly claim that the sensors control the process. Only one mark would be awarded for the whole part.

Exam-style questions

4 A pharmaceutical company uses synthetic gloves to protect scientists when carrying out work in a glovebox. The gloves used have a limited operational life (a 'use by' date) and must be regularly checked and changed if necessary. As part of the monitoring system, each glove has a unique barcode stamped on it which contains the part number (0123111) and use by date (22/10/2025):

012311122102025

   a) Describe how the barcode is read and how it could be used to indicate whether the glove needs to be changed. [3]

   b) The barcode has the number 012311122102025.
Modulo-11 is used to generate a check digit. Calculate the check digit for this barcode, showing all your working. [3]

   c) Give **two** advantages to the site managers of using barcodes to track the age of gloves. [2]

   d) To improve the system further, the managers are considering the introduction of QR codes to replace barcodes.
      i) Describe the differences between the methods used to read barcodes and to read QR codes. [2]
      ii) Suggest additional information the QR could hold. Give a reason for your answer. [2]
      iii) Give **one** disadvantage of using QR codes. [1]

5 Mobile phones use touchscreen technology.
   a) Name **one** type of touchscreen technology.
   b) Describe the advantages and disadvantages of the touchscreen technology named in part a). [5]

6 Name a suitable output device for each of the following applications.
   a) Produce a working model of a new toy during its development stages.
   b) Advertising a new product on a billboard on the approach road to a large city. The billboard will show moving images.
   c) Very thin screen which can be attached to a curved tunnel wall at a Metro station. The screen will show an animated advertising display.
   d) Projection of a computer image onto a large screen to be shown to a large audience.
   e) Production of 10 000 high quality colour flyers to advertise a new product.
   f) Production of a one-off calendar using 12 photos from a user's photo library. The calendar will be printed on semi-gloss photographic paper.
   g) Computerised control of a water valve in an industrial process. Opening and closing of the valve is under computer control.
   h) Output device that allows a partially-sighted person to check if a word processed document has been entered correctly. [8]

7 a) Explain the difference between **monitoring** and **control**. [2]
   b) An apartment has an air conditioning system which is controlled by sensors and a microprocessor. The temperature and humidity levels are constantly measured and, if either fall outside a set range, the air conditioning unit is switched on.
Name suitable sensors for this application. Describe how sensors, actuators and a microprocessor interact to control the air conditioning unit. You may wish to draw a diagram of your system. [5]

3.3 Data storage

REVISED

Memory and storage can be split into two groups:

- primary memory
- secondary storage.

Random access memory (**RAM**) and read-only memory (**ROM**) are usually referred to as primary memory. Both memories are fairly small and relatively expensive per GiB, so it is necessary to also have secondary storage (see later).

- ROM chips are typically 4 to 8 MiB in size.
- RAM chips are typically 1 to 256 GiB in size.
- Secondary storage is typically 2 TiB or larger.

Unlike secondary storage, primary memory is directly addressable by the CPU. If data on secondary storage is needed by the CPU, it must first be loaded into RAM before the CPU can use the data.

Secondary storage devices can be external or internal to the computer.

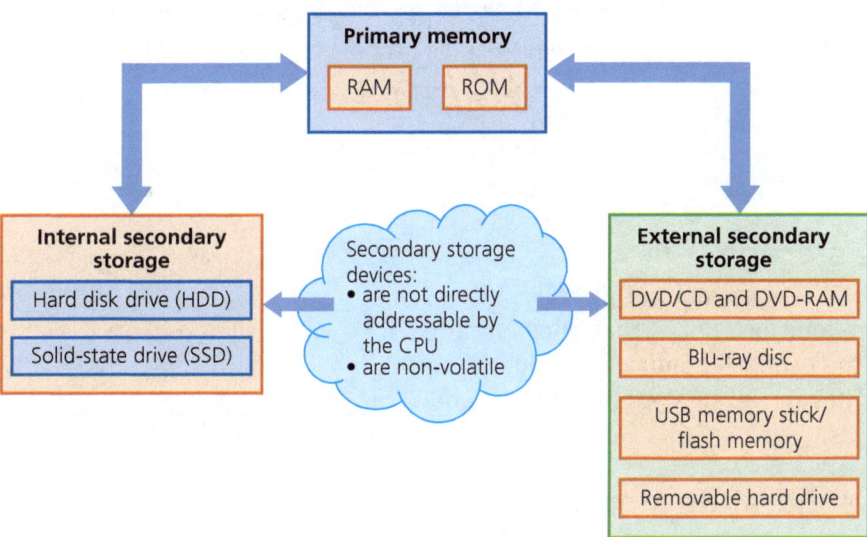

3.3.1 Primary memory

The following diagram shows how primary memory is split into RAM and ROM and the two types of RAM commonly used. The cache memory is also shown; this is an extension to primary memory. Cache is high speed RAM that holds a copy of only the most frequently used data or instructions – cache is first checked when the CPU wants to access data/instructions from the primary memory.

> The larger the RAM the faster the CPU will operate; as RAM becomes 'full', the CPU has to continually access secondary storage to overwrite old data on RAM with new data – increasing RAM size reduces this requirement making the CPU more efficient.

Computers need both RAM and ROM. RAM is the working area of the computer where data currently being used is temporarily stored; ROM contains data that can't be changed and needs to be stored permanently (for example, start-up routines).

The following table summarises the differences between RAM and ROM.

RAM	ROM
Temporary memory device.	Permanent memory device.
Volatile memory.	Non-volatile memory device.
Can be written to and read from.	Data stored cannot be altered.
Used to store data, files, programs, part of operating system (OS) currently in use.	Always used to store BIOS and other data needed at start-up.
Can be increased in size to improve operational speed of a computer.	

RAM can be two types: dynamic RAM (DRAM) or static RAM (SRAM).

DRAM	SRAM
Consists of a number of transistors and capacitors.	Uses **flip flops** to hold each bit of memory.
Needs to be constantly refreshed.	Doesn't need to be constantly **refreshed**.
Less expensive to manufacture than SRAM.	Has a faster data access time than DRAM.
Has a higher memory capacity than SRAM.	CPU memory cache makes use of SRAM.
Main memory is constructed from DRAM.	
Consumes less power than SRAM.	

3.3.2 Secondary and offline storage

Secondary storage includes storage devices that are not directly addressable by the CPU. They are non-volatile devices that allow data to be stored for as long as required by the user. All applications, operating system, devices drivers and general files (for example, photographs and music) are stored on secondary devices.

3.3.3 Magnetic, optical and solid-state storage

There are three common technologies used in secondary storage devices: magnetic, solid state and optical.

Magnetic storage devices

The most common example of magnetic storage is the **hard disk drive (HDD)**. HDDs can be fixed or **removable**.

Data is stored on platters that are made from aluminium, glass or ceramic and each surface is coated in a magnetisable material. The platters spin at about 7000 times per second and read/write (electromagnetic) heads float a fraction of a millimetre above the surface; these heads permit writing and reading of data. Disk drives can have several platters; both sides of the platter are used and each surface has its own read/write head.

Blocks of data are stored in sectors and tracks. The read/write heads are constantly moving in and out to find blocks of data; the time it takes to find and access the required data block is known as **latency**. Once the sector containing the required data block is found, the data in a sector is read sequentially (in order); however, actual data access is direct.

After a lot of use, data on an HDD can suffer from **fragmentation**, which can seriously affect the performance of the storage device.

Solid-state storage devices

Solid-state drives (SSDs) are rapidly replacing HDDs as the main secondary storage. SSDs operate by controlling the movement of electrons within NAND or NOR chips. The data is stored as 0s or 1s in millions of tiny transistors. At each junction in a solid-state NAND matrix, there is one transistor called a floating gate and another called a control gate; this forms a non-volatile rewritable memory store.

When a voltage is applied to the control gate, electrons from an electron source are attracted to it. The control gate is coated in a dielectric material causing electrons to be trapped in the floating gate which gives control of the bit value stored at each junction.

Memory sticks, **flash memories**, SD cards and SSDs all use solid-state technology. Memory sticks are primarily used to store data that can be transferred between computers or for backing up files, such as photographs. Flash memory is a general term for devices that use solid-state technology; they are used in mobile phones and tablets as a form of storage. SD cards are used primarily to store data on digital cameras, but can also be used to expand the storage capacity of mobile phones, dashcams or drones (dashcams and drones use micro SD cards – these are about half the size of a normal SD card).

SSDs have the following benefits and drawbacks compared to HDD; the benefits indicate why SSD is gradually replacing HDD in all computer applications.

Benefits of SSDs compared to HDDs	Drawbacks of SSDs compared to HDDs
<ul><li>More reliable (no moving parts).</li><li>Much lighter weight.</li><li>No need to 'get up to speed' before data access.</li><li>Less power consumption.</li><li>Run much cooler.</li><li>Very thin due to solid-state technology.</li><li>Much faster data access.</li></ul>	<ul><li>Longevity (**SSD endurance**) is still an issue (but this situation continues to improve).</li><li>The memory chips in a solid-state storage device have a limited number of write cycles – this can lead to unrecoverable data loss.</li><li>If the controller chip, memory cache, or one of the NAND memory chips has been damaged, it may be impossible to recover the data.</li></ul>

Optical media

CDs and **DVDs** are **optical storage** devices that use red laser light to read and write data on the disk surface. The surface of the optical disk is coated in a special light alloy or light-sensitive dye – the coating is sensitive to red laser light. CDs and DVDs have one spiral track and data is stored in pits and lands, which can be read by an optical head. DVDs often use **dual-layering** to increase capacity.

Blu-ray discs use blue laser light to read and write data. Since the wavelength of blue light is much shorter than the wavelength of red light, this increases the storage capacity of Blu-ray discs, making Blu-ray suitable for 4K high-definition movies. Blu-ray discs have built-in encryption and a much faster data transfer rate than DVDs. They can also automatically search for empty space on the disk surface, preventing over-recording. Blu-ray discs allow for greater interactivity than DVDs.

> The most common use of DVDs and Blu-ray discs is to supply movies or games. As televisions move to 4K and 8K, Blu-ray becomes the only media large enough to store a movie.

The following table summarises the difference between optical media.

(Note: nm = 10^{-9} m and μm = 10^{-6} m):

Disk type	Laser colour	Wavelength of laser light, in nm	Disk construction	Track pitch (distance between tracks, in μm)
CD	red	780	single 1.2 mm polycarbonate layer	1.60
DVD (dual-layer)	red	650	two 0.6 mm polycarbonate layers	0.74
Blu-ray (single layer)	blue	405	single 1.2 mm polycarbonate layer	0.30
Blu-ray (dual-layer)	blue	405	two 0.6 mm polycarbonate layers	0.30

3.3.4 Virtual memory

If the amount of RAM available is exceeded due to multiple programs running at the same time (and competing for available memory), then **virtual memory** can help resolve this issue. RAM is known as the physical memory and virtual memory is the RAM plus swap space (which is allocated storage space on an HDD or SSD).

New data is loaded into RAM from the HDD/SSD whenever required and 'old' data is moved out to HDD/SSD as and when required. Memory mapping is used to keep track of where data is. Part of memory mapping is called **paging**, which is used by memory management to store and retrieve data (a **page** is a fixed length **contiguous** block of data utilised in virtual memory systems).

Virtual memory gives the illusion of unlimited RAM; even when RAM is 'full', pages of data can be moved to and from HDD/SSD to give the illusion that RAM is always available.

Benefits of virtual memory

- With virtual memory, programs can be larger than physical RAM and still be executed.
- Virtual memory reduces the need to buy and install extra RAM (which is expensive).

If a hard disk drive is being used with virtual memory, **disk thrashing** can become an issue since pages are being constantly moved to and from HDD. This causes so many head movements to be made that a **thrash point** can be reached (the thrash point is when the system is so busy moving data to and from HDD that very little actual execution is done). SSDs aren't affected in the same way since they have no moving parts.

3.3.5 Cloud storage

Cloud storage is the storing of vast quantities of data on remote physical servers. Some of the larger cloud providers use server capacities in excess of 1 exbibyte (2^{60} or 1.2×10^{18} bytes). There are three types of cloud storage.

- Public cloud – the client and cloud storage provider are different companies.
- Private cloud – a dedicated system behind a firewall where the client and storage provider operate as a single entity.
- Hybrid cloud – a combination of public and private cloud provider where the most sensitive data is stored on the private cloud.

When using cloud storage, the same data is stored on more than one server in case of maintenance/repair – this is called **data redundancy**.

The benefits and drawbacks of cloud storage are considered in this table.

Benefits of cloud storage	Drawbacks of cloud storage
• Customer/client files stored on the cloud can be accessed at any time from any device anywhere in the world provided internet access is available. • There is no need for a customer/client to carry an external storage device with them, or even use the same computer to store and retrieve information. • The cloud provides the user with remote **back-up** of data with obvious benefits to alleviate data loss/disaster recovery. • If a customer/client has a failure of their hard disk or back-up device, cloud storage will allow recovery of their data. • The cloud system offers almost unlimited storage capacity.	• If the customer/client has a slow or unstable internet connection, they would have many problems accessing or downloading their data/files. • Costs can be high if large storage capacity is required; it can also be expensive to pay for high download/upload data transfer limits with the customer/client internet service provider (ISP). • The potential failure of the cloud storage company is always possible – this poses a risk of loss of all back-up data. • Data security issues – how safely stored and protected is the data from hacking, natural disasters and malware?

Sample question and answer

REVISED

Use the following words to complete the paragraph that follows. Each word may be used once, more than once or not at all.

bit value	intersection	NAND
control gate	lasers	negative
electrons	leak away	positive
floating gate	matrix	transistor
insulator	moving parts	volatile

Solid-state devices control the movement of < .... > within a < .... > chip.

The device is made up of a < .... > and at each < .... > there is a < .... > and a < .... > transistor.

< .... > are attracted towards the < .... > when a voltage is applied.

This gives control over the < .... > stored at each intersection.

After 12 months, the charge can < .... > which means the device needs to be used at least once a year.

One of the main advantages of solid-state devices is there are no < .... > to wear out. [6]

> ### Tips
> These type of questions need to be tackled very carefully since some of the words in the list are intended to throw you off the track. Read the paragraph very carefully and then read it again and try to fit in your own answers then check your answers against those in the given list, filling in any gaps. Any differences between your answers and those given in the list need to be carefully reconsidered. Remember some of the words can be used more than once or even not at all.

Sample high-level answer

(gaps filled using these words, in this order):

electrons; NAND; matrix; intersection; floating gate; control gate; electrons; control gate; bit value; leak away; moving parts

Sample low-level answer

(gaps filled using these words, in this order):

electrons; volatile; matrix; intersection; NAND; volatile; electrons; positive; electrons; leak away; moving parts

Teacher's comments

The first answer shows a clear understanding of how solid-state memories work and used clear logic to determine the missing words/phrases. The second answer has clearly made a guess at several of the answers and only got half of them right. But they were correct in their strategy by at least making an attempt at each part of the question.

Exam-style questions

8 Six statements are shown on the left, and six computer terms are shown on the right.
By drawing lines, connect each statement to the correct term. [5]

Statement	Term
Refers to RAM and ROM	Secondary storage
Made up of many tiny transistors in a matrix; has a control gate and floating gate at each intersection	Solid-state memory
Frequent moving of the read-write heads on a HDD during read-write operations can lead to this	Primary memory
Memory/storage not directly addressable by the CPU	Virtual memory
Contains a physical memory and a swap space on HDD or SSD	Cloud storage
Remote servers where clients/customers can store their data so it can be accessed from anywhere	Thrashing

9 **a)** Describe the main differences between RAM and ROM. [3]
   b) Discuss the advantages and disadvantages of increasing the size of RAM in a computer. [3]
   c) Describe the differences between DVDs and Blu-ray discs. [3]

10 A firm of architects has decided to store client drawings on the cloud thus enabling clients and architects to access the drawings (and other data) whenever they want.
   a) Which type of cloud storage would be most appropriate in this application?
      Explain your choice. [2]
   b) **i)** Give **two** advantages to the architects of using cloud storage.
      ii) Give **one** disadvantage to the architects of using cloud storage. [3]
   c) The architect's firm have 500 TiB of cloud storage. Some of the drawings are over 50 GiB in size.
      Describe any possible issues that might arise from the size of the stored files. [2]

3.4 Network hardware

REVISED

3.4.1 Network interface cards

A **network interface card (NIC)** is needed to allow a device to connect to a network (for example, the internet). The NIC contains the **Media Access Control (MAC) address**, generated at the manufacturing stage. Wireless NICs (WNICs) can also be used; these plug into the USB port or can be part of an internal integrated circuit.

3.4.2 Media Access Control addresses

MAC addresses identify a device connected to a network. They are made up of 48 bits written in groups of six hex digits.

NN — NN — NN — DD — DD — DD
manufacturer's code / device serial number

MAC addresses can be Universally Administered MAC addresses (UAAs) set at the manufacturing stage, or they can be altered by the user as Locally Administered MAC Addresses (LAAs) – these can be reset by the user if all devices on a network need a certain MAC format.

3.4.3 Internet Protocol addresses

When a device connects to a network, a router assigns the device an Internet Protocol (IP) address, via a **Dynamic Host Configuration Protocol (DHCP)** server, which is unique to that network. There are two versions of IP address:

- IPv4 (32-bit address with the format A.B.C.D where A, B, C and D can take the values 1 to 255; for example, 215.180.1.80)
- IPv6 (128-bit address with the format eight groups of four hex digits; for example, A8FB:7A88:FFF0:0FFF:3D21:2085:66FB:F0FA).

IPv6 removes the risk of IP address collisions and allows for more efficient packet switching; IPv6 also has built-in authentication checks.

IP addresses can be **static** or **dynamic**. The following table compares static and dynamic IP addresses.

Dynamic IP address	Static IP address
Changes every time a device connects to a network.	Permanently assigned.
Greater privacy since it changes each time a user logs on.	Since static IP addresses don't change, it allows each device to be fully traceable.
Dynamic IP addresses can be an issue when using, for example, Voice over Internet Protocol (VoIP) since this type of addressing is less reliable as it can disconnect and change the IP address causing the VoIP connection to fail.	Allows for faster upload and download speeds.
	More expensive to maintain since the device must be constantly running so that information is always available.

The following table summarises the differences between a MAC address and an IP address.

MAC address	IP address
Identifies the physical address of a device on the network.	Identifies the global address on the internet.
Unique for device on the network	May not be unique.
Assigned by the manufacturer of the device and is part of the NIC.	Dynamic IP address is assigned by the ISP using DHCP each time the device connects to the Internet (see later).
Can be universal or local.	Dynamic IP addresses change every time a device connects to the internet; static IP addresses don't change.
When a packet of data is sent and received, the MAC address is used to identify the sender's and recipient's devices.	Used in routing operations as it specifically identifies where the device is connected to the internet.
Uses 48 bits.	Uses either 32 bits (IPv4) or 128 bits (IPv6).
Can be UAA or LAA.	Can be static or dynamic.

3.4.4 Routers

Routers enable **data packets** to be routed between different networks, for example a local area network (LAN) to a wide area network (WAN). Routers take data transmitted in one format (protocol) from network 'A' and convert the data to another format (protocol) that network 'B' understands. This allows communication between networks to take place.

Routers inspect data packets sent to it from another device or network. Every device on the same network has the same part of an IP address (for example, 215.164.10.XX) so the router can send data packets to an appropriate **switch**. The switch then directs the data packet to the correct device on the network.

Sample question and answer

REVISED

Explain the different function of a MAC address and an IP address of a device connected to the internet. Also include any similarities in the two types of addressing. [4]

> **Sample high-level answer**
>
> A MAC address identifies the physical address of a device on the internet, whereas the IP address identifies the device's global address on the internet.
>
> MAC addresses are unique for each device; however, IP addresses are not necessarily unique since all devices on a network share the same part of an IP address.
>
> MAC addresses can be set by the manufacturer but can also be changed by the user; IP addresses can also be dynamic or static (an IP address is usually assigned by the DHCP server).
>
> MAC addresses are used to identify a data packet's sender and recipient; IP addresses are used in routing operations as they specifically identify where the device is connected to the internet.

> **Sample low-level answer**
>
> MAC addresses are used to identify a device on a network. An IP address is used to identify the location of a device. Both MAC and IP addresses are set at the factory and can't be changed.

Tips

Since this is an 'explain' question, and it refers to differences, some comparison of features is expected. Avoid giving opposites (for example, IP addresses are global, but MAC addresses aren't global) since it is necessary to explain what the difference is (for example, MAC addresses can be local or universal). If you can think of any similarities these should be included as well, but you could gain all four marks for describing the differences.

Teacher's comments

The first answer covers four distinct points and would gain the maximum mark available. The second answer is a little too brief, but would probably still gain two marks for the statements that MAC addresses identify a device and IP addresses indicate the location of a device. The second point starts off partially correct but then the candidate makes an incorrect statement – both IP and MAC addresses can be changed and the IP address isn't set at the factory during manufacture.

> **Exam-style questions**
>
> 11 Five descriptions of network terms are given below. In each case, name the network term being described.
>   a) Hardware component (on a circuit board) or chip that allows a device to connect to a network, such as the internet.
>   b) Unique identifier that acts as a network address for a device; takes the form NN-NN-NN-DD-DD-DD.
>   c) Server that automatically provides and assigns an IP address to a device when it first connects to the internet.
>   d) Device that allows data packets to be moved between different networks.
>   e) Address given to a device so that its global position on a network is known. [5]

4 Software

Key objectives

The objectives of this chapter are to revise:
- types of software and interrupts:
  - system software and application software
  - role and function of operating systems
  - need for hardware, firmware and operating systems when running apps
  - role and operation of interrupts
- types of programming language, translators and integrated development environments (IDEs):
  - advantages and disadvantages of high-level languages and low-level languages
  - assembly languages
  - advantages and disadvantages of compilers and interpreters
  - role and function of IDEs when writing programming code

4.1 Types of software and interrupts

REVISED

4.1.1 System software and application software

All computer systems are made up of hardware, system software and application software.

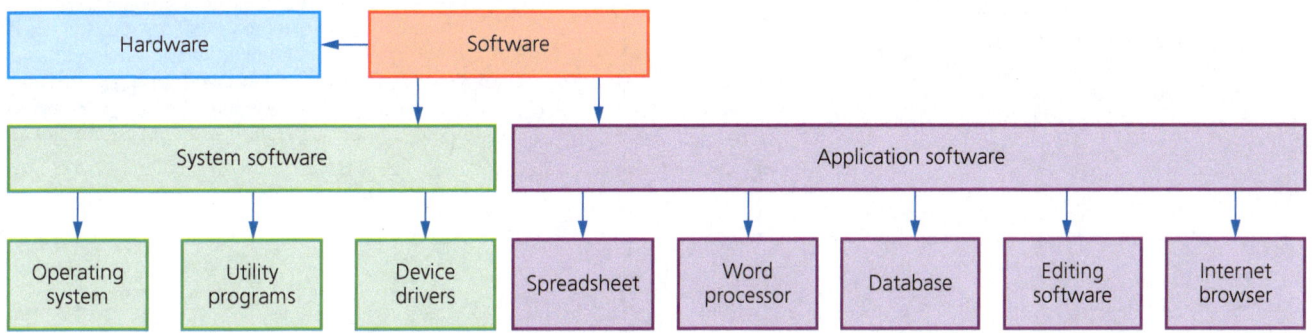

The following table summarises the features of system software and applications software together with the reasons why both types of software exist.

General features of system software	General features of application software
• Controls and manages the operation of the computer hardware. • Provides a platform on which all software can run properly. • Provides a human computer interface (HCI). • Controls the allocation and usage of resources (software and hardware).	• Used to perform various tasks on a computer. • Allows the user to perform specific tasks on a computer. • Meets the requirements of the user.

Application software allows various tasks to be performed on a computer using applications (apps). The software can be a single program or a suite of programs. The user simply needs to open the software from the main screen as and when required. The following diagram summarises the typical application software found on computers.

Hodder & Stoughton Limited © David Watson and Helen Williams 2022

4.1 Types of software and interrupts

Application Software
These are programs that allow the user to do specific tasks

WORD PROCESSOR:
Word processing software is used to manipulate a text document, such as an essay or a report. Text is entered using a keyboard and the software provides tools for copying, deleting and various types of formatting. Some of the functions of word processing software include:
- creating, editing, saving and manipulating text
- copy and paste functions
- spell checkers and thesaurus
- import photos/images into a structured page format
- translation into a foreign language.

SPREADSHEET:
Spreadsheet software is used to organise and manipulate numerical data (in the form of integer, real, date and so on). Numbers are organised on a grid of lettered columns and numbered rows. The grid itself is made up of cells, and each cell is identified using a unique combination of columns and rows, for example, B6. Some of the functions of spreadsheets include:
- use of formulas to carry out calculations
- ability to produce graphs
- ability to do modelling and 'what if' calculations.

DATABASE:
Database software is used to organise, manipulate and analyse data. A typical database is made up of one or more tables. Tables consist of rows and columns. Each row is called a 'record' and each column is called a 'field'. This provides the basic structure for the organisation of the data within the database. Some of the functions include:
- ability to carry out queries on database data and produce a report
- add, delete and modify data in a table.

CONTROL AND MEASURING SOFTWARE:
Control and measuring software is designed to allow a computer or microprocessor to interface with sensors so that it is possible to:
- measure physical quantities in the real world (such as temperatures)
- control applications (such as a chemical process) by comparing sensor data with stored data and sending out signals to alter process parameters (e.g. open a valve to add acid and change the pH).

APPS:
Apps is short for applications – a type of software. They normally refer to software which runs on mobile phones or tablets. They are normally downloaded from an 'app store' and range from games to sophisticated software such as phone banking. Common examples of apps include:
- video and music streaming
- GPS (global positioning systems – help you find your way to a chosen location)
- camera facility (taking photos and storing/manipulating the images taken).

PHOTO EDITING SOFTWARE:
Photo editing software allows a user to manipulate digital photographs stored on a computer, for example, change brightness, change contrast, alter colour saturation or remove 'red eye'. They also allow for very complex manipulation of photos (e.g. change the features of a face, combine photos, alter the images to give interesting effects and so on). They allow a photographer to remove unwanted items and generally 'touch up' a photo to make it as perfect as possible.

VIDEO EDITING SOFTWARE:
Video editing software is the ability to manipulate videos to produce a new video. It enables the addition of titles, colour correction and altering/adding sound to the original video. Essentially it includes:
- rearranging, adding and/or removing sections of video clips and/or audio clips
- applying colour correction, filters and other video enhancements
- creating transitions between clips in the video footage.

GRAPHICS MANIPULATION SOFTWARE:
Graphics manipulation software allows bitmap and vector images to be changed. Bitmap images are made up of pixels which contain information about image brightness and colour. Bitmap graphics editors can change the pixels to produce a different image. Vector graphic editors operate in a different way and don't use pixels – instead they manipulate lines, curves and text to alter the stored image as required. Both types of editing software might be chosen depending on the format of the original image.

4 Software

The following diagram summarises the typical system software found on computers.

COMPILERS:
A compiler is a computer program that translates a program written in a high-level language (HLL) into machine code (code which is understood by the computer) so that it can be directly used by a computer to perform a required task. The original program is called the *source code* and the code after compilation is called the *object code*. Once a program is compiled, the machine code can be used again and again to perform the same task without re-compilation. Examples of high-level languages include: Java, Python, Visual Basic, Fortran, C++ and Algol.

LINKERS:
A linker (or link editor) is a computer program that takes one or more object files produced by a compiler and combines them into a single program which can be run on a computer. For example, many programming languages allow programmers to write different pieces of code, called modules, separately. This simplifies the programming task since it allows the program to be broken up into small, more manageable sub-tasks. However, at some point, it will be necessary to put all the modules together to form the final program. This is the job of the linker.

DEVICE DRIVERS:
A device driver is the name given to software that enables one or more hardware devices to communicate with the computer's operating system. Without drivers, a hardware device (for example, a computer printer) would be unable to work with the computer. All hardware devices connected to a computer have associated drivers. As soon as a device is plugged into the USB port of a computer, the operating system looks for the appropriate driver. An error message will be produced if it can't be found. Examples of drivers include: printers, memory sticks, mouse, CD drivers and so on.

OPERATING SYSTEMS (OSs):
The operating system (OS) is essentially software running in the background of a computer system. It manages many of the basic functions. Without the OS, most computers would be very user-unfriendly and the majority of users would find it almost impossible to work with computers on a day-to-day basis.
For example, operating systems allow:
- input/output operations
- users to communicate with the computer (e.g. *Windows*)
- error handling to take place
- the loading and running of programs to occur
- managing of security (e.g. user accounts, login passwords).

System Software
These are programs that allow the hardware to run properly and allow the user to communicate with the computer

UTILITIES:
Utility programs are software that are designed to carry out specific tasks on a computer. Essentially, they are programs that help to manage, maintain and control computer resources. Examples include:
- antivirus (virus checkers)
- anti-spyware
- back-up of files
- disk repair and analysis
- file management and compression
- security
- screensavers
- disk defragmenter/defragmentation software.

4.1 Types of software and interrupts

Utility programs
Utility software (utilities) provides a number of useful programs to protect the computer and the user and also give the user software tools to carry out some of the day-to-day maintenance.

Virus checker
A small program that replicates itself and can delete or modify important files. Antivirus software looks for **malware** 'clues' or recognises it from a database of known viruses. Virus checkers run in the background and need to be regularly updated. They make use of **heuristic checking** (this looks for software behaviour that could indicate a possible virus). Once an infected files is discovered it is **quarantined** and then deleted.

Defragmenter
Defragmentation software tidies up the hard disk drive as it begins to reach its maximum capacity. A **disk defragmenter** works by rearranging blocks of data (by removing space left from the earlier deletion of data) so that they can now become **contiguous** (rather than randomly stored across various sectors). This frees up disk space and also makes location of data a faster process.

Disk repair
Disk repair software verifies if an error has been found in the disk directory; it will then attempt to correct the error if possible. The repair process will remove or bypass damaged/corrupted data/disk sectors and then link blocks of data together to allow files to be read (some data may be lost in the process).

File compression
File compression can either be lossy or lossless. With lossy file compression, the original file cannot be reconstructed following the compression process. With lossless file compression, the original file can once again be reconstructed. Lossy file sizes are much smaller than lossless files.

Utility programs
Software tools that allow the user and computer to do specific tasks to maintain the computer

Back-up software
Back-up files are essential in case files/data become corrupted or lost and are needed to recover the data. They are either done automatically or initiated by the user. Many OS offer the ability to restore a computer status to a point in the past using backed up data.

Security
The security system manages access control to a computer. It links into other software such as virus checkers and firewalls, and uses a firewall to protect the computer when automatic software updates are requested. It makes use of encryption to safeguard data.

Device drivers
Device driver is the name given to software that enables one or more hardware devices to communicate with a computer's operating system. All hardware devices connected to computers have an associated device driver. As soon as the device is plugged into one of the USB ports, the OS looks up the appropriate driver or the user will be instructed to download an appropriate driver from the internet (or from an accompanying DVD). All USB device drivers contain information known as **descriptors** (these include vendor ID, product ID and unique serial number). If a device has no serial number (one of the required descriptors), the OS will treat it as a new device every time it is plugged into the computer.

Screensavers
Screensavers are moving or still images on a computer screen that are initiated after a period of inactivity. They are part of the security system since screensavers automatically log out a user if they have left the computer unlocked and there has been no activity for, for example, 5 minutes; the user then needs to log back in. They are often used to activate background tasks, such as virus scans, when initiated.

4.1.2 Operating systems
To enable a computer system to function correctly and allow users to communicate with the computer, system software known as an **operating system** is used. Operating systems provide both the environment in which applications (apps) can be run and enable a human computer interface to function in a non-complex way. They disguise the complexity of software and hardware. Operating systems ensure there is a platform for running all applications in a safe and secure manner.

The operating system operates in the background carrying out tasks such as those shown in this diagram.

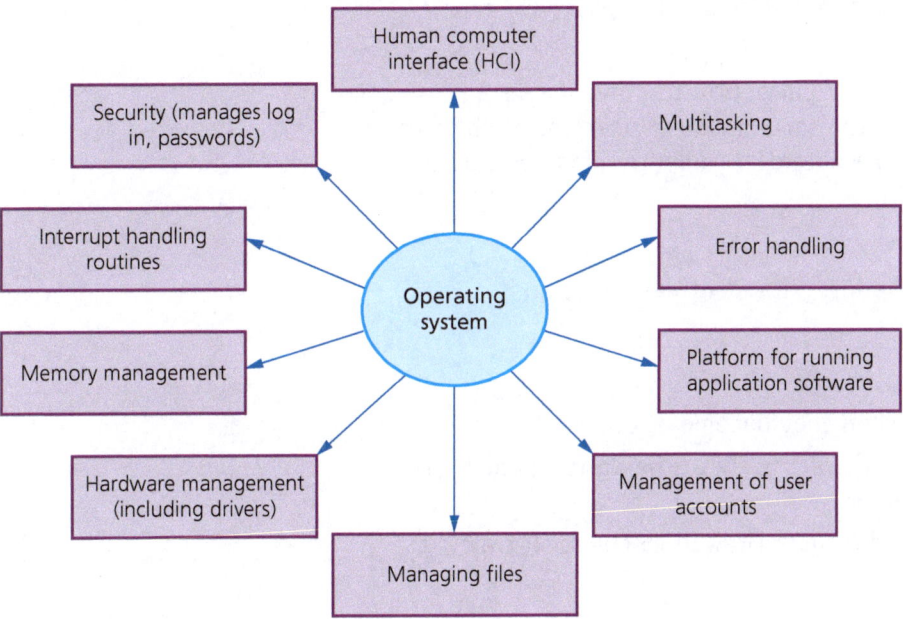

Human computer interface

The **human computer interface (HCI)** is necessary to allow a human being to communicate with a computer. The two most common types of HCI are the **command line interface (CLI)** and **graphical user interface (GUI)**.

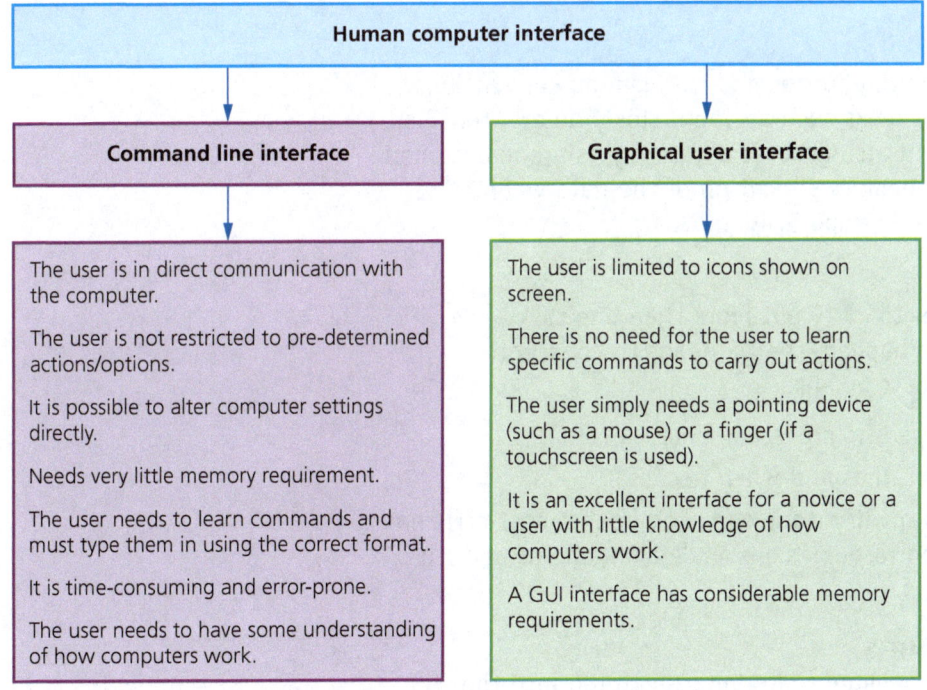

GUI interfaces are examples of a **windows, icons, menu and pointing device (WIMP)** environment. More recently, devices such as smartphones and tablets invariably use touchscreens that require a **post-WIMP** interface – this allows actions such as pinching and rotating which would be impossible in a WIMP environment using a mouse.

Memory management
Memory management is essentially management of the primary storage (RAM) and the data being moved between RAM and HDD/SSD. It keeps track of all the memory locations.

This part of the OS carries out memory protection to prevent two competing applications from using the same memory locations at the same time. This would otherwise lead to a potential computer crash, security issues or loss or corruption of data.

Security management
Security management ensures the integrity, confidentiality and availability of data.

This can be achieved by:

- overseeing software updates when they become available
- ensuring the latest version of software is always being run (which often contains revised security fixes
- running **antivirus software** and using a firewall to check all traffic to and from the computer
- maintaining access rights for all users
- carrying out data recovery and system restore.

Hardware peripheral management
Hardware management uses **device drivers** to allow input and output to take place. It manages the queues and **buffers** to ensure data is being handled correctly and that the CPU performs to its maximum.

File management
File management maintains file directories and file naming conventions. It can perform file maintenance tasks such as open, close, delete, rename, copy and so on. File management also ensures access rights are maintained as part of security and correct memory allocation of the data when it is read from the HDD/SSD and saved temporarily in RAM.

Multitasking
Multitasking allows a computer to carry out more than one task simultaneously. To allow this to happen, the OS needs to constantly monitor the status of each process by ensuring:

- all resources are allocated specific processor time
- all processes can be interrupted as and when necessary
- priorities are used so that a given resource is used in the most efficient manner and that the required resources are made available as and when necessary.

Management of user accounts
User account management allows more than one user to log into the computer by ensuring each user's data is stored in a separate part of memory. Each user logging onto a computer is given a user account area, which is protected by a username and a password. Each user can customise their screen layout and manage their own files and folders. An **administrator** oversees the management of user accounts.

Multi-access hierarchy levels are used to ensure access to certain data stored on the computer system is only allowed if a user has the correct hierarchy clearance level.

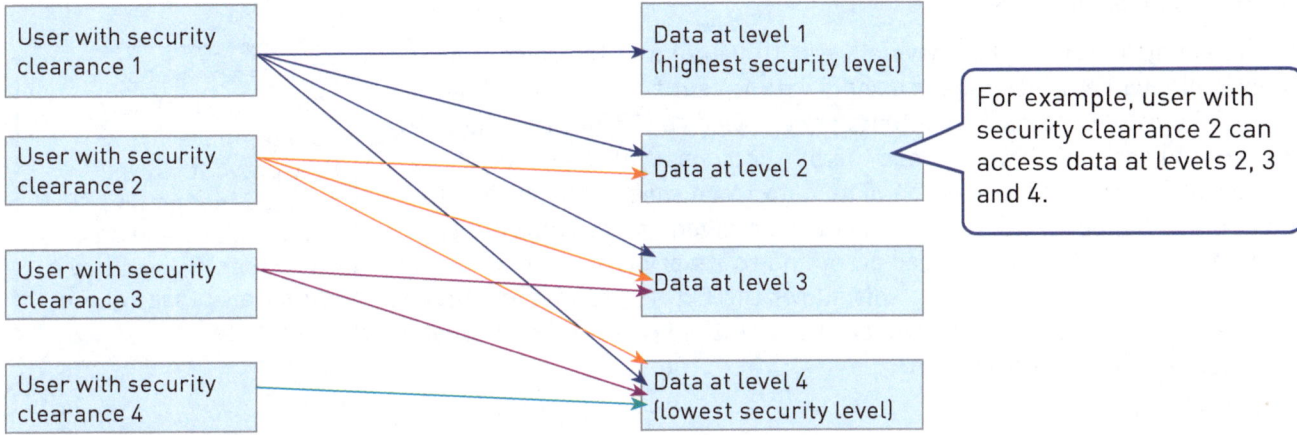

4.1.3 Running of applications

When a computer starts up, part of the operating system is loaded into RAM (this is called **booting up** the computer). This routine is handled by the Basic Input Output System (BIOS) which is a type of **firmware** – a program that provides low-level control of devices. The BIOS is stored on a flash memory chip called an **EEPROM** (electrically erasable programmable ROM) and its task is to tell the CPU where the operating system can be found.

Although BIOS is stored on EEPROM, BIOS settings are stored on a **complementary metal oxide semi-conductor (CMOS)** chip, which is always connected up to a power supply (battery). The user is allowed to alter the factory settings by changing CMOS contents, such as changing the clock speed.

Apps are under the control of the operating system and need to access system software, such as device drivers. Different parts of the operating system may need to be loaded in and out of RAM as software runs.

4.1.4 Interrupts

An **interrupt** is a signal sent from a device or software (or it can be an internal signal) to the microprocessor. This will cause the microprocessor to temporarily stop what it is doing so it can service the interrupt. Causes of interrupts include those shown below.

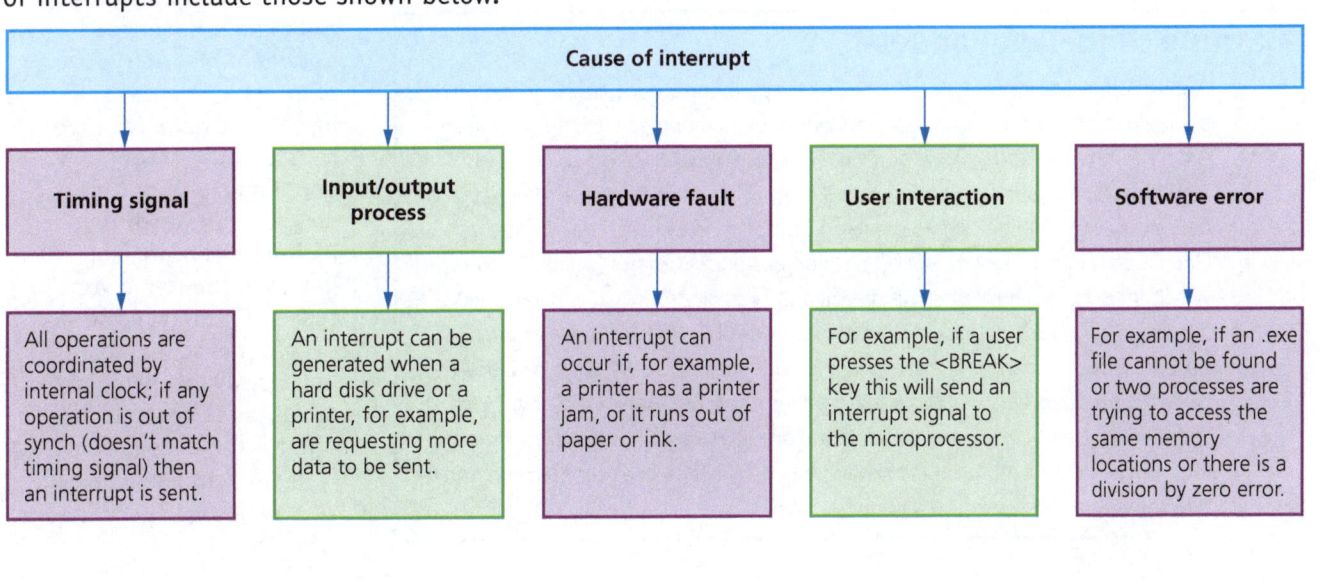

4.1 Types of software and interrupts

Once an interrupt signal is received, the microprocessor either continues with its existing task or temporarily pauses the task in order to **service** the interrupt. To determine the order of servicing interrupts, each interrupt is given an **interrupt priority**.

Buffers are also used to allow several tasks to be done at the same time. For example, while printing a document, data is sent to a buffer to hold it temporarily. While the buffer contents are emptied to the printer, the CPU can carry on with other tasks. Once the buffer is empty, the printer sends an interrupt to the CPU requesting more data to be sent to the buffer. To allow this to happen, all interrupt requests are given an interrupt priority. The interrupt will then be serviced according to its priority using an **interrupt service routine (ISR)**. This allows the CPU to stop its existing task, service the interrupt from the printer, and then restore the original task once the interrupt is cleared.

> Buffers are areas of memory that hold data temporarily; they prevent slower processes affecting CPU performance and also allow the CPU to carry out several tasks at the same time.

Examples of interrupts include:

- software interrupts (e.g. divide by zero error, can't find .exe file, two processes trying to access the same memory location at the same time)
- hardware interrupts (e.g. a printer has paper jam or has run out of ink)
- timing signal error (this usually means there has been a clock issue and operations are not synchronised)
- input/output hardware processes (e.g. a HDD is requesting new data)
- user interaction (e.g. pressing keyboard keys, clicking a mouse button, and so on).

Sample questions and answers

REVISED

a) Human computer interfaces (HCIs) are sometimes referred to as WIMP and post-WIMP.
   i) Explain the difference between WIMP and post-WIMP
   ii) Describe the relative advantages and disadvantages of the two types of interface.
b) Explain the term screensaver. Include, in your answer, the reasons why screensavers are used.
c) Apart from HCIs, name **three** other functions carried out by a typical operating system. [9]

> **Tips**
>
> Part a)i) of this question involves 'explain'. Your answer needs to show the main differences between the two types of interface. In part a) ii), you are asked to give relative advantages and disadvantages so your answer must include a comparison between the two given types of interface. Be careful not to include any disadvantages and advantages compared to other interfaces (such as CLI) since this would gain you no marks.

Sample high-level answer

a) i) A WIMP environment involves the use of a pointing device, such as a mouse, to navigate a screen and select options from a menu or 'click on' an icon. With post-WIMP, the user doesn't need a pointing device since this only works with a touchscreen. The user simply uses their finger or stylus to carry out movement such as pinch and rotate, as well as selections.

   ii) Due to situations like the 2020 pandemic, touchscreens (which use post-WIMP interfaces) have obvious disadvantages since they can allow the transfer of viruses and bacteria between people who touch the same screen. However, their big advantage is that no input devices are needed, such as a mouse, which could equally transfer viruses and bacteria. Post-WIMP also allows actions such as pinch or rotate which would be almost impossible using a mouse. One advantage of WIMP is that any screen can be used and it doesn't require a touchscreen.

b) A screensaver is a moving or still image which appears on a user's screen following a period of inactivity (for example, 5 minutes). The screensaver automatically logs out a user and is therefore being used as part of the security since the user will need to supply a valid username and password to use the computer again. Some screensavers use face ID which means the computer unlocks again as soon as a valid user faces the screen again.

c) Examples of OS functions include: multitasking, user account management, file management, hardware management, memory management, interrupt handling and security.

> **Tips**
>
> Part b) requires an explanation of a computer term, but it also requires you to include reasons why screensavers are used. Your reasons should not contradict any part of your explanation. Finally, in part c), you are asked to name three functions of an OS; no description or explanation is needed but be careful about your spelling of the terms since this could be crucial (for example, user account manager is different from user account management).

Sample low-level answer

a) i) WIMP means windows, icons, mouse and pointer device which means a mouse is used to select items from a windows environment. Post-WIMP refers to tablets and mobile phones where touchscreens are used to allow fingers to zoom in and out of photos, swipe from page to page and so on.

ii) You can't use a mouse to do some of the post-WIMP functions. Also touchscreens get quite dirty.

b) Screensavers protect screens from burning where a logo, for example, is permanently burnt into the screen.

c) Examples include: memory management, running security software and looking after user accounts.

> **Teacher's comments**
>
> The first answer gives very comprehensive explanations and has also included examples to help further with their explanations. It is very hard to fault their answers since they seem to have followed tips correctly.
>
> The second answer is less satisfactory. In part a)i), their definition of WIMP is not entirely correct but the description of post-WIMP is adequate to get a mark. In part a)ii) they have not really explained why the named functions are an advantage or a disadvantage. In part b), their use of a screensaver is no longer true; they were originally developed to protect old cathode-ray tube (CRT) monitors from 'phosphor burn' but this is no longer an issue, so it would be impossible to award any marks. However, they have redeemed themselves in part c) by correctly naming three OS functions.

Exam-style questions

1 Tick (✓) the appropriate column, in the following table, to indicate whether the named software is either system software or application software. [5]

Software	System	Application
Screensaver		
Antivirus software		
Printer driver		
Video editing software		
Compiler		
QR code reader		
On-screen calculator		
Operating system software		
Interrupt handling routine		
Photo editing software		

2 a) Explain what is meant by a **virus**. [1]
  b) Explain how a virus checker detects and removes viruses. [2]

3 Operating systems are used to oversee the efficient and correct operation of a computer system.
  Describe the functions of the following parts of a typical operating system.
  a) Memory management
  b) User account management
  c) Security management [6]

4.2 Types of programming language, translators and integrated development environments

4 a) Explain why device drivers are needed. In your answer, include what information is contained in a device driver and why that information is needed. [3]

b) Describe how buffers and interrupts are used when data is being transferred from a camera (through a USB port) to a computer. [3]

5 The following paragraph has several terms missing. A list of possible terms is given below. By writing the correct term in the spaces provided, complete the paragraph.
Each term in the list may be used once, more than once or not at all.

attention	download	quarantine
buffer	file	RAM
compensate	interrupt	service
deleting	microprocessor	signal
descriptor	permanently	software
device driver	printer	streaming
disk drive	priority	temporarily

An interrupt is a < .... > sent from a hardware device or < .... > to the < .... > requesting < .... >.

This causes the < .... > to temporarily halt what it is doing and to < .... > the interrupt.

To determine the order in which an < .... > is dealt with, it is given a < .... >.

When data is sent to a printer, it is first stored in a < .... > where data is held < .... >.

This allows the < .... > to get on with other tasks.

If the printer runs out of ink or there is a paper jam, it sends an < .... > to the < .... >.

When < .... > data from the internet, a < .... > is used to < .... > for the difference between < .... > speeds and the computer's data requirements. [8]

4.2 Types of programming language, translators and integrated development environments

REVISED

A **computer program** is a list of instructions that enable a computer to perform a specific task. Programmers use many different programming languages to communicate with computers. Computer programs can be written in **high-level languages (HLLs)** and **low-level languages (LLLs)**.

4.2.1 High-level languages and low-level languages

High-level languages are used by the majority of programmers as they make it much easier and quicker to develop and maintain programs. Examples of high-level languages include Visual Basic, Python and Java.

Low-level languages are used by programmers who need to develop special routines that make best use of memory, the computer's instruction set and hardware. Most programs are written in **assembly language**, which is translated into **machine code**.

4 Software

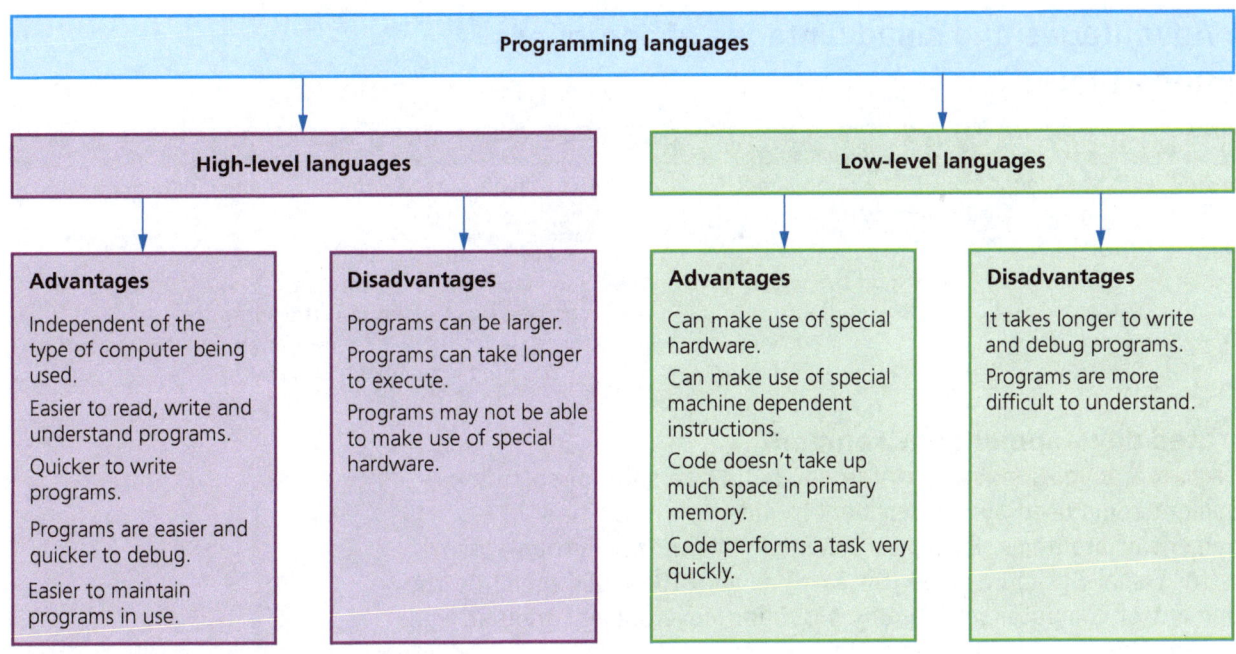

4.2.2 Assembly languages

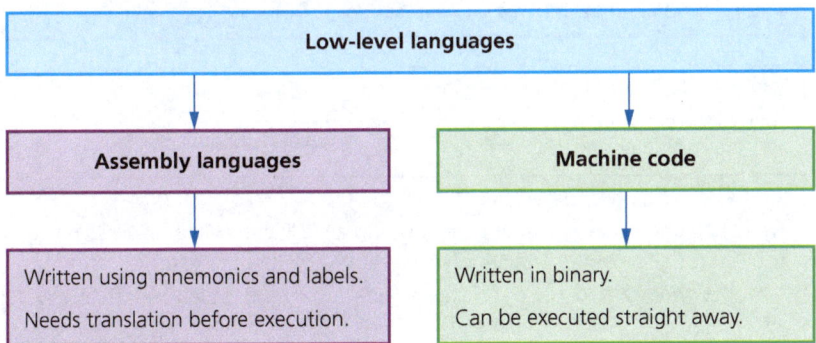

4.2.3 Translators

Programs are written in a form that computer programmers can understand. Computers use programs with binary instructions so programs must be translated into binary for the computer to follow them. A **translator** is a utility program. There are several types of translator program performing different tasks.

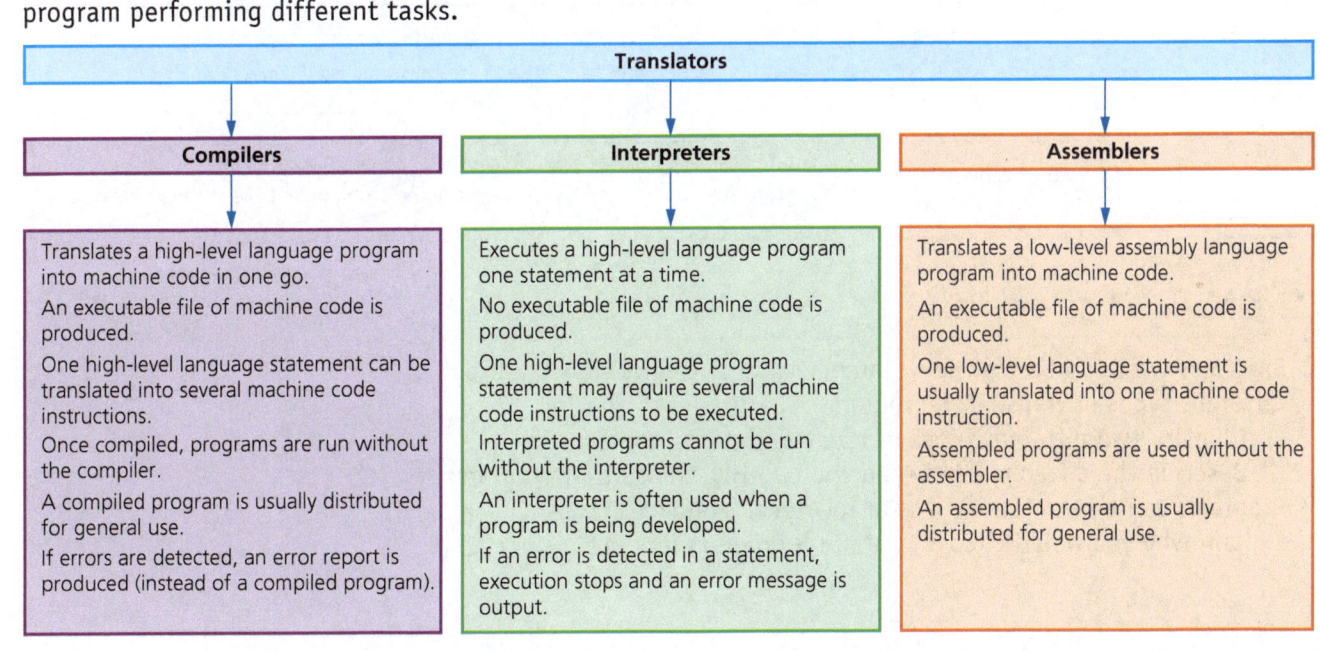

4.2 Types of programming language, translators and integrated development environments

4.2.4 Advantages and disadvantages of compilers and interpreters

Translators	Disadvantages	Advantages
Interpreter	Takes longer to write, test and debug programs during development.	Easier and quicker to debug, test and edit programs during development.
Compiler	Programs: • cannot be run without the interpreter • can take longer to execute.	A compiled program: • can be stored ready for use • can be executed without the compiler • takes up less space in memory when it is executed • is executed in a shorter time

Integrated development environment

An **integrated development environment** (IDE) is a suite of software development tools used by programmers to aid the writing and development of programs. Examples include PyCharm (for Python), Visual Studio (for Visual Basic) or BlueJ (for Java) as your IDE. IDEs speed up the development of computer software by providing development tools in one application. They usually have several features.

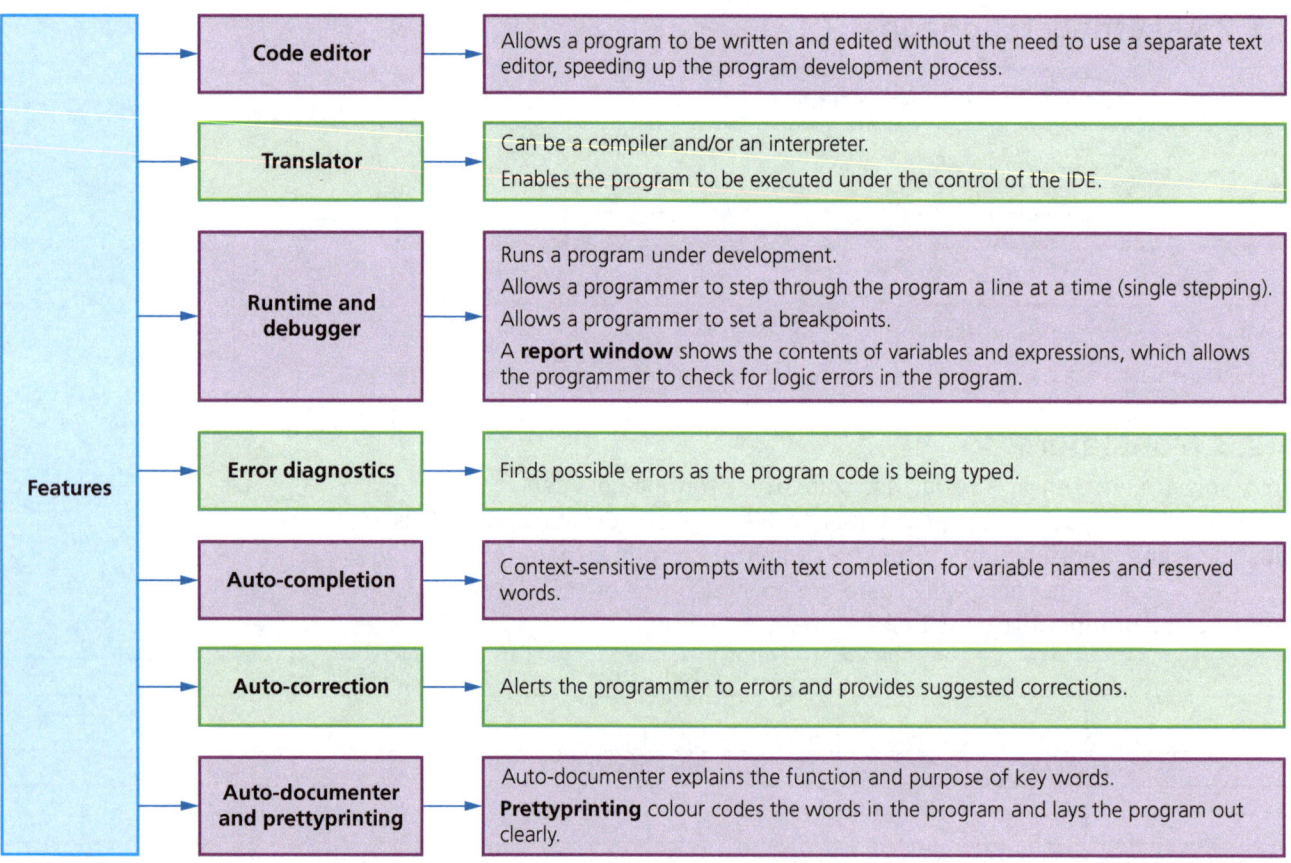

Sample questions and answers

REVISED

a) Programs written in a high-level language (HLL) can be translated by different types of translation programs.
   i) Identify **two** different types of HLL translation program.
   ii) Describe the difference between the two HLL translation programs.
b) Programs can be written in HLLs or low-level languages (LLLs). Explain why you would choose to write a program in a LLL. [6]

60 Cambridge IGCSE™ and O Level Computer Science Study and Revision Guide Second Edition

Sample high-level answer

a) i) Compiler and interpreter.
   ii) A compiler translates the whole program at once and produces a file to be executed later, whereas an interpreter translates each statement then executes it before moving on to the next statement.
b) A program is written in a low-level language when it needs to perform a task very quickly or includes special machine dependent instructions to operate hardware.

Sample low-level answer

a) i) Pycharm and Idle.
   ii) Pycharm, gives me more help than Idle and completes my key words for me.
b) Nobody writes programs in a low-level language anymore as it is too hard as you have to learn special commands for each computer.

Tip

Part a)i) of this question involves 'identify'. Your answer must either name the two types of translation program or clearly identify each one with a short statement. The question specifies HLL translation programs, so be careful not identify a LLL translation program as this would be incorrect and not gain a mark.

In part a)ii), you are asked to describe the difference; this means your answer must include a comparison between the two translators given in part a)i). Make sure it is clear which translator you are describing when making your comparison.

Part b) requires an explanation of why a program would be written in a LLL; be careful to not explain how a LLL program would be written. The reader must see the reasons for choosing a LLL.

Exam-style questions

6 Tick (✓) the appropriate box in the table below to indicate whether the description applies to an assembler, a compiler and/or an interpreter. You may need to tick more than one column in each row.

Description	Assembler	Compiler	Interpreter
Translates a program written in a LLL.			
Translates a program written in a HLL.			
Identifies errors.			
Does not produce an executable file.			
Allows editing during execution.			

[5]

7 In this question you will be given a statement followed by **four** possible answers.
   Select which of the four answers you think is correct and tick (✓) the box next to your answer.
   a) What is meant by the term **assembly language**?
      ☐ A language that is dependent on computer hardware and needs to be translated into binary before it is executed.
      ☐ A low-level programming language written in binary.
      ☐ A translator that translates programs into binary.
      ☐ An example of a binary program.
   b) What is meant by the term **debugging**?
      ☐ Correcting syntax errors in a computer program.
      ☐ Finding errors in a computer program by running the program.
      ☐ Highlighting syntax errors in a computer program.
      ☐ Stopping translation of a program when an error is found.
   c) What is meant by the term **high-level programming language**?
      ☐ A language that is dependent on computer hardware.
      ☐ A language that is independent of computer hardware.
      ☐ A language that is written in binary.
      ☐ A language that is written in hexadecimal. [3]

8 a) Explain what is meant by an **integrated development environment (IDE)**.
   b) Describe **two** features of an IDE. [6]

9 Explain why an integrated development environment (IDE) is needed. In your answer, identify the features that are included in an IDE and the reasons why a programmer finds these features useful. [8]

Teacher's comments

The first answer would gain full marks since two types of translators and the difference between them have been correctly identified. The explanation of why a LLL would be chosen is clear.

The second answer would only gain one mark. The translators are examples of available IDEs. The student has attempted to explain why a LLL would not be used; in doing this they have included a valid reason for using a LLL.

5 The internet and its uses

Key objectives

The objectives of this chapter are to revise:
- the internet and World Wide Web (WWW):
  - differences between the internet and the World Wide Web
  - meaning of uniform resource locator (URL)
  - purpose and operation of hypertext transfer protocols (http and https)
  - purpose and function of a web browser
  - how web pages are located, retrieved and displayed
  - types of cookie
- digital currencies:
  - how digital currencies are used
  - the process of blockchaining and how it is used to track digital currency transactions
- cyber security:
  - cyber security threats: brute force attacks, data interception, distributed denial-of-service (DDoS) attacks, hacking, malware, phishing, pharming and social engineering
  - ways of preventing or mitigating the risks of cyber security threats

5.1 The internet and World Wide Web (WWW)

REVISED

5.1.1 Differences between the internet and World Wide Web (WWW)

The differences between the **internet** and **World Wide Web (WWW)** are summarised in the following table.

Internet	World Wide Web
Users can send and receive emails.	A collection of multimedia web pages and other information on websites.
Allows online chatting (via text, audio and video).	http(s) protocols are written using hypertext mark-up language.
Makes use of transmission protocols (TCP) and internet protocols (IPs).	Uniform resource locators are used to specify the location of web pages.
A worldwide collection of interconnected networks and devices.	Web resources are accessed by web browsers
	WWW uses the internet to access information from web servers.

5.1.2 Uniform resource locators

Web browsers (often simply referred to as 'browsers') are software that allow users to access and display web pages or play multimedia from websites on their devices. The browser interprets **hypertext mark-up language (HTML)** sent from the websites.

Uniform resource locators (URLs) are text addresses used to access websites in the format:

protocol://website address/path/filename

- http or https
- made up of domain host (www), domain name (website name), domain type (.com, .org, .gov), and country code (.uk, .de, .cy)
- web page (often omitted)
- name of item on web page

For example:

https://www.hoddereducation.co.uk/cambridge-igcse-computerscience

5.1.3 http and https
Hypertext transfer protocol (http) is a set of rules that must be obeyed when transferring files across the internet. If some form of security is employed, it becomes http**s** (**s** = secure) and you may also see a green padlock in the browser address window.

5.1.4 Web browsers
Browsers interpret (translate) HTML from websites and show the results of the translation (either as a website page or play multimedia). The main features of a typical browser include:

- a home page and address bar
- the ability to store favourite websites and web pages (bookmarks)
- keeping a history of websites visited (user history)
- the ability to allow the user to navigate forwards and backwards through a website
- allowing many web pages to be open at the same time by using multiple tabs
- making use of cookies
- using **hyperlinks** to navigate between websites:
  - either the website is underlined and requires <ctrl> + <click> to follow the link (for example, www.hoddereducation.com)
  - or a small, pointed finger shows under the name of the website link to highlight it for example:
  www.hoddereducation.com/

  <u>www.hoddereducation.com</u>

- data stored as a cache (see Section 5.1.5)
- make use of JavaScript.

5.1.5 Retrieval and location of web pages and websites
To retrieve pages from a website, a browser needs to know the IP address. A **domain name server (DNS)** is used to find the IP address from the domain name in the URL typed into the browser window. The DNS process involves converting a URL, such as:

hoddereducation.co.uk/cambridge-igcse-computerscience

into an IP address the computer can understand, such as:

107.162.140.19

5.1 The internet and World Wide Web (WWW)

The following diagram shows how the DNS is used to locate and retrieve web pages from a website.

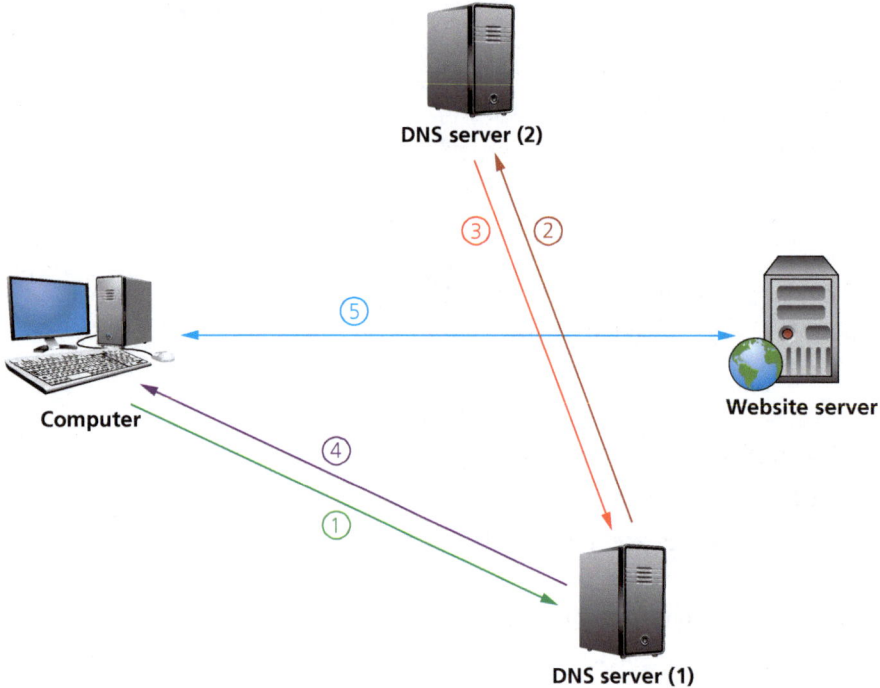

(1) The user opens their browser and types in the URL (www.hoddereducation.co.uk) and the browser asks the DNS server (1) for the IP address of the website.

(2) In this case, let us assume the DNS server can't find www.hoddereducation.co.uk in its database or its cache, so it sends out a request to DNS server (2).

(3) The DNS server (2) finds the URL and can map it to 107.162.140.19; this IP address is sent back to the DNS server (1) which now puts this IP address and associated URL into its cache/database.

(4) This IP address is then sent back to the user's computer.

(5) The computer now sets up a communication with the website server and the required pages are downloaded. HTML files are sent from the website server to the computer. The computer's browser interprets the HTML, which is used to structure content, and then displays the information on the user's computer.

5.1.6 Cookies

Cookies are small files or code stored on a user's computer (permanently or temporarily). Cookies are sent by a web server to the browser on a user's computer.

A cookie behaves like a small look-up table which allows the cookie to track data about the user's internet activity. Every time the user re-visits a website, it checks if it has set cookies on the browser before.

There are two types of cookie – **session cookies** and **persistent cookies** – as shown in this table.

Session cookie features	Persistent cookie features
• Stored temporarily on the user's computer. • Once the browser is closed, the website session ends and the cookie is deleted.	• Remember user's log in details. • Cookies are stored on user's hard drive until expiry date reached or user deletes them. • Remain in operation even after browser closed or website session terminated.

Session cookies

- Used for making online purchases.
- Used for virtual shopping baskets.
- Stored temporarily only for the single website session and are deleted when the user leaves the website.
- Don't collect and information about the user and don't identify who they are.

Persistent cookies

- Allow websites to remember user passwords, email addresses and so on; permitting faster log in.
- Serve as a memory, enabling the website to recognise users every time they visit the website.
- Save user's items in a virtual shopping basket/cart.
- Track user's browsing habits and website history.
- Allow targeting of specific users with advertising based on previous buying/surfing habits.
- Storing user preferences.
- Used in online transactions.
- Allow social networking sites to recognise certain preferences and browsing history.
- Allow different languages to be used on the web pages automatically as soon as users log in.

Sample questions and answers   REVISED

a) Define what is meant by a **cookie**. [2]
b) Describe the differences between a session cookie and a persistent cookie. [2]
c) Give **three** uses of persistent cookies. [3]

> **Tip**
>
> Part a) asks for an explanation of the term 'cookie'; this requires a precise definition of the term. Part b) is a description where the differences between the two types of cookie is required. Avoid answers such as 'session cookies are temporary whereas persistent cookies are permanent' – this would not be regarded as a description of the difference. To answer the question fully, explain what is meant by the word temporary (for example, deleted at the end of a website session) and the word persistent (for example, stored on user's computer until deleted or expiry date reached). Part c) needs three briefly described uses of persistent cookies (one sentence for each example would be adequate).

5.1 The internet and World Wide Web (WWW)

Sample high-level answer

a) Cookies are small files or code stored on a user's computer; they can track data about a user, such as IP addresses and browsing activity.

b) **Session cookies:**
   - This type of cookie is stored temporarily on a user's computer.
   - They don't collect any information from the user's computer and don't identify the user.
   - They cease to exist on a user's computer once the browser is closed or the website session is ended.

   Persistent cookies:
   - This type of cookie is stored on the user's HDD or SSD until the expiry date is reached or the user deletes it.
   - They remain in operation on the user's computer even after the browser is closed or the website session is ended.
   - They remove the need to type in log in details every time a certain website is visited; this is achieved by storing user preferences.

c)
   - Remember passwords and email addresses about a user.
   - Recognise user each time they visit a website.
   - Save user's items in a virtual shopping basket/cart.
   - Track internet habits and user history/favourites.
   - Target user with adverts which match previous buying habits.
   - Show user preferences (for example, language used).

Sample low-level answer

a) A cookie is used when a user visits a website each time.
b) Session cookies only last while the user visits the website and a persistent cookie is one which is always there.
c) Three uses would be: recognise user preferences, putting things in a virtual basket and targeting user with specific adverts.

Teacher's comments

The first answer is very clear and concise; although the use of bullet points make the answers easy to read, many students may prefer to write their answer in an essay format. Parts a) and b) don't specify how many points need to be raised, but a minimum of three or four is recommended to ensure all the available marks can be awarded.

The second answer is much briefer. The answer to part a) doesn't really define a cookie and only explains its use by the website. The second part gets one mark for a rather brief explanation of a session cookie, but the statement about persistent cookies is just too unclear. In part c), three uses have been given and is probably worth full marks.

Exam-style questions

1. A URL is being entered as:
   https://www.frage-eins-beispiel.org.de/example-page
   Identify:
   a) the domain name
   b) the domain type
   c) file name
   d) protocol being used. [4]

2. The following table contains features of the internet and World Wide Web (WWW). Indicate in the right-hand column, by writing 'internet' or 'WWW' which features refer to the internet and which features refer to the WWW. [8]

Feature	Internet or WWW?
Ability to send and receive emails.	
Makes use of http and https protocols.	
Uses URLs to specify locations of websites and web pages.	
Resources can be accessed by using web browsers.	
Makes use of TCP and IP protocols.	
Allows online chatting (via text, audio and video).	
Collection of multimedia web pages and other information on websites.	
Physical infrastructure that allows networks and devices to connect to each other.	

Cambridge IGCSE™ and O Level Computer Science Study and Revision Guide Second Edition

5 The internet and its uses

5.2 Digital currencies

REVISED

5.2.1 What is digital currency?

Digital currency exists purely in a digital format and has no physical form unlike fiat currency (for example, £, $, €, ¥). It relies on a central banking system (centralisation); however, this makes it difficult to maintain confidentiality and security.

Cryptocurrency is a type of digital currency that overcomes security and confidentiality issues. Unlike other types of digital currency, cryptocurrency has no state control and transactions are publicly available and can be fully tracked. Cryptocurrency uses **cryptography** to track transactions; the use of cryptography was introduced to address the security problems sometimes associated with the centralisation of digital currency.

5.2.2 Blockchaining

Cryptocurrency makes use of **blockchaining**. Blockchain is a decentralised database; when a new transaction takes place, all networked computers in the system get a copy of the transaction, removing security risks such as hacking.

When a new transaction takes place, a new **block** is created. The new block contains data, a new hash value (a unique value generated by an algorithm) and a previous hash value pointing to the preceding block. The hash value is unique to each block and includes a **timestamp**, which identifies when the creation of the block took place. In a blockchain the first block is called the genesis block.

If a block has been accessed illegally (for example, by a hacker) the hash value will change; this means the link to all the following blocks is now broken. A **proof-of-work** is used to prevent high speed number crunching (using a computer) from altering all of the block hash values by a cybercriminal; the proof-of-work takes ten minutes to complete thus preventing cyberattacks. Cryptocurrency is 'policed' by **miners**; these are special network users who get a commission for each new block created.

Apart from cryptocurrency, other uses of blockchain include:

- smart contracts
- in research – for example, development of new drugs
- in politics
- in many areas of education.

Sample question and answer

REVISED

Describe the main differences and any similarities between digital currency and cryptocurrency. **[3]**

> **Tip**
>
> To answer this question fully, at least three distinct differences (or similarities) between the two types of currency need to be described. Avoid answers such as 'digital currency is centralised whereas cryptocurrency is not centralised'. Such answers don't explain the difference and just state opposites which is insufficient to gain any marks.

5.2 Digital currencies

Sample high-level answer
- Both types of currency are in a digital format and have no physical form unlike traditional money, such as £, $, € and ¥.
- Digital currency relies on a central banking system to make a transaction, whereas cryptocurrency has no state control and there is no need for a central banking system.
- Cryptocurrency uses a method known as blockchaining.

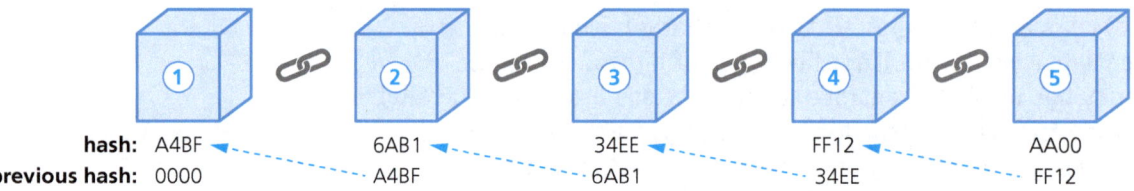

hash: A4BF	6AB1	34EE	FF12	AA00
previous hash: 0000	A4BF	6AB1	34EE	FF12

- Due to centralisation, digital currencies have security and confidentiality issues; cryptocurrency transactions are all publicly available to all members on the network – all transactions can therefore be tracked using blockchaining thus making all transactions transparent and removing risks such as hacking.

Sample low-level answer
Cryptocurrency is just one of many examples of digital currency. There are several different digital currencies but they all have the same features. Basically, no physical money passes in a transaction and it is only electronic transactions that occur.

Teacher's comments
The first answer has three parts to it: it gives similarities between the two types of currency, it gives differences between the two types of currency, but it also gives a very detailed description of why the two are different. A very clear answer worth full marks.

The second answer makes a very common mistake – cryptocurrency isn't the same as digital currency; there are many differences between the two. No marks could be awarded since the actual similarities have not been explained. However, one mark might be awarded for the last sentence since it is true that both don't use physical currency.

Exam-style questions
3 a) Explain what is meant by the term **blockchaining**. [1]
   b) Apart from monetary transactions, name **three** other uses of blockchaining. [3]
4 A blockchain has seven blocks.
   a) Draw a diagram to show how these seven blocks are all interconnected to form a blockchain. Include any values in your diagram. [2]
   b) Describe what would happen if block 3 was hacked to change a sum of money or an attempt was made to divert money to a different block. [2]

5.3 Cyber security

REVISED

5.3.1 Cyber security threats
Cyber security refers to systems put in place to defend computers (or electronic devices), web servers, mobile phones and networks (and their associated data) from an attack by a cybercriminal. There are a number of cyber security threats that need to be considered:

- brute force attacks
- data interception
- distributed denial of service (DDoS) attacks
- hacking
- malware
- phishing
- pharming
- social engineering.

Brute force attacks
A **brute force attack** is a method where all combinations of letters, numbers and other symbols (such as !, &, @) are tried to generate passwords. The method relies on the high speed of computer processing, therefore longer, more complex, passwords make the task of the cybercriminal much harder.

There are ways brute force attack criminals try to make cracking passwords an easier task:

- check if the password is in a list of commonly used passwords (such as, 123456, ABCD123, querty, and so on)
- if it isn't a common password, the criminal can then check a word list (this is a text file containing a collection of words that have been used in passwords by certain groups of people or organisations) – while the word list can still be very long, they do save a lot of time.

Data interception
Data interception is the stealing of data by tapping into a network. This can be done by **packet sniffers**, which examine all data packets on a network and read the data being moved across the networks.

War driving (also known as **access point mapping**) is a method that intercepts Wi-Fi (wireless) signals; the method requires a laptop, smartphone or tablet, an antenna, a GPS device, and software to gather the data from the wireless network.

> To safeguard against war driving, **Wired Equivalency Privacy (WEP) encryption protocol** is used – this gives a wireless LAN the same level of security as a wired network.

Distributed denial-of-service attacks
A **distributed denial-of-service (DDoS)** attack is an attempt to prevent anyone accessing part of a network, for example, a specific web server. The system uses a network of computers to carry out an attack. It is slightly different to a **denial-of-service (DoS)** attack, which only uses a single computer to carry out the attack; DoS is therefore much easier to identify and remove the risk.

DDoS can also be used to attack an individual's computer by preventing them accessing their emails, certain websites or online services. The attack can be carried out by sending out masses of spam emails which overload a server or fill up a user's inbox. It is possible to mitigate the risk of DDoS by using up-to-date malware checkers, ensuring there is a firewall running to filter out **spam** and applying email filters to filter out unwanted traffic.

Hacking

Hacking is gaining illegal access to a computer system without the user's permission. It can lead to identity theft, gaining personal information or the loss/corruption of key data.

Hacking is not prevented by using measures such as encryption, but can be mitigated against by using a firewall, usernames and frequency changed strong passwords; anti-hacking software also exists. Some hacking is referred to as **ethical hacking**, where companies employ staff to try and hack into their systems to check how strong their security measures are.

Malware

Malware is one of the biggest risks to the integrity and security of data on a computer system. The following are examples of malware.

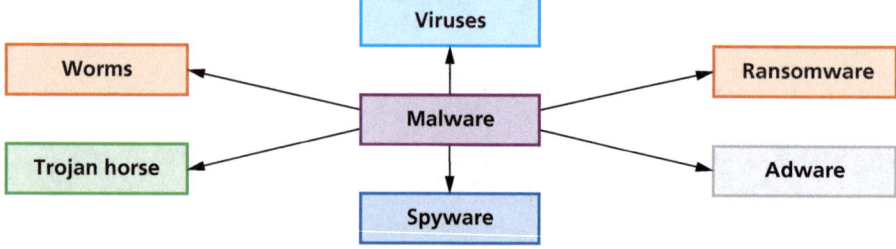

Here is a summary of the types of malware.

Viruses are programs (or program code) that can replicate or copy themselves with the intention of deleting or corrupting files, or causing the computer to malfunction. They need an **active host** program on the target computer or an operating system that has already been infected before they can run. Viruses are often part of an email attachment and they require the user to take some action (for example, click on a link in the attachment) for the virus to infect their computer.
Worms are types of stand-alone viruses that can replicate themselves with the intention of spreading to other computers. They often use networks to search out computers with weak security that are prone to such attacks. Worms can spread throughout a network without any action by an end user; this potentially makes them more dangerous than viruses.
Trojan horses are malicious programs often disguised as legitimate software. They replace all or part of the legitimate software with the intent of carrying out some harm to the user's computer system. A Trojan horse needs to be executed by an end user and they often arrive as an attachment to an email/message or can be downloaded from an infected website (they are frequently transmitted via a fake antivirus website).
Spyware is software that gathers information by monitoring, for example, all the activity on a user's computer and captures personal data. The gathered information is then sent back to the person who sent the software (sometimes the software monitors key presses and it is then referred to as key logging software).
Adware is software that floods a user's computer with unwanted advertising, usually in the form of pop-ups. It can frequently appear in the browser address window redirecting the browser to a fake website which contains the promotional adverts. Adware is not necessarily harmful, but it can highlight weaknesses in a network's security, and be difficult to remove since anti-malware doesn't see them as harmful.
Ransomware are programs that encrypt the data on a user's computer, so a decryption key is needed. The key is sent to the user once they pay a sum of money (a ransom). The ransomware is often sent via a Trojan horse or by social engineering.

Phishing

Phishing is the sending out of legitimate-looking emails to users; they may contain links to or attachments to fake websites. They require the user to take some action to initiate the phishing attack, for example, by clicking on the link in the email or attachment. Once a link is established, the user's browser is taken to a fake website where personal information can be stolen.

Another type of phishing is called **spear phishing** – a cybercriminal targets specific individuals/companies to get access to financial data or for industrial espionage. Normal phishing isn't usually specific in who it targets.

Phishing attacks can be mitigated against by:

- awareness training of users
- not clicking on links in emails unless you are 100% certain they are genuine
- running the anti-phishing tool in the browser
- using up-to-date browsers and run up-to-date firewalls
- closing down 'pop-ups' by selecting the small 'x' in the top right corner
- getting information about the email sender by clicking on the information symbol (a letter 'i' in a small circle); the actual email address from the sender will indicate whether or not it is from a genuine source.

Pharming

Pharming is malicious code installed on a user's computer or web server without their knowledge. The user doesn't need to take any action to initiate the pharming attack; it is initiated automatically by the stored code. The creator of the malicious code can gain information by sending the user's browser to a fake website without their knowledge.

Pharming redirects the user's browser to a fake/malicious website often by using **DNS cache poisoning** (cache poisoning changes genuine IP addresses on an infected website to fake IP addresses that take the browser to the fake website).

Pharming attacks can be mitigated against by:

- modern browsers alerting the user to potential phishing and pharming attacks
- running up-to-date virus checkers which will look for malicious code stored on the user's computer or on the web server
- checking the spelling of websites (for example, Amozon) to see if they are genuine
- getting information about the email sender by clicking on the information symbol (a letter 'i' in a small circle); the actual email address from the sender will indicate whether or not it is from a genuine source.

Social engineering

Social engineering occurs when a cybercriminal creates a social situation that can lead to a potential victim 'dropping their guard'. It involves the manipulation of people into breaking their normal security procedures. No hacking is required since the user willingly gives the cybercriminal the necessary access or information to carry out an attack. There are five types of social engineering threats that commonly exist.

5.3 Cyber security

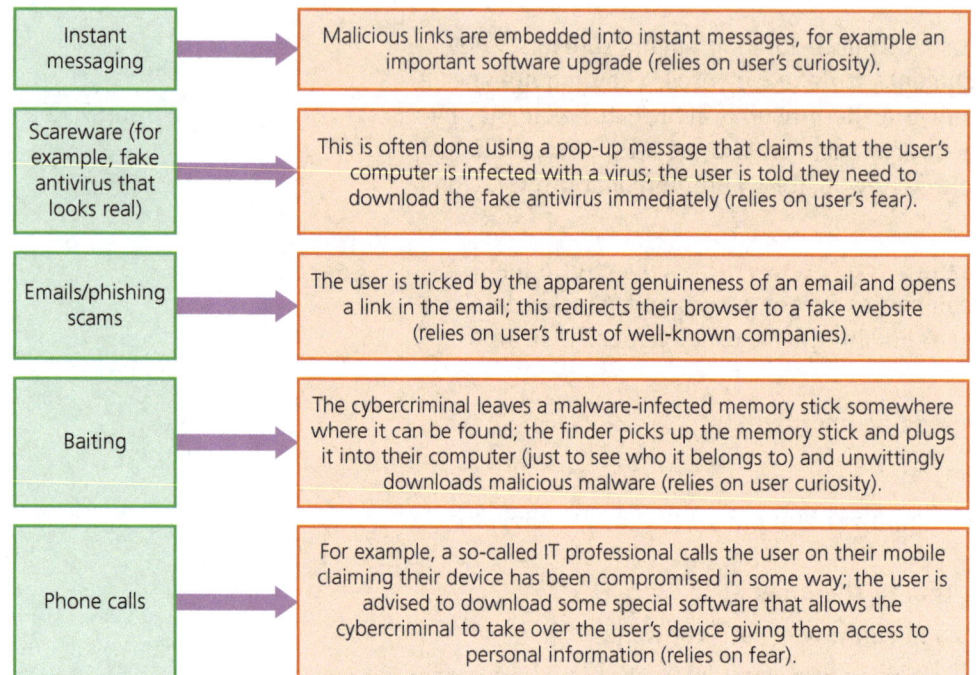

It is clear from the five examples that social engineering links into many other types of malware, and is an effective method of introducing malware. The whole idea is based on the exploitation of certain human emotions. The three most common emotions exploited are shown here.

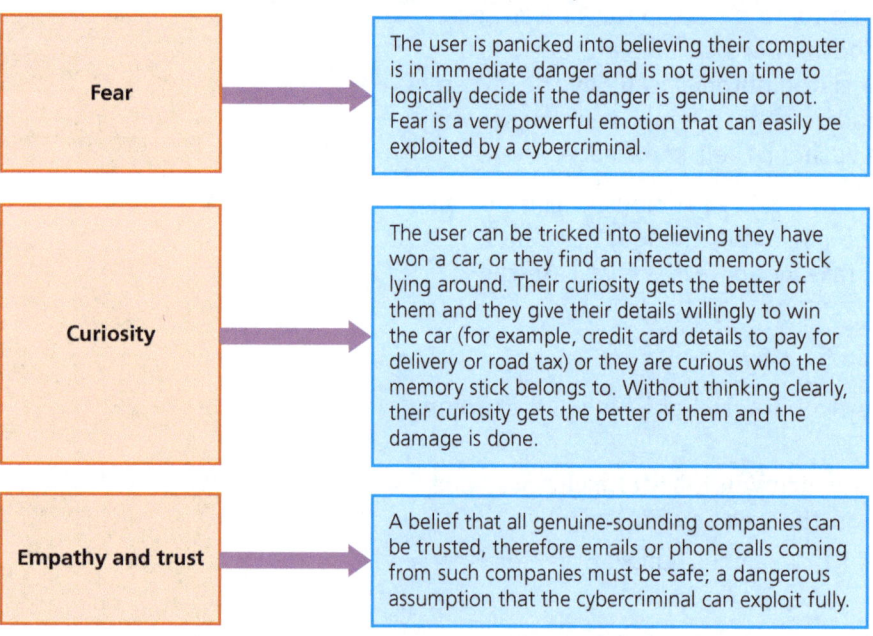

5.3.2 Keeping data safe from security threats

Use of access levels

User accounts can be used to control a user's rights. This involves a number of **levels of access**, each protected by a username and password. This prevents, for example, a hospital cleaner gaining access to patient records. Access levels are used by social network sites in privacy settings to protect a user against potentially dangerous activity.

> Refer to Section 4.1 for a diagram showing access levels.

Anti-malware

The most common types of anti-malware are antivirus and **anti-spyware**. Anti-spyware software detects and removes spyware using two methods.
1. Rules – looks for certain features associated with spyware.
2. File structures – looks for file structures common to spyware software.

> Refer to Chapter 4 for information on antivirus software.

The general features of anti-spyware include the following.

- Detects and removes spyware from user's HDD/SSD.
- Prevents the downloading of spyware.
- Encrypts files making data more secure in case spyware becomes installed on user's computer.
- Encrypts keyboard strokes.
- Blocks access to user's webcam and microphone if suspicious activity detected.
- Scans for signs that the user's personal information is being stolen and warns the user.

Authentication

Authentication refers to the ability of a user to prove who they are. There are three factors used in authentication.

- Something you know (for example, a password or PIN).
- Something you have (for example, a mobile phone or tablet).
- Something unique to the user (for example, biometrics).

Passwords are the most common form of authentication (they are often associated with usernames). Passwords should:

- be changed regularly
- not be easy to guess (for example, date of birth is a very weak password)
- be strong (at least eight characters including numbers, lower case letters, upper case letters and other keyboard symbols, for example, T7%%asR3£Sc is very strong but pas5word is very weak).

If passwords are forgotten or need resetting, this can be resolved by using an email sent to the user if password reset has been requested; the email contains a link where the password can be reset safely. Passwords are often entered twice (verification) and show up on screen as **********.

Biometrics

Biometrics can be used as a type of password and are based on certain unique human characteristics, such as:

- fingerprint scans
- retina scans
- face recognition
- voice recognition.

The following table summarises the four common types of biometrics.

5.3 Cyber security

Benefits	Drawbacks
Fingerprint scans	
• One of the most developed biometric techniques. • Very easy to use. • Relatively small storage requirements for the biometric data created.	• Very intrusive for some, since it is still related to criminal identification. • Can make mistakes if the skin is dirty or damaged (for example, cuts).
Retina scans	
• Very high accuracy. • No known way to replicate a person's retina.	• Very intrusive. • Can be relatively slow to verify a retina scan using stored scans. • Very expensive to install and set up.
Face recognition	
• Non-intrusive. • Relatively inexpensive.	• Can be affected by changes in lighting, the person's hair, change in age, and if the person is wearing glasses.
Voice recognition	
• Non-intrusive. • Verification takes less than five seconds. • Relatively inexpensive.	• A person's voice can be recorded and used for unauthorised access. • Low accuracy. • Illness, such as a cold, can change a person's voice, making absolute identification difficult or impossible.

Applications of biometrics include:

- door security systems (only allows access to a building if fingerprint scan is positive)
- some mobile phones use fingerprint scans and/or face recognition, rather than a PIN, to unlock the phone for use.

Two-step verification

Two-step verification is used as a method of authentication where two different types of authentication are needed to identify someone, for example:

- a user logs onto a website using username and password and decides to use their credit card to buy something
- as part of the security, an 8-digit PIN is sent back to the user either in an email or as a text message to a mobile phone number already registered on the website (this is known as a one-time pass code (OTP))
- this 8-digit PIN is entered on the website proving the user's identity.

> The mobile phone is something the user has and the PIN is something the user knows.

Automatic software updates

Automatic updates of software keep a device secure. The updates will contain **patches** that could include updated virus checkers, software improvements and bug fixes. Updates are often done overnight, for example, when a device is charging. Doing the updates overnight also causes less disruption to the user since many devices can't be used while certain software (such as an operating system) is being updated.

Check spelling and tone of communication and of URL links

Users should take the following actions when they receive an email.

- Look out for suspicious links; destination address should match rest of the email (for example, name of the company in website address and in any email addresses).

- Check the spelling in the email itself and any links (for example, Am**o**zon or Go**g**gle) – these misspellings are intended to make the website look like a genuine company and are known as **typo squatting**.
- Check the tone of the message and language used (for example, 'we have receive your tax calculation which show you are due a tax repayment of 240 USD' – the English used here is clearly incorrect and should raise suspicion).
- Check email addresses; no legitimate company would use an email address such as @gmail.com; if you are unsure, click on the information symbol which will give you the full email address of the sender.

Firewalls

Firewalls can be either software or hardware; they sit between the user's computer and an external network. They are the primary defence to any computer system (either a stand-alone computer or a device which is part of a network) protecting it from potential cybercriminal activity.

The main features of firewalls are as follows.

- Examine the 'traffic' between the user's computer and an external network (for example, the internet).
- Check if incoming or outgoing data meets certain criteria; if the data fails the criteria, the 'traffic' is blocked, and the user is given a warning that there may be a security issue.
- Can prevent access to certain undesirable websites; they keep a list of all undesirable IP addresses.
- Can help prevent viruses or hackers.
- Maintain a log so a user can interrogate the daily activity to and from their computer.

It is important to consider circumstances where firewalls cannot prevent potentially harmful traffic, as per the following examples.

- If individuals use their own hardware on networks and bypass the network's firewall.
- Employee misconduct or carelessness (for example, poor control of passwords).
- Stand-alone computers can choose to disable a firewall allowing harmful traffic to enter the network.

Proxy servers

Proxy servers are an intermediate between a user and a web server.

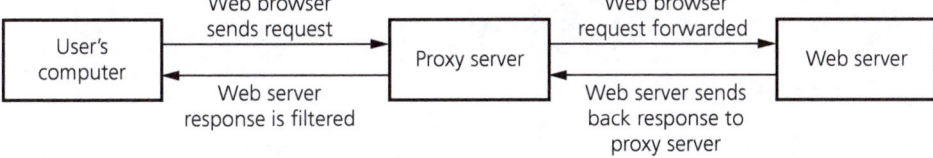

The main features of proxy servers are as follows.

- Filter internet traffic, blocking access to websites if necessary.
- Keep user's IP addresses secret.
- Can block requests from certain IP addresses.
- Prevent direct access to a web server by sitting between user and server.

5.3 Cyber security

- If a cyberattack is launched, the proxy server is affected instead of the web server, thus leaving the web server secure.
- Can direct invalid traffic away from the server.
- Using a 'cache' speeds up access to a website; the website home page is stored in a cache on the proxy server – next time the user visits the website, the proxy server cache is first checked and the home page is found.
- Can act as a firewall.

Privacy settings

Privacy settings are controls available on web browsers, social networks and other websites; they are designed to limit who can access and see a user's personal profile (data). Features of privacy settings include:

- a 'do not track' setting that stops websites collecting browsing data
- a check to see if the payment methods have been stored on websites, thus preventing the need to type in financial details each time a website is visited
- privacy options (browsing history, storing cookies)
- advertising opt-outs preventing unsolicited adverts from websites
- preventing apps sharing your location.

Secure sockets layer

Secure sockets layer (SSL) is a type of protocol used by computers to communicate securely with each other across networks. When a user logs onto a website, SSL encrypts the data; the user knows if SSL has been applied when they see https and/or the green padlock on the browser address bar.

The address window in the browser when the https protocol is being applied, rather than just the http protocol, is quite different.

The following diagram shows what happens when a user wants to access a secure website and receive from it and send data to it.

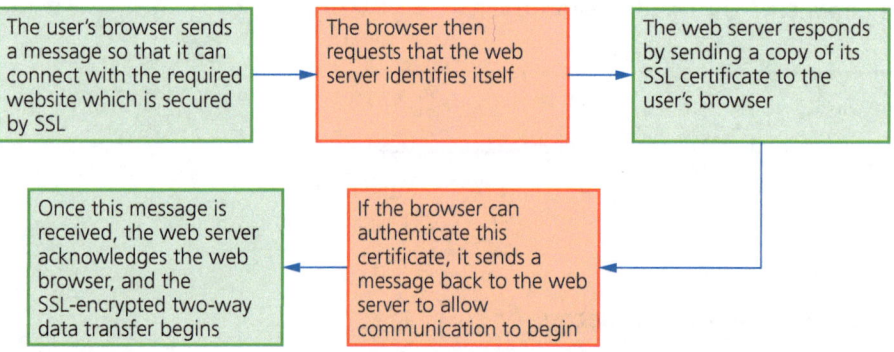

SSL certificates are a form of digital certification used to authenticate a website. SSL could be used when doing online banking, online shopping, sending/receiving emails, using cloud storage, using VoIP or instant messaging.

5 The internet and its uses

Sample question and answer

REVISED

John wants to access his bank account. Apart from username and password, John's bank also uses one-time passcodes (OTPs). Explain how OTP would be used in this application and also explain why it would be used. [4]

High-level sample answer

John logs on to his bank's website using his username and password. The bank sends John an 8-digit PIN either to his email address or to a mobile phone number registered as 'safe' on the bank website. John then types in the 8-digit PIN on the bank's website. If the PIN matches the one sent out by the bank, then John is allowed access to his bank account.

The process is time limited otherwise John will have to repeat the process. It is a form of authentication (the mobile phone is something John possesses and the PIN is something he knows).

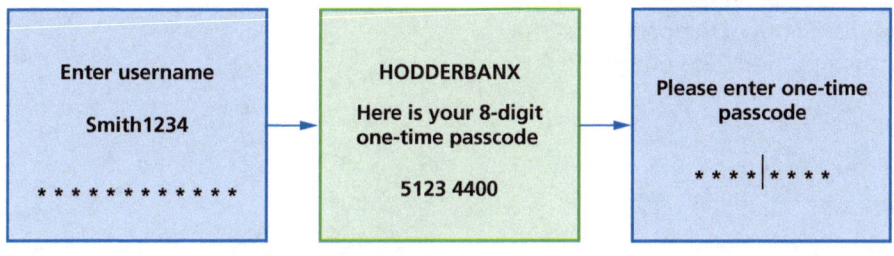

Sample low-level answer

When John accesses his website he has to type in a PIN to gain access. This extra level of security makes the website more secure. If John has three tries at entering the wrong PIN, he will be logged out of the system for several hours before being allowed to try again.

Tips

A full description of how OTP works is required here. Remember to refer to the given scenario, avoiding generic answers. The best way to answer the question is to go through the OTP steps and remember to include at least one reason why OTP is used by the bank.

Teacher's comments

The first answer goes through the OTP process very systematically, which makes it easy to follow. The diagram also helps since this reinforces the answer and can also help if any of the explanation is a little vague.

The second answer is unfortunately on the wrong track. The student clearly thought this was a simple PIN entry requirement and has failed to recognise the significance of OTP. This is a classic example of a student not reading the question carefully and missed the key aspect of the question.

Exam-style questions

5. a) Explain why passwords are used when logging onto websites. [1]
   b) Give **three** features you would expect to see in a strong password. Also give one example of what should be avoided when deciding on a password. [4]
   c) Mikael uses a password and also uses his email address as a username to log into a secure website. Unfortunately, he has forgotten his password.
   Explain how Mikael can reset his password securely. [2]
6. Name the **eight** computer terms being described below (a different answer is required for all eight parts).
   a) A user is granted access to a website only after successfully presenting two pieces of evidence to verify their identity.
   b) Makes use of a cache to speed up access to web pages on a website.
   c) Controls that are used on social networks and other websites to allow users to limit who can access data from their stored personal profile.

5.3 Cyber security

d) Protocol that is used to allow data to be sent securely over a network, such as the internet.

e) Software or hardware that sits between a computer and an external network; it monitors and filters all incoming and outgoing traffic.

f) Use of unique human characteristics (such as face recognition) to identify a user as a form of authentication.

g) Manipulation of people into breaking normal security procedures and best practices to gain illegal access to a user's computer and steal or corrupt data.

h) Malicious code stored on a user's hard drive or on a web server used to redirect a browser to a fake website without the user's knowledge. [8]

7 You have been asked to write an article on cyber security threats to a computer connected to the internet.
Describe **four** different examples of cyber security threats and explain how the risks can be mitigated against. [8]

8 Automatic software updates are used by many mobile phone companies. The following flowchart shows the procedure for updating mobile phone software automatically overnight.

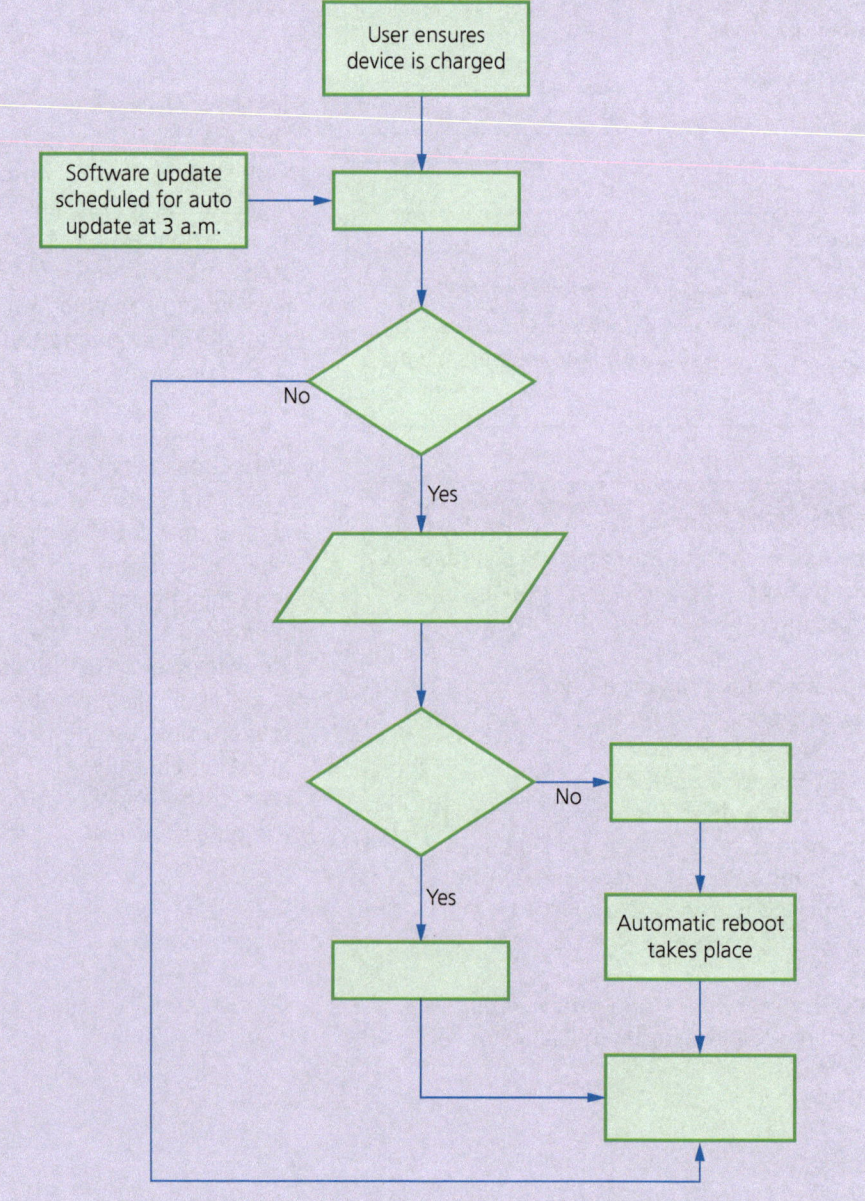

Seven of the boxes in the flowchart are incomplete. Use the following list of items to complete the flowchart. (You only need to write the item numbers, 1–7, in your answer.)

1	Installation of update takes place
2	Is a manual reboot of the mobile phone needed?
3	Do you need to reboot the mobile phone?
4	Output 'WARNING! Your phone will reboot in 10 minutes'
5	System waits ten minutes before rebooting
6	Update of mobile phone software is complete
7	User manually reboots mobile phone

[7]

9 Five statements are shown on the left, and eight computer terms are shown on the right.
By drawing lines, connect each statement to the correct computer term (three of the computer terms won't be used). [5]

Statements (left):
- A type of stand-alone virus that can replicate itself; they often use networks to search out computers with weak security that are prone to attack.
- Malicious programs often disguised as legitimate-looking software; replaces all or part of the legitimate software code with the intention of causing harm to the user's computer.
- Software that floods a user's computer with unwanted advertising, usually in the form of pop-ups but can also appear in a browser's address window redirecting the browser to a website that contains promotional material.
- Legitimate-looking emails that contain links to fake websites; when the user opens a link, the web browser is sent to a website where the user's personal details can be stolen or altered.
- The real IP address is changed to an IP address of a fake website thus redirecting the browser to this fake website.

Computer terms (right):
- Virus
- DNS cache poisoning
- Adware
- Worm
- Ransomware
- Trojan horse
- Phishing
- Pharming

10 Describe **three** ways to check whether an email is from a legitimate source. [3]

6 Automated and emerging technologies

Key objectives

The objectives of this chapter are to revise:
- automated systems:
  - use of sensors, microprocessors and actuators in automated systems
  - advantages and disadvantages of using automated systems in a given scenario
- robotics:
  - what is meant by robotics
  - characteristics of a robot
  - roles, advantages and disadvantages of robots
- artificial intelligence (AI):
  - what is meant by AI
  - the main characteristics of AI
  - the basic operation and components of AI systems to emulate intelligence behaviour

6.1 Automated systems

REVISED

6.1.1 Sensors, microprocessors and actuators

An **automated system** is a combination of hardware and software that is designed and programmed to work automatically without the need for any human intervention. Refer back to Section 3.2 (page 31) for more information on the role of sensors, microprocessors and actuators in the control of processes.

6.1.2 Advantages and disadvantages of automated systems

The *Cambridge IGCSE and O Level Computer Science Second Edition* Student's Book has a number of examples of automated systems. In this revision book, the key examples identified in 6.1 of the Student's Book have been summarised in a table on pages 82 and 83 Student's Book.

The applications covered in the following table include industrial, transport, weather, gaming and lighting. For an example on agriculture, refer to the high-level answer in the sample question. No examples for science have been given here, but automated systems can control experiments and research much more safely and accurately; they can also lead to faster results which is very important in drug development (refer to the example in the Student's Book page 228).

6 Automated and emerging technologies

Automated system	Sensors used in the automated system	Function of the actuators in the automated system	Function of the microprocessor in the automated system	Additional information
Industrial				
Nuclear power station	temperature, pressure, flow level (gas) and radiation level	To operate water pumps/valves, operate gas pumps/valves, automatic shutdown of process.	The microprocessor takes sensor readings and checks against stored parameters and sends signals to actuators to open/close relevant valves (pumps) or initiate shutdown of process.	At the centre of the system is a **distributed control system (DCS)**, a very powerful computer. The whole process is monitored from a control room where a schematic of the whole process can be seen; the supervisor can over-ride the computer system if necessary.
Paracetamol manufacture	temperature, pH, infrared and pressure	To operate heating elements, open/close valves to allow ingredients to be added to reaction vessels, recognise the presence of a tablet and measure the hardness of a tablet.	The microprocessor takes sensor readings and checks against stored parameters and sends signals to actuators to open/close valves, to operate heating elements and give warnings if tablets are out of specification (or missing).	The whole process is monitored from a central control room where a schematic of the process can be seen; the supervisor can over-ride the computer system if necessary.
Transport				
Adaptive cruise control	infrared laser sensors, cameras	To operate the brakes, accelerator and steering box.	Sensors pulse laser beams of infrared light from the front bumpers and the laser beams are reflected back to sensors from the vehicle in front. The microprocessor calculates time between sending and receiving these laser signals and then calculates the distance between the two vehicles. If distance less than safe distance, then the microprocessor sends a signal to the actuators to operate the brakes. If distance greater than safe distance the microprocessor sends a signal to operate the accelerator to bring the car up to the set speed.	This can be part of an autonomous system where the vehicle requires no human input. Sensor readings, cameras and **LiDaR** all give the vehicle information about the surroundings. This is a much safer system as it allows more cars per kilometre of road space. The downsides include the over-reliance on the technology, and dirty sensors and cameras can make the system malfunction.
Self-parking cars	infrared laser sensors and cameras	To operate brakes and accelerator and also to operate the steering wheel.	Sensors pulse laser beams of infrared light from the bumpers and the laser beams are reflected back to sensors from the surroundings. The microprocessor calculates the time between sending and receiving laser signals and calculates any distances. It then sends signals to operate the brakes, accelerator and steering wheel, moving the vehicle into the parking space. The sensors and camera allow the microprocessor to work out the distance from the kerb	Sensors and cameras give a 3D image of the surroundings, allowing the vehicle to park safely. The cameras also show the driver the surroundings so they can over-ride the system if necessary. Cars can fit into smaller parking spaces and parking is safer. However, faulty/dirty sensors and cameras can cause problems, and it is an expensive option that

				and the distance between any other vehicles in the parking space. Sensors also check if any objects are in the way (such as lamppost or human, etc.)	doesn't necessarily save the driver any money.
Weather					
Weather stations	thermometer (temperature), anemometer (wind speed), hygrometer (humidity sensor), barometer (air pressure sensor), level sensor (measure rainfall) and light sensor (hours of sunlight)	To measure rainfall, rain is collected in a 'bucket' and at the end of the day, an actuator is used to operate a piston to tip the water in the bucket into a vessel where level sensors can measure the amount of rainfall.		The microprocessor takes the sensor readings and stores them in a central database. It also analyses the sensor data and sends out weather reports on a regular basis (for example, to a nearby airport). It sends signals to operate the actuator to operate the piston to tip the collected water in the 'bucket' into a vessel where rainfall can be calculated for the last 24 hours.	Since data is collected 24 hours a day, seven days a week, automated systems are essential and also safer in bad conditions, which could be hazardous to human operators.
Gaming					
Gaming and simulations	**accelerometers** (response to tilting and movement of input devices) and proximity sensors (used in smart touchpads)	If a simulator is being controlled (for example, flight simulator), readings from sensors are used by the microprocessor to control the movement of the simulator (signals are sent to actuators to operate motors etc.).		The microprocessor takes sensor readings and compares them to stored data (for example, sensor readings indicate that the simulated airplane is stalling) and sounds signals to give realism to the simulator. The microprocessor also sends signals to actuators to move pistons and start/stop motors to give simulated motion of an airplane cockpit. In a game, the microprocessor takes accelerometer and proximity sensor readings to alter on-screen movement and images in accordance with the user's inputs.	Games and simulators are much more realistic if sensors are used to gather actual data from the user's actions.
Lighting					
Lighting systems	light sensors and infrared sensors	Actuators are only used if the lighting system is part of a display (for example, a water and light fountain); the actuators will operate pumps and switches.		The microprocessor compares the light sensor readings. When the lighting level in a room < stored value, the microprocessor sends signals to switch on lights automatically. If the lighting system is part of a security system, the infrared sensor detects movement and the microprocessor takes action if the received signal indicates an intruder (for example, switch on an external light).	Automated systems reduce energy consumption since lights only come on when necessary and this also increases bulb life.

6 Automated and emerging technologies

The following table gives a general indication of the advantages and disadvantages of automated systems.

Advantages of automated systems	Disadvantages of automated systems
• Faster than humans taking any necessary action. • Safer if automated system is part of a hazardous system. • System is more likely to run under optimum conditions. • Less expensive in the long run/more energy efficient. • Can be a more effective use of materials and resources. • May increase overall productivity. • Results are more consistent.	• Often expensive to set up and purchase initially. • There is always the possibility for a set of conditions to occur which weren't considered during the development stage. • The constant fear of cyberattacks (hacking, viruses, and so on). • Automated systems need enhanced maintenance to operate correctly; this can be very expensive.

Sample questions and answers

REVISED

The irrigation (watering) of crops in large areas of Brazil is now fully automated due to the vast areas covered by farms.

The following diagram shows how sensors, actuators and microprocessors can be used to automatically control the irrigation system.

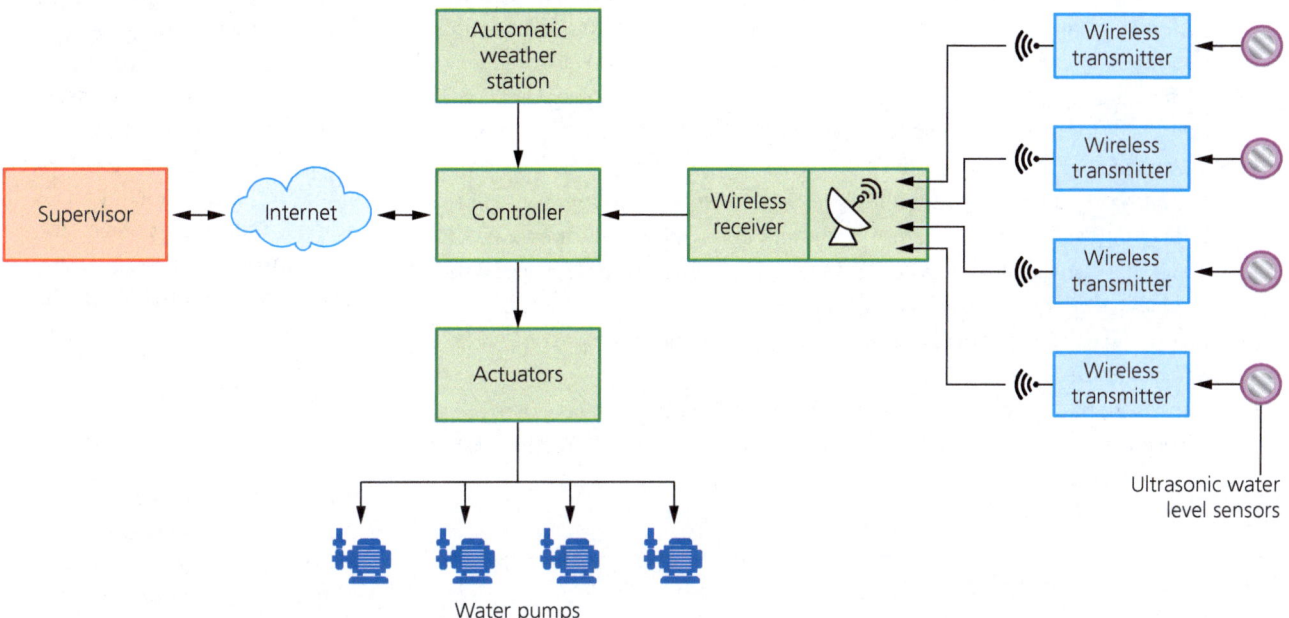

a) Using the diagram, explain how sensors, actuators and a microprocessor (controller) are used to monitor and control this irrigation system. [5]
b) Describe the advantages and disadvantages of using this automated irrigation system. [5]

> **Tips**
>
> All the information you need to answer the question is given in the diagram supplied. Use this information, together with your knowledge of other automated systems, to describe how the irrigation process will work. Do not be generic with your answers and constantly make reference to the given scenario. In part b), give at least three advantages and three disadvantages to gain the full marks. Again, you need to be specific and reference this application (for example, if a virus is planted in the system causing it to crash, then whole crops could be destroyed if the irrigation system stops working).

6.1 Automated systems

Sample high-level answer

a) Data from an automated weather station is received by the controller. The weather station gives a forecast about future conditions; will it be dry or wet. Data from the ultrasonic water level sensors is used to measure the amount of water in the irrigation channel. This sensor data is sent to the controller via wireless transmission, due to vast size of the area. The controller uses the sensor data and data from the weather station to decide whether to start or stop the water pumps. The water pumps are controlled by signals sent to actuators from the controller. A supervisor can watch the whole process remotely and can oversee several irrigation systems at the same time from a single control room (which will have a schematic of each irrigation system on computer screens). The supervisor can over-ride the controller if necessary.

b) Advantages:
- Reduced labour costs since system only needs a supervisor to monitor vast areas.
- More efficient/effective control of the irrigation process.
- There is a better control of scarce resources, such as water.
- Faster response than a human if anything goes wrong; there are many kilometres of channels to check which would take humans a long time.
- Safer; the temperatures could be over 40 °C in the fields and some crops need vast amounts of water which could also pose a risk to humans.
- Different crops need different conditions; it is possible to program the controller for a specific crop to ensure optimum yield.

Disadvantages:
- Expensive system to set up initially (expensive equipment and testing the system/modelling the system is both time-consuming and expensive).
- There are high maintenance costs associated with automated systems (and the need for specialist technicians).
- Increased need to maintain water channels to ensure the system works effectively at all times.
- The risk of hacking or viruses in the system; this could lead to a system failure which could cause considerable damage to crops before the system was repaired.

Sample low-level answer

a) The sensors, actuators and controller will work together to monitor and control the irrigation system. When the water level changes, the sensors will then send data to the actuators telling them to open valves or close valves to control the water levels in the irrigation channels. The sensor data will be sent wirelessly due to the large distances involved.

b) The advantages include: it is safer, it will stop fields becoming dry, water can be added faster and there is no need for any maintenance.
The disadvantages are it will be expensive and there is the risk of hackers from foreign countries altering things to destroy the crops.

Teacher's comments

The first answer is a model answer and very few students would be expected to have this level of knowledge. Full marks would be given since only five points would be needed on both parts to gain full marks and this was exceeded in the answers to both part a) and part b).

The second answer is a good attempt but they have made the common mistake of thinking sensors only send data when something happens. Sensors constantly send data and it is up to the controller/microprocessor to take the necessary actions. It was also incorrect to say that sensor data is sent to the actuators. Marks could be gained for mentioning the need for data conversion to binary. Part a) would gain one mark overall by the student. For part b), again this was very brief but a mark could be gained for safety aspects (advantages) and a mark for security issues (disadvantages). The comment about being expensive needs to be expanded a bit to get any marks.

Exam-style questions

1. A laboratory experiment involves the use of a burette 'A' adding acid to a solution in a conical flask 'B'. As the reaction proceeds, the colour of the solution changes from yellow to red. The colour change is picked up by a sensor called a colorimeter.

   The amount of acid to be added is measured using two level detectors; the opening and closing of the burette tap is controlled by an actuator.

   As soon as the solution in 'B' turns red, the whole process is stopped. A microprocessor controls the whole process, as shown in the diagram.

   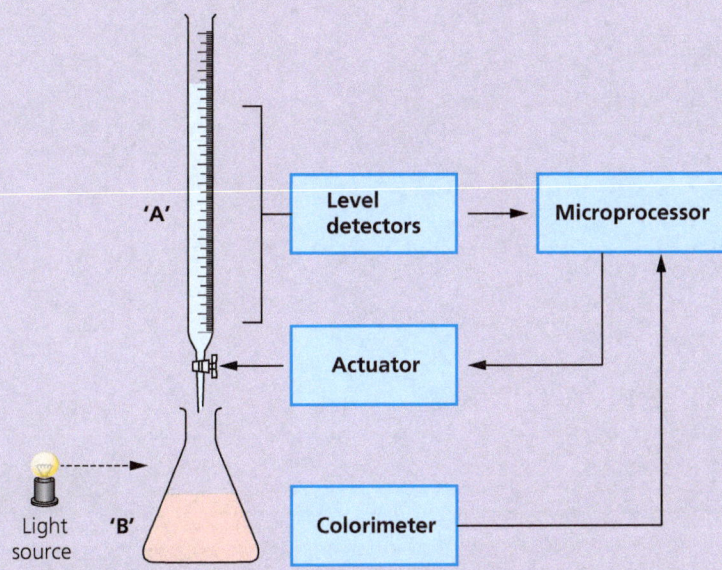

   a) Explain how sensors, actuators and a microprocessor are used to control the experiment to ensure the final product (red colour) is always produced. [4]
   b) Describe the advantages and disadvantages of using an automated system in this experiment. [3]

2. a) Name suitable sensors for each of the following automated systems.
   i) Manufacture of a new vaccine which requires the mixing of four liquids in the ratio 1:2:3:4 as a single batch. The four liquids must be totally mixed and the temperature must be maintained at 35 °C (± 1 °C) which is a critical temperature.
   ii) A lighting display has been set up in one room of an art gallery. A random sequence of different coloured lights is under microprocessor control. The display in the room only switches on when visitors walk into the room; at the same time, the room lights are also dimmed to give the most dramatic effect of the light display.
   iii) A train uses automatic twin-doors. Both doors open automatically when the train stops. Both doors close again when no one is still boarding or leaving the train. The doors have a safety mechanism so that a passenger cannot become trapped between the two closing doors. The train can only move off when every door on the train has been safely closed. [6]
   b) For each application in part a), give **one** advantage and **one** disadvantage of using automated systems. [4]

3 The eight statements on the left-hand side of the table are either true or false.

Tick (✓) the appropriate box to indicate which statements are true and which statements are false.

Statement	True	False
Automated systems lead to less consistent results or less consistent products.		
Automated systems are more expensive to set up than traditional manual systems.		
Automated systems would be quickly overwhelmed by the amount of data presented to them.		
Automated systems are inherently less safe than manual systems.		
Automated systems generally require enhanced maintenance when compared to manual systems.		
Automated systems allow processes to run at optimum conditions at all times.		
Software failures, due to unforeseen conditions, are unlikely to impact on an automated system.		
Automated systems will react more quickly to unusual process conditions.		

[8]

6.2 Robotics

REVISED

6.2.1 What is robotics?

Robotics is a branch of (computer) science that brings together the design, construction and operation of robots.

Some examples of the uses of **robots** in factories include:

- welding metal parts in a factory (for example, car body panels)
- spray painting panels
- laser cutting of patterns (for example, in metal, plastic, leather) with a high precision and very little waste
- bottling and canning in the food and drinks industry
- warehouse logistics (for example, location of items and loading onto correct lorry).

There are also several areas where robots are used in the home, such as:

- **autonomous** floor sweepers
- autonomous lawn mowers
- automatic window cleaning
- in home entertainment ('friend' robots).

Drones are another example of robotics, used in:

- reconnaissance (for example, aerial photography)
- parcel deliveries (particularly in busy cities)
- flying in dangerous areas where there is a danger to human life (for example, carrying out a survey following a hazardous chemical spillage or nuclear incident).

6.2.2 Characteristics of a robot
The following three characteristics are used to evaluate if a machine can be termed a robot.

Ability to sense their surroundings
- Use sensors and cameras as input to the robot.
- Use sensors to recognise the immediate environment by building up a 3D picture to determine the size, shape and weight of an object, for example.
- All sensor data is sent to a microprocessor or computer.

Have a degree of movement
- Use of wheels, cogs, pistons, gears and so on, to carry out functions such as turning, twisting, moving backwards/forwards and gripping or lifting.
- Mechanical structures made up of motors, hydraulic pipes, actuators and circuit boards.
- Contain many electrical components.
- Able to use **end-effectors** – different attachments to carry out a number of tasks.

Must be programmable
- Have a **controller** that determines the actions that need to be taken to carry out a task automatically.
- Controllers are programmable so that the robot can be 'trained' to do various tasks.

Many robots don't possess artificial intelligence (AI) since they are often used to do repetitive tasks rather than requiring adaptive human characteristics.

All of the above notes refer to physical robots; but there are also software robots in existence, such as search engine bots or **web crawlers** and **chatbots** (web crawlers roam the internet scanning websites and categorising them so that they can be recognised by a search engine; chatbots are programs that pop up on websites and seem to have a conversation with the web user).

Neither web crawlers nor chatbots are true robots, since they don't meet all of the three characteristics necessary to be defined as a robot.

Physical robots can be classified as independent or dependent.

Independent robots	Dependent robots
Have no direct human control (autonomous).	Have a human interfacing with the robot (for example, a control panel).
Can replace human activity totally.	Can supplement, rather than replace, the need for human activity.

6.2.3 The role of robots and their advantages and disadvantages
The *Cambridge IGCSE and O Level Computer Science Second Edition* Student's Book has a number of detailed examples of applications that use robots (pages 232–239). In this revision book, the key parts of each system have been summarised in the following table.

6.2 Robotics

Application	Advantages of using robots in the application	Disadvantages of using robots in the application
Industry		
Welding car bodies and spray painting body panels. Manufacturing microchips or electrical goods. Makes use of end-effectors to do many different tasks. Used in many production facilities (car manufacturing, bottling/canning, testing circuit boards and so on).	Robots can work in conditions that may be hazardous to humans (noisy, dusty, chemicals and so on). Robots can work 24/7 with no breaks except for occasional maintenance. Using robots is less expensive in the long run. Robots are usually more productive than humans. In manufacturing, using robotics usually produces a more consistent product. Robots are better suited to boring and repetitive tasks.	It can be difficult to get the robot to handle 'non-standard' tasks without some human intervention. Using robots can lead to higher unemployment. Risk of deskilling since the robots take over tasks previously done by humans. Factories can be moved overseas (advantage to company but a disadvantage to the workforce); it is relatively easy to dismantle robots and reassemble them in another country. Robots are expensive to buy and set up initially.
Transport		
Autonomous cars, vans, buses, trams and trains.	Safer since human error is removed when operating vehicles. Better for the environment since vehicles will operate more efficiently and energy consumption is minimised. Leads to less traffic congestion as autonomous road vehicles can move more efficiently in cities and on motorways at busy times (due to increased lane capacity). Stress-free environment for drivers and passengers. Improves punctuality and frequency of public transport, such as buses, trams and trains. Reduction in running costs (due to more efficient operation). Easier to alter the bus, tram or train schedule at short notice (if some event makes this necessary).	Very expensive to set up in the first place (high technology requirements). Needs constant maintenance to work effectively, securely and safely (cleaning of sensors and cameras). Ensuring the good behaviour of passengers (especially at peak times) can lead to problems (for example, jamming doors, too many people trying to board at once and so on). Need a good, reliable control system (for example, CCTV); this can be expensive to maintain. Emergency situations may be difficult to deal with. Driver and passenger reluctance to use the new technology.
Agriculture		
Harvesting. Weed control (AI can distinguish between weed and crop). Phenotyping – observing plant growth/health. Seed planting and fertiliser spraying using drones. Automatic fruit picking, grass mowing, pruning.	More accurate and less likely to damage crops/fruit. Potentially higher yields since seeding, fertiliser application and so on is more efficient; leads to optimum conditions for growth and health. Less labour needed (for example, automatic weeding, fruit picking and so on). Plant health monitored better, and problems can be identified earlier and rectified. Less waste of seeds, fertilisers and so on.	Expensive systems to set up initially and to maintain. Risk of cybercriminal activity (such as hacking, viruses and so on). Risk of deskilling, since key farming skills could be lost (over-reliance on technology).

Medicine		
Surgical procedures. Monitoring patients. Disinfecting rooms and operating theatres. Taking blood samples. Micro bots used in target therapy. Prosthetic limbs are mini-robots.	Operations can be quicker and safer to carry out (fewer errors will be made). Leaves doctors/surgeons available to do more complex surgery and leaves nurses to do more skilled work. Taking blood samples is less painful to the patient; nurses and doctors are not subjected to potentially hazardous blood samples (for example, some viruses are very contagious). Target therapy causes less damage to surrounding tissues. Prosthetic limbs can now mimic human limb movement more precisely.	Robotic surgery is very expensive to set up and maintain. Difficult to make sure robots are fully disinfected before doing surgical work. Risk of cybercriminal activity (for example, hacking and viruses). Reluctance by the general population to robotic surgery. The all-important human factor is missing.
Domestic robots		
Autonomous vacuum cleaners. Autonomous grass cutters. Personal assistants.	Leave people free to do other (more interesting) tasks. More than one task can be completed at the same time. Can be programmed to work at a specific time of the day. Can be operated remotely (for example, using mobile phone app). Can automatically empty the dust bag/grass bag and automatically park and connect to the mains supply to recharge internal batteries. Allow linking together of several devices in the home and can also carry out certain useful tasks (for example, get flight information or weather forecasts for the next day). Can be programmed to turn on lights at random times at night if a house is unoccupied thus helping with security (there are many such tasks).	Expensive devices to buy initially and require regular expert servicing (sensors and cameras need specialist technicians). Unable to deal with unusual circumstances as well as a human (for example, a tree has fallen on the grass). Battery life can be short. Sometimes can't reach into corners where dust/long grass accumulates and requires human action. Takes much longer to do the tasks (up to three times longer than doing hoovering or grass cutting manually). Personal assistants could make people lazy rather than looking up for information themselves. Personal assistants can be annoying if used frequently. Digital assistants can be hacked into remotely; this can result in a breach of the user's privacy. Digital assistants can collect and process user's personal data without their knowledge.
Entertainment		
Theme parks and arenas/large venues (robotic characters are used to interact with visitors). Film and TV industry (operate cameras, stunt actions, special effects).	Greater realism to theme park characters, increasing entertainment factor. Music festivals can be more immersive (robot-controlled lighting and animation); effects can be synchronised with music. Control of cameras leads to better results (smoother action and always correctly focused). Better and more realistic animation and more effective cross-over with animation and actual actors.	Very expensive system to set up initially and to maintain. Risk of deskilling since many of the tasks done by skilled humans are now done by robots (for example, camera work).

6.2.4 Using sensors, actuators and microprocessors together

Example 1: Spraying car body with paint

The above table considers the role of robots in a number of different areas. The following is an example of the use of robots in industry. It considers the interaction between a robot arm, sensors, actuators and controller/microprocessor. The robot arm has the task of spraying a car body with paint.

- When a car body arrives, sensors detect it is in the correct position ready for spraying.
- The sensor data is constantly fed back to a controller/microprocessor in the body of the robot arm.
- The controller/microprocessor sends signals to actuators in the robot arms to move the arms in the correct programmed sequence to ensure the whole car body is painted.
- The sensors are used to make sure spraying cannot occur if there is no car body present or it is wrongly orientated.

Example 2: Control of opening/closing doors on a train

The following example shows how sensors, actuators and a microprocessor are used in the automatic opening and closing of train doors.

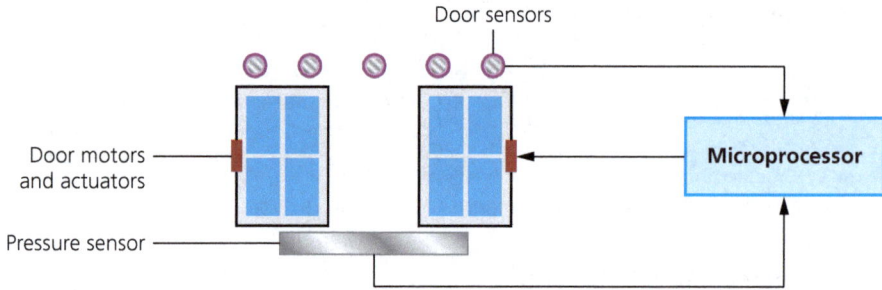

- Sensors above the doors detect the presence of passengers waiting to enter or leave the train; a pressure sensor is also used to detect passengers standing between the doors (to prevent the doors closing if a passenger is 'in the way').
- The sensor data is constantly sent back to a microprocessor in a central location.
- The microprocessor determines if it is safe to open or close doors by checking sensor data; the whole system is automatic.
- Data is sent to actuators to operate the motors closing and opening the doors.

Sample questions and answers

a) Describe the **three** characteristics that must be shown by a device for it to be regarded as a robot. [6]
b) Explain the difference between **dependent** and **independent** robots. [2]
c) Describe briefly **two** examples of software robots. [2]

High-level sample answer

a) Robots must have the ability to sense their surroundings. They need to use a number of different sensors and various types of camera to gain a 3D image of their immediate surroundings, enabling the ability to determine shape, size or weight of any object within sensor range.

Robots must have a high degree of movement. They can use wheels, cogs, pistons, gears (and so on) to carry out movement such as turning, twisting/rotating, move backward/forward, gripping an object (without breaking it or dropping it) or lifting an object.

Robots must be programmable. The robot uses a controller (a microprocessor system) to determine its action and how to perfectly perform a task. Controllers must be programmable (this can be done either remotely or by connecting to a device such as a memory stick)

b) Independent robots are autonomous and don't need any human interaction. Dependent robots need a human to interface and can therefore supplement, rather than replace, the need for a human operator.

c) Two examples of software robots are web crawlers and chatbots. Web crawlers roam the internet scanning websites characterising them so that they can be recognised by a search engine. Chatbots pop-up on websites and provide some form of 'intelligent' conversation with the web user.

Sample low-level answer

a) Robots must be made from metal and be able to move on their own. They should understand verbal commands and have in-built routines not to harm humans. Most robots carry out tasks that humans don't want to do.

b) Independent robots can work on their own whilst dependent robots need some help.

c) One type of software robot is the type used when doing online chatting.

Tips

In part a) it is necessary to give as many examples as possible to enable a full description of all three characteristics. Part b) is a comparison; it is necessary to give clear differences between the two types of robot. Part c) asks for brief descriptions; so only give a very short mention of the key features of typical software robots.

Teacher's comments

The first answer gives a full description of the three characteristics that define a robot. They have also correctly explained what is meant by an independent robot and a dependent robot – the difference is very clear. In part c), the student has correctly recognised two of the most common types of software robot.

The whole of the second answer is very vague and very sci-fi influenced and worth no marks. In part b), there is not enough for any marks; none of it is incorrect, it is not enough. The last part will gain a mark for its reference to chatbots.

Exam-style questions

4   Use the following words to complete the paragraph that follows.

actuators	end-effectors	microprocessor	repetitive
adaptive	environment	physical	sensors
controller	intelligence	programs	system

Robots can collect data from their surroundings by using < .... >.

The data is then sent to a < .... > to allow the robot to build up an image of its < .... >.

Robots can do various tasks by using different < .... >.

The 'brain' of the robot is often called a < .... >, which contains < .... > to allow it carry out various tasks automatically.

Many robots are not (artificially) intelligent, since they only do < .... > tasks rather than requiring < .... > human characteristics.

[4]

5 Autonomous robots are used in space exploration and in undersea exploration. These robots have to either work in the near vacuum of space or the very high pressures under the oceans. They need to be equipped with many sensors and cameras to carry out their remote tasks.
   a) The undersea robots are being used to investigate shipwrecks.
      Describe how the sensors and cameras could be used to photograph the shipwrecks. Also describe the role of the microprocessor and actuators in taking photographs and any samples needed from the shipwreck for further investigation. [3]
   b) A space exploration robot has been sent on a mission to Mars. The robot needs to move around the surface of the planet safely, taking photographs and taking soil/rock samples for later analysis.
      i) Describe how sensors, actuators and a microprocessor can be used to take samples from the planet's surface.
      ii) Describe **three** uses of the cameras on this autonomous robot. [5]
   c) Describe the advantages of using autonomous robots in both undersea and outer space exploration. [3]
   d) Give **two** other examples of where autonomous robots could be used. [2]
6 Autonomous buses, trams and trains are being introduced to many cities around the world.
   a) Explain what is meant by the term **autonomous**. [1]
   b) Autonomous trains make use of many sensors to enable functions, such as closing and opening doors, to be done automatically.
      Describe **three** sensors that might be used by the train to control the opening and closing of doors. In your description, explain the function of the sensors and how they would interact with actuators and a central microprocessor. [5]
   c) Give **two** advantages and **two** disadvantages of using autonomous buses in a city centre. [4]

6.3 Artificial intelligence

REVISED

6.3.1 Introduction

Artificial intelligence (AI) is a branch of computer science dealing with the simulation of intelligent human behaviour by a computer. This is often referred to as **cognitive** functions of the human brain. All these cognitive functions can be replicated in AI and can be measured against human benchmarks such as reasoning, speech and the senses (such as sound, sight, touch and smell).

6.3.2 Characteristics of AI

AI is a collection of rules and data, together with the ability to reason, learn and adapt to external stimuli. There are three categories of AI: narrow AI, general AI and strong AI.

- **Narrow AI:** a machine has superior performance to a human in one specific task.
- **General AI:** a machine is similar, but not superior, in its performance in doing one specific task.
- **Strong AI:** a machine has superior performance to humans in many tasks.

Reasoning is the ability to draw reasoned conclusions based on given data. Deductive reasoning is where a number of correct facts are built up to form a set of rules that can be applied to other problems. For example, if AI has been 'trained' to make a cup of tea, the rules can then be applied to making a cup of coffee or hot chocolate, by modifying the existing rules as necessary.

Examples of AI include:
- news generation based on live news feeds
- smart home devices/assistants (such as Amazon Alexa or Apple Siri)
- use of chatbots that interact through instant messaging
- autonomous vehicles
- facial expression recognition.

6.3.3 AI systems

There are two types of AI system that need to be considered at IGCSE: expert systems and machine learning.

Expert systems

Expert systems are a form of AI developed to mimic human knowledge and experience. They use knowledge and inference to solve problems by analysing responses to a series of questions thus mimicking a human expert.

An expert system consists of a number of components, as shown in the diagram below.

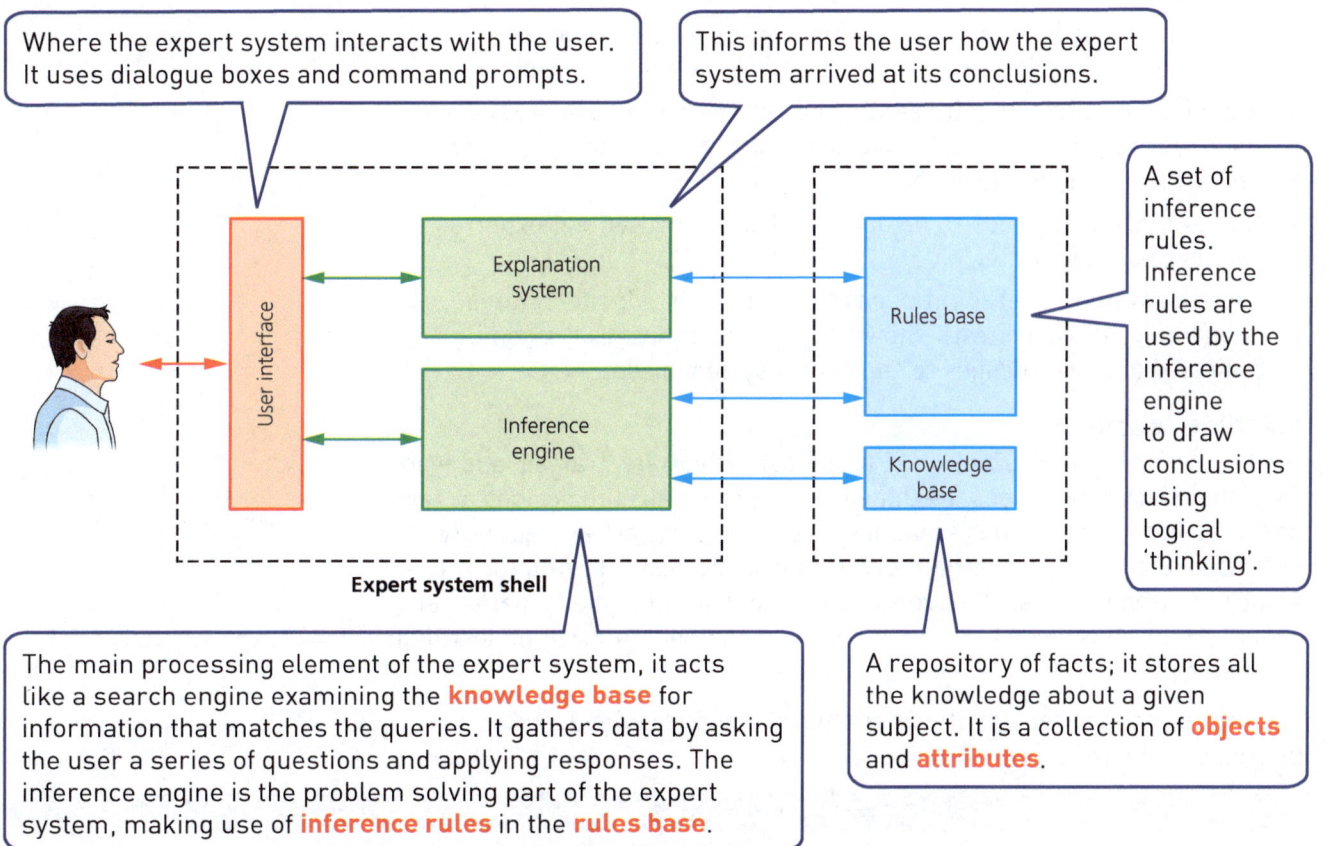

Where the expert system interacts with the user. It uses dialogue boxes and command prompts.

This informs the user how the expert system arrived at its conclusions.

A set of inference rules. Inference rules are used by the inference engine to draw conclusions using logical 'thinking'.

The main processing element of the expert system, it acts like a search engine examining the **knowledge base** for information that matches the queries. It gathers data by asking the user a series of questions and applying responses. The inference engine is the problem solving part of the expert system, making use of **inference rules** in the **rules base**.

A repository of facts; it stores all the knowledge about a given subject. It is a collection of **objects** and **attributes**.

There are many applications of expert systems.
- Oil and mineral prospecting.
- Diagnosis of a patient's illness.
- Fault diagnostics in mechanical and electrical equipment.

- Tax and financial calculations.
- Strategy games (for example, chess).
- Logistics (for example, most efficient parcel deliveries).
- Identification of plants, animals and chemical compounds.

This table summarises the advantages and disadvantages of expert systems.

Advantages of expert systems	Disadvantages of expert systems
<ul><li>High level of expertise and very accurate.</li><li>Give consistent results.</li><li>Can store vast amounts of information.</li><li>People can be trained to use the systems even if they are not experts in a particular field.</li><li>Can make traceable logical solutions/diagnostics.</li><li>Can have multiple expertise.</li><li>Very fast response time.</li><li>Unbiased reporting.</li><li>Give the probability of the solution or suggestion being correct.</li></ul>	<ul><li>Users need training to operate them correctly.</li><li>Set up and maintenance is costly and time-consuming (it takes time to populate the knowledge base, for example).</li><li>Tend to give 'cold' responses that may not be appropriate in certain circumstances (for example, when diagnosing a patient's illness).</li><li>Only as good as the information entered into the knowledge base.</li><li>Users sometimes make the dangerous assumption that expert systems are infallible.</li></ul>

Setting up an expert system

- Information needs to be gathered from human experts or from written sources such as textbooks, research papers or the internet.
- Information gathered is used to populate the knowledge base which needs to be first created.
- A rules base needs to be created; this is made up of a series of inference rules so that the **inference engine** can draw conclusions.
- The inference engine itself needs to be set up; it is a complex system since it is the main processing element making reasoned conclusions from data in the knowledge base.
- The user interface needs to be developed to allow user and expert system to communicate.
- Once the system is set up, it needs to be fully tested; this is done by running the system with known outcomes so that results can be compared and any changes to the expert system made.

Machine learning

Machine learning is a subset of AI where algorithms are 'trained' and learn from their past experiences. Machine learning can make predictions or take decisions based on previous scenarios. They can offer fast and accurate outcomes due to very powerful processing capabilities. A key factor is the ability to manage and analyse considerable volumes of complex data that could take humans years to complete without the help of machine learning technology.

The differences between artificial intelligence and machine learning can be summarised as follows.

AI	Machine learning
Represents simulated intelligence in machines.	The practice of getting machines to make decisions without being programmed to do so.
Aim is to build machines which are capable of thinking like humans.	Aim is to make machines that learn through data acquisition, so that they can solve new problems.

6 Automated and emerging technologies

Examples of machine learning include the following.

- In search engines where machine learning is used to improve on the search engine's ability to select relevant websites based on the search criteria. Web crawlers are used to 'train' the software/algorithms so that the search engine 'hits' are all listed on the first page of the search results.
- Categorising emails as spam by analysing 'cleaned' emails after **stop words** like 'the', 'and' and 'a' have been removed. Certain key words and phrases are used to determine if emails could be spam. A machine learning model is built and a 'training data set' is used to 'train' the model so it can learn from previous emails which were known to be spam.
- Recognising a user's buying history on the internet; this makes use of **collaborative filtering**. It is a process of comparing a customer's shopping behaviour to a new customer who has similar shopping behaviour, which allows the system to recommend products to the new customer; this system is also used to generate music playlists based on a user's criteria.
- Detection of fraudulent internet activity uses **web scraping** (this is information about a customer's shopping habits used to predict credit/debit card activity) to identify any unusual spending patterns and thus spot potentially fraudulent activity.

Sample questions and answers

REVISED

The following table contains ten descriptions. Complete the table by writing the computer term being described in the right-hand column.

Description	Computer term
Attachment to a robot arm that allows it to carry out a specific task, such as welding a car body.	
A type of search engine used in an expert system that examines the knowledge base for information that matches the queries.	
General name of any robotic device that can operate independently without any need for human input.	
A subset of AI in which algorithms are 'trained' and learn from past experiences.	
A combination of software and hardware designed and programmed to work automatically without the need for any human intervention.	
A collection of rules and data that leads to the ability to reason, learn and adapt to external stimuli.	
Pop-up robots found on websites that appear to enter into a meaningful conversation with the website user.	
The mental process of the human brain whereby it acquires knowledge and understanding through thought, experience and the senses.	
Something that defines the objects stored in the knowledge base of an expert system.	
Repository of facts, in an expert system, that is a collection of objects and attributes.	

[10]

Sample high-level answer

(Table filled with following terms, from top to bottom):

end-effector; inference engine; independent or autonomous robot; machine learning; automated system; artificial intelligence; chatbot; cognitive; attribute; knowledge base

6.3 Artificial intelligence

> **Sample low-level answer**
>
> (Table filled with following terms, from top to bottom):
>
> extension; Google; independent; expert system; autonomous; rules base; chatbot; thought; table; memory

Exam-style questions

7 a) Describe the term **machine learning**. [2]
   b) Explain how machine learning and artificial intelligence (AI) differ. [3]
   (c) Describe how a search engine might use machine learning to determine the most appropriate results based on a user's search criteria. [2]

8 a) Explain each of the following terms used in machine learning.
      i)   Stop words
      ii) Collaborative filtering
      iii) Web crawlers
      iv) Web scraping [4]
   b) Describe how machine learning can help to categorise an email as spam. [2]

9 Six statements are shown on the left, and nine computer terms are shown on the right.

   By drawing lines, connect each statement to its correct term. Not all computer terms will be used. [6]

Statements (left):
- Branch of computer science where cognitive behaviour of the human brain is studied.
- When a machine shows superior performance to a human in many tasks.
- Application that uses knowledge and inference to solve problems that would require human expertise.
- Repository of facts that is a collection of objects and their attributes.
- Contains the inference rules used to determine any matches between input data and stored data.
- Subset of AI in which the algorithms are 'trained' and learn from past experiences and examples.

Terms (right):
- Rules base
- Search engine
- Strong AI
- Artificial intelligence
- Machine learning
- Robotics
- Expert system
- Knowledge base
- User interface

Tips

It is necessary to be very careful when answering questions of this type. Many descriptions can be very similar and you need to pick out key words/phrases to ensure you pick the correct term being described. Also be very careful with the spelling of the term.

Teacher's comments

The first student has clearly revised all of the definitions since they scored the maximum mark here.

The second student has clearly made a number of guesses and manged to get two marks overall. It is very important that definitions are well revised before going into the exam, since a percentage of all marks are based on recalling facts (you are advised to check the breakdown of how marks are allocated by reading the syllabus to see how many of the marks are just for recollection and so on).

10 This diagram shows a schematic of an expert system.
  a) Name each of the components, 1–4. [4]

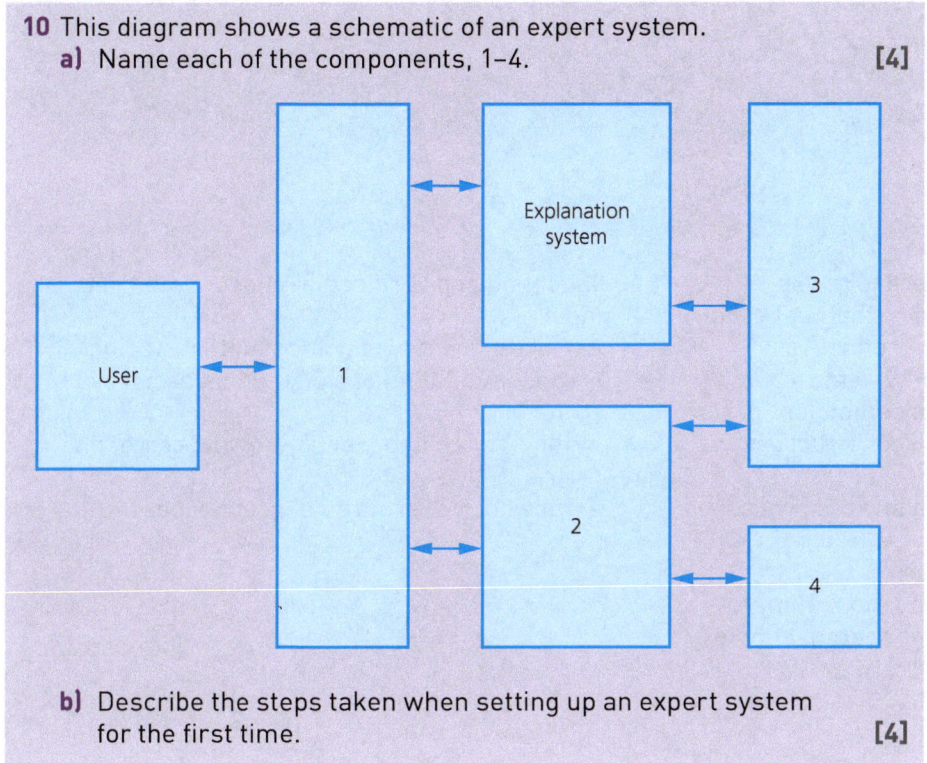

  b) Describe the steps taken when setting up an expert system for the first time. [4]

7 Algorithm design and problem solving

Key objectives

The objectives of this chapter are to revise:
- the stages in the program development cycle:
  - analysis, design, coding, testing
- computer systems and sub-systems
- problem decomposition into component parts
- methods used to design and construct solutions to problems
- the purpose of an algorithm and the processes involved in it
- standard methods of solution:
  - totalling, counting, finding maximum, minimum, average, linear search, bubble sort
- validation and verification checks when data is input
- use of different types of test data including:
  - documentation of a dry run using a trace table
- writing, amending identifying, and correcting errors in:
  - flowcharts, programs, pseudocode

7.1 Program development life cycle

REVISED

The program development life cycle is divided into five stages: **analysis**, **design**, **coding**, **testing** and **maintenance**.

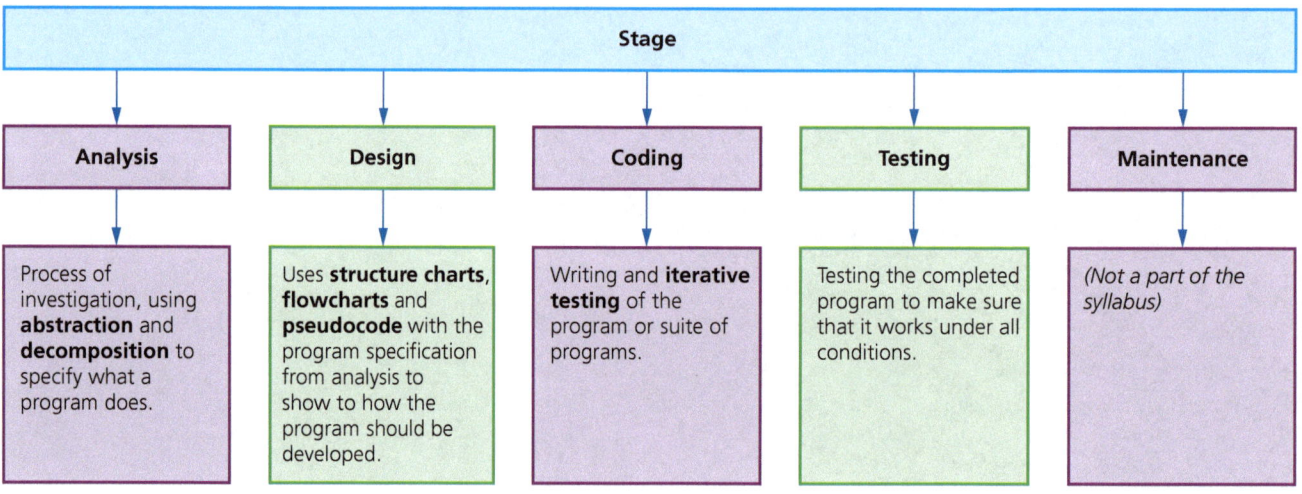

Sample questions and answers

REVISED

The program development life cycle is divided into different stages. Analysis is the first stage.
a) Describe the purpose of analysis.
b) Identify and describe **two** other stages of the program life cycle.   [6]

98 Cambridge IGCSE™ and O Level Computer Science Study and Revision Guide Second Edition

Sample high-level answer

a) Analysis is used to investigate the problem that requires a solution and find out what the program needs to do to provide that solution.

b) Two other stages are:
design – document the tasks required for the solution using structure charts and pseudocode
coding – write the programs that are required.

Sample low-level answer

a) A systems analyst will use interviews and questionnaires to find out what is needed.

b) The stages of program development are analysis, design, coding and testing. There is lots to do as the programs need to be written and fully tested.

Tips

Part a) of this question asks for the purpose, so your answer must state why the analysis stage is needed, not what actions are to be performed. It is always very important to read the question carefully. Part b) of this question involves 'identify'. This means your answer must either name the two stages of the program life cycle or clearly identify each one with a short statement.

Teacher's comments

The first answer would gain full marks since there is a clear description of the purpose of analysis. Two other stages of types of the program life cycle have been identified and described with each description clearly shown for the stage identified.

The second answer would gain one mark for part a) since the statement 'analysis is to find out what is needed' partially describes the purpose of analysis. Including the methods used answered a different question about how analysis is carried out. For part b) all the stages of the program life cycle are identified not just the two required. There is a description of the actions required but it is unclear which stage these apply to. A maximum of two marks could be awarded.

7.2 Computer systems, sub-systems and decomposition

REVISED

Each **computer system** is made up of software, data, hardware, communications and people. Each computer system can be divided up into a set of sub-systems and each sub-system can be further divided into sub-systems and so on until each sub-system just performs a single action. The process of **decomposition** into sub-systems so that a system can be more easily represented and understood is the basis of **top-down design**.

Any problem that uses a computer system for its solution needs to be decomposed into its component parts. These are **inputs**, **processes**, **outputs** and **storage**. The methods used to design and construct a solution are:

- structure diagrams
- flowcharts
- pseudocode.

7.2 Computer systems, sub-systems and decomposition

7.2.1 Structure diagrams

A **structure diagram** shows hierarchically how each computer system can be divided up into a set of sub-systems.

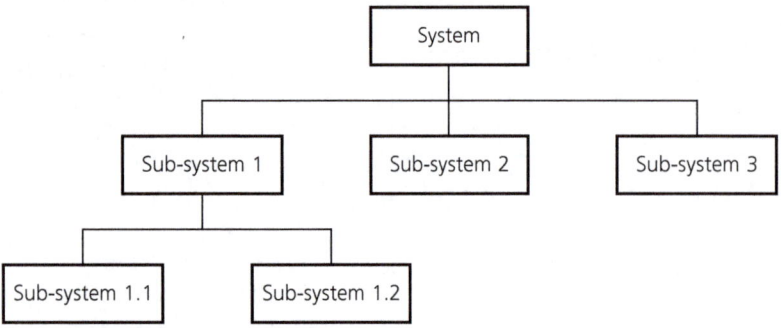

7.2.2 Flowcharts

A **flowchart** shows diagrammatically the steps required to complete a task and the order that they are to be performed. These steps, together with the order, are called an **algorithm**.

Flowcharts are drawn using standard flowchart symbols as shown in this table.

Use	Symbol	Description
Terminator Start/Stop	START STOP	Used at the beginning and end of each flowchart. At least two outputs.
Process	A ← 0 B ← 0	Used to show actions, for example, when values are assigned to variables.
Input/output	INPUT X	The same flowchart symbol is used to show the input of data and output of information.
Decision	x > B?	Used to decide which action is to be taken next. These can be used for selection and repetition/iteration. There are always two outputs from a decision flowchart symbol.
Flow lines	⟶	Used to show the direction of flow.

7.2.3 Pseudocode

Pseudocode is a simple method of showing an algorithm. It describes what the algorithm does by using English key words that are very similar to those used in a high-level programming language and meaningful identifier names.

Mathematical operators

Operator	Action
+	Add
−	Subtract
*	Multiply
/	Divide
^	Raise to the power
( )	Group

7 Algorithm design and problem solving

Pseudocode statements

Pseudocode statement	Examples

Assignment
 	
A value is assigned to an item/variable using the ← operator.
	`Cost ← 10`
	
	`SellingPrice ← Price + Tax`

Conditional 1
 	
A condition that can be true or false: `IF … THEN … ENDIF` or `IF … THEN … ELSE … ENDIF`
 	
For an `IF` condition the `THEN` path is followed if the condition is true, and the `ELSE` path if it is false (an `ELSE` may not be required). The end of the statement is followed by `ENDIF`
	`IF Age < 18`
	`  THEN`
	`    OUTPUT "Child"`
	`  ELSE`
	`    OUTPUT "Adult"`
	`ENDIF`

Conditional 2
 	
A choice between several different values: `CASE OF … OTHERWISE … ENDCASE`
 	
For a `CASE` statement, the value of the variable decides the path taken. Several variables are usually specified. `OTHERWISE` path is taken for all other values. The statement is ended by `ENDCASE`
	`CASE OF Grade`
	`  "A" : OUTPUT "Excellent"`
	`  "B" : OUTPUT "Good"`
	`  "C" : OUTPUT "Average"`
	`  OTHERWISE OUTPUT "Improve"`
	`ENDCASE`

Iteration 1
 	
`FOR … TO … NEXT` a variable is set up, with a start value and an end value, this variable is incremented in steps until the end value is reached and the iteration finishes.
	`FOR Counter ← 1 to 10`
	`  OUTPUT "*"`
	`NEXT Counter`

Iteration 2
 	
`REPEAT … UNTIL` is used when the number of repetitions/iterations is not known, and the actions are repeated `UNTIL` a given condition becomes true. The actions in this loop are always completed at least once.
	`Counter ← 0`
	`REPEAT`
	`  OUTPUT "*"`
	`  Counter ← Counter + 1`
	`UNTIL Counter >= 10`

Iteration 3
 	
`WHILE … DO … ENDWHILE` is used when the number of repetitions/iterations is not known, and the actions are only repeated `WHILE` a given condition is true. If the `WHILE` condition is untrue then the actions in this loop are never performed.
	`Counter ← 0`
	`WHILE Counter < 10 DO`
	`  OUTPUT "*"`
	`  Counter ← Counter + 1`
	`ENDWHILE`

Input `INPUT` used for data entry.	`INPUT Name` `INPUT StudentMark`
Output `OUTPUT` or `PRINT` used to display information.	`PRINT "Your name is", Name` `OUTPUT Name1, "Ali", Name3`

Nesting 1
 	
Nested `IF` makes use of two `IF` statements; the second `IF` statement is part of the first `ELSE` or `THEN` path
	`IF Age < 18`
	`  THEN`
	`    OUTPUT "Child"`
	`  ELSE`
	`    IF Age > 65`
	`      THEN`
	`        OUTPUT "Senior"`
	`      ELSE`
	`        OUTPUT "Adult"`
	`    ENDIF`
	`ENDIF`

Pseudocode statement	Examples

Nesting 2
 	
Nested iteration makes use of two loops; the second loop is inside the first loop.
	FOR Number ← 1 to 10
	  OUTPUT Number
	  FOR Counter ← 1 to Number
	    OUTPUT "*"
	  NEXT Counter
	NEXT Number

Comparison operators

Operator	Comparison
>	Greater than
<	Less than
=	Equal
>=	Great than or equal
<=	Less than or equal
<>	Not equal
AND	Both
OR	Either
NOT	Not

Sample questions and answers

REVISED

a) A computer system can be decomposed into its component parts. One of the parts is input.
   Identify **two** other component parts.
b) Formal methods are used to show a proposed solution.
   i) Identify the formal methods shown.

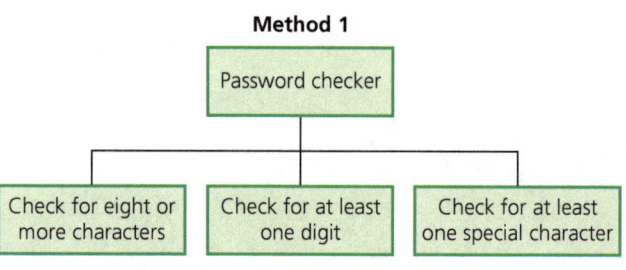

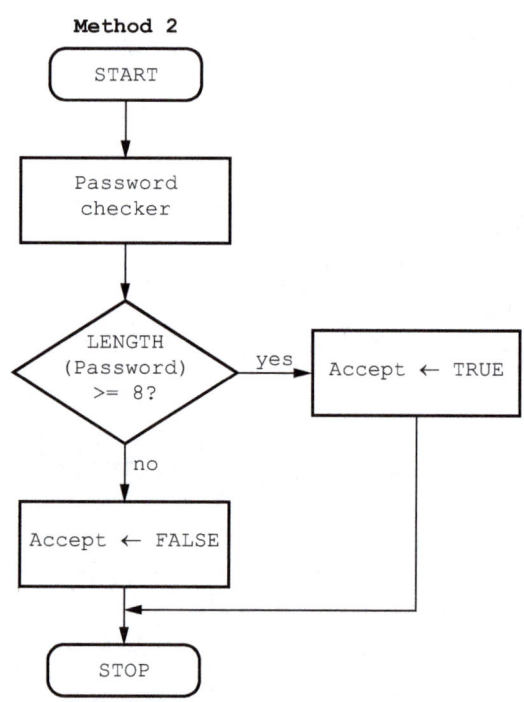

   ii) Identify another formal method that could be used to check if the password has more than eight characters.
   iii) Use the formal method you identified in part b)ii) to show the same routine to check if the password has more than eight characters.
   [8]

Cambridge IGCSE™ and O Level Computer Science Study and Revision Guide Second Edition

7 Algorithm design and problem solving

> **Tip**
>
> Part a) of this question asks for two **other** component parts; you must not use the part mentioned in the question. It is surprising how many students do this and throw away a mark. Part b)i) and ii) of this question involves 'identify'. This means your answer must either name the methods or clearly identify each one with a short statement. Part b)iii) needs the same routine to be rewritten using pseudocode, not a programming language.

Sample high-level answer

a) Process and output
b) i) The two methods are:
   Method 1 – structure diagram
   Method 2 – flowchart
   ii) Pseudocode
   iii)
```
IF LENGTH (Password) >= 8
     THEN Accept ← TRUE
     ELSE Accept ← FALSE
ENDIF
```

Sample low-level answer

a) input and output
b) i) The two methods are:
   Method 1 – structure chart
   Method 2 – flow diagram
   ii) Code
   iii)
```
IF Pwd.length > 8:
     OK = Yes
ELSE: OK = No
```

Teacher's comments

The first answer would gain full marks since two other components are identified, the methods are identified correctly, and the routine rewritten exactly matched the flowchart given and used the same identifiers, Password and Accept.

The second answer would gain one mark for part a) since only one other method was identified. For part b)i) the methods are identified, but the terminology used was not accurate, so one mark. For parts b)ii) and iii) code is used for the actual solution and the student has gone on to write a solution in Python that did not exactly match the flowchart. A maximum of two marks could be awarded.

7.3 Explaining the purpose of an algorithm

REVISED

An algorithm sets out the steps to complete a given task. This is usually shown as a flowchart or pseudocode, so that the purpose of the task and the processes needed to complete it are clear to those who study it.

Worked example

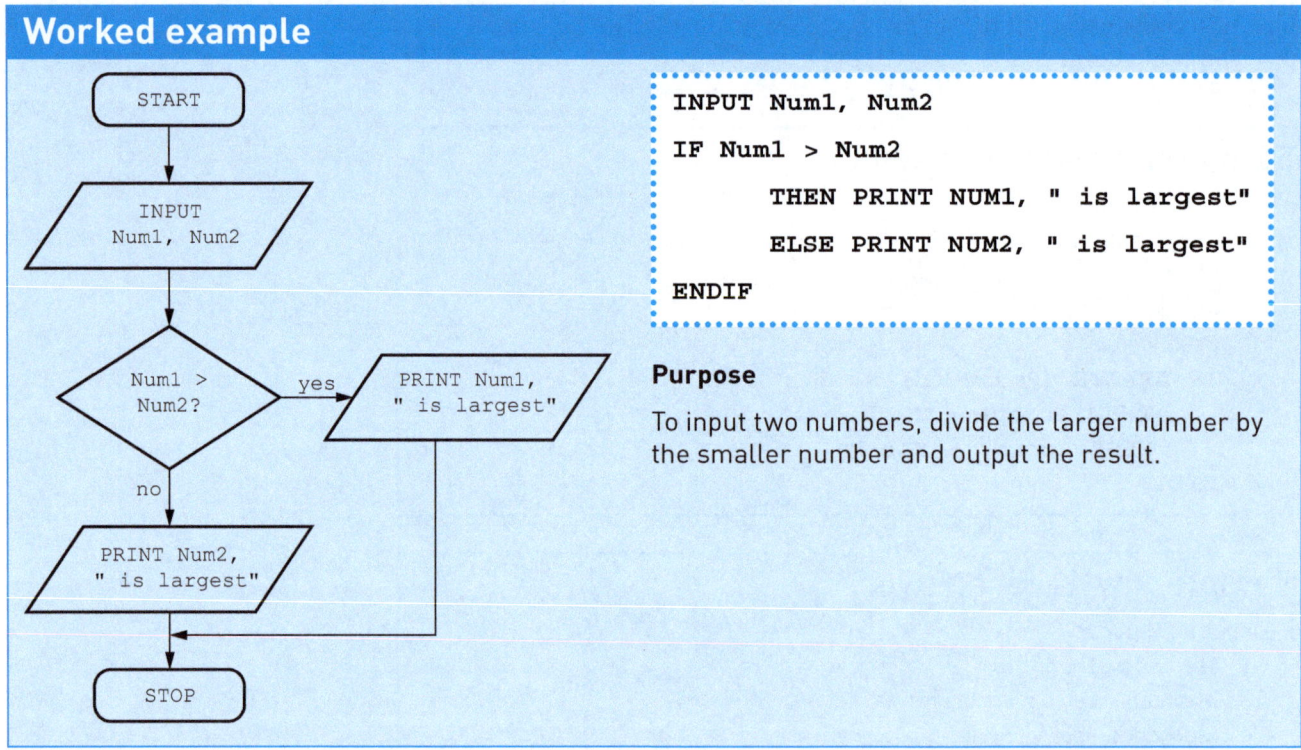

```
INPUT Num1, Num2
IF Num1 > Num2
      THEN PRINT NUM1, " is largest"
      ELSE PRINT NUM2, " is largest"
ENDIF
```

Purpose

To input two numbers, divide the larger number by the smaller number and output the result.

7.4 Standard methods of solution

REVISED

You need to be able to use and understand these standard methods used in algorithms.

Totalling

Sample pseudocode	Notes

Total ← 0
FOR Count ← 1 TO ClassSize
  INPUT Mark
  Total ← Total + Mark
NEXT Count
	Totalling adds up all the marks for students in the class.
	When totalling, the total is increased by the value of the mark.
	Always set the total to zero before checking the mark input.

Counting

Sample pseudocode	Notes

PassCount ← 0
FOR Counter ← 1 TO ClassSize
  INPUT Mark
  IF Mark > 50
    THEN
      PassCount ← PassCount + 1
  ENDIF
NEXT Counter
	Counting counts the number of students whose mark is over 50.
	When counting the counter is always increased by 1.

Finding maximum, minimum, average

Sample pseudocode	Notes
| ```
Total ← 0
MaxMark ← 0
MinMark ← 100
FOR Count ← 1 TO ClassSize
  INPUT Mark
  IF Mark > MaxMark
    THEN
      MaxMark ← Mark
  ENDIF
  IF Mark < MinMark
    THEN
      MinMark ← Mark
  ENDIF
  Total ← Total + Mark
NEXT Count
Average ← Total / ClassSize
``` | To find the maximum and minimum values every value must be checked. To find the average all values must be totalled then divided by the number of values.<br><br>Always set the minimum value to the largest value possible, always set the maximum value to the lowest value possible, before checking the mark input. |

Linear search

Sample pseudocode	Notes
| ```
OUTPUT "Enter name to find "
INPUT Name
Found ← FALSE
Counter ← 1
REPEAT
  IF Name = Name[Counter]
    THEN
      Found ← TRUE
    ELSE
      Counter ← Counter + 1
  ENDIF
UNTIL Found OR Counter > ClassSize
IF Found
  THEN
    OUTPUT Name, " found"
  ELSE
    OUTPUT Name, " not found."
ENDIF
``` | A **linear search** inspects each name in a list in turn to see if the name matches the name that was input.<br><br>The search stops as soon as the name is found. |

7.6 Test data

Bubble sort

Sample pseudocode	Notes
| ```
First ← 1
Last ← ClassSize
REPEAT
  Swap ← FALSE
  FOR Index ← First TO Last - 1
    IF Name[Index] > Name[Index + 1]
      THEN
        Temp ← Name[Index]
        Name[Index] ← Name[Index + 1]
        Name[Index + 1] ← Temp
        Swap ← TRUE
    ENDIF
  NEXT Index
  Last ← Last -1
UNTIL (NOT Swap) OR Last = 1
``` | A **bubble sort** compares each name in the list is with the next name and swaps them if the names are in the wrong order, starting from the first name and finishing with the next to last name.<br><br>The last name is in the right place once the list has been checked, this is repeated, decreasing the size of list by one, until no names are swapped or there are no names left to be swapped. |

7.5 Validation and verification

REVISED

For data entry, **validation** ensures that only data that is reasonable is accepted. **Verification** is used to check that the data does not change as it is being entered. Different types of checks may be used on the same piece of data.

> For check digits, please see Section 2.2.3 on page 21, where they are covered more fully.

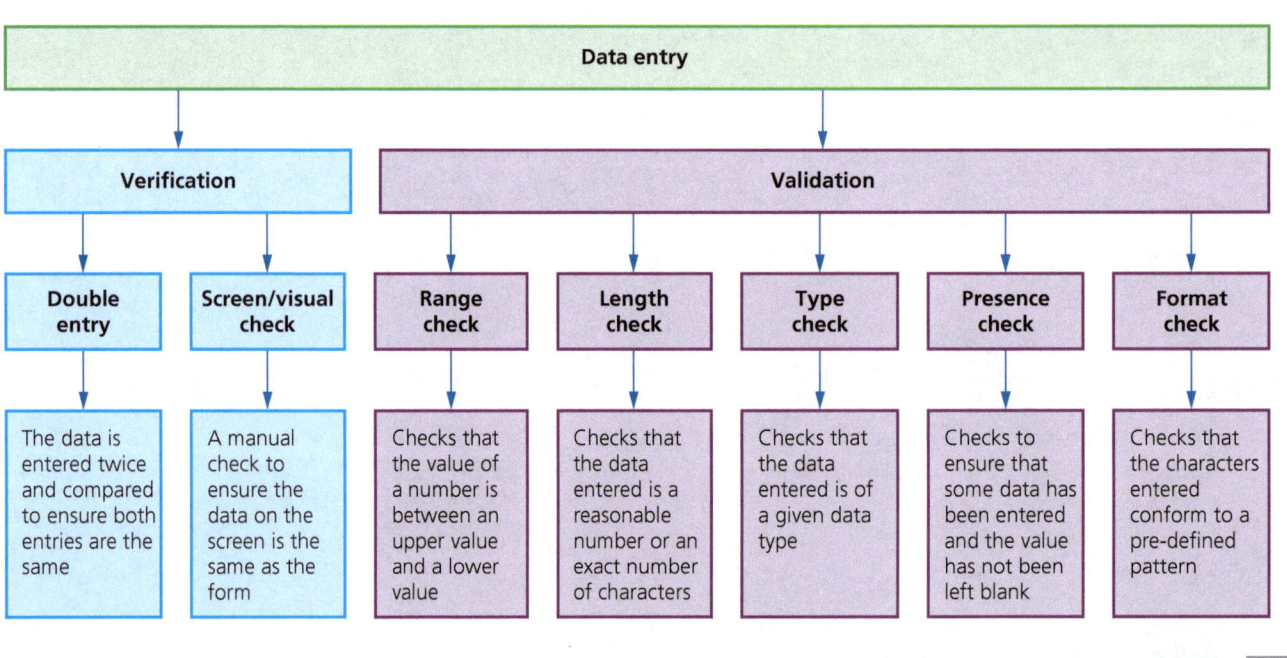

7.6 Test data

REVISED

Test data ensures that an algorithm works as expected, completing all parts of the solution with no errors. It is used with trace tables to check pseudocode and flowcharts work as expected. **Sets of test data** are used with programs to ensure outputs are as expected.

It is illegal to photocopy this page

106 Cambridge IGCSE™ and O Level Computer Science Study and Revision Guide Second Edition
```

7 Algorithm design and problem solving

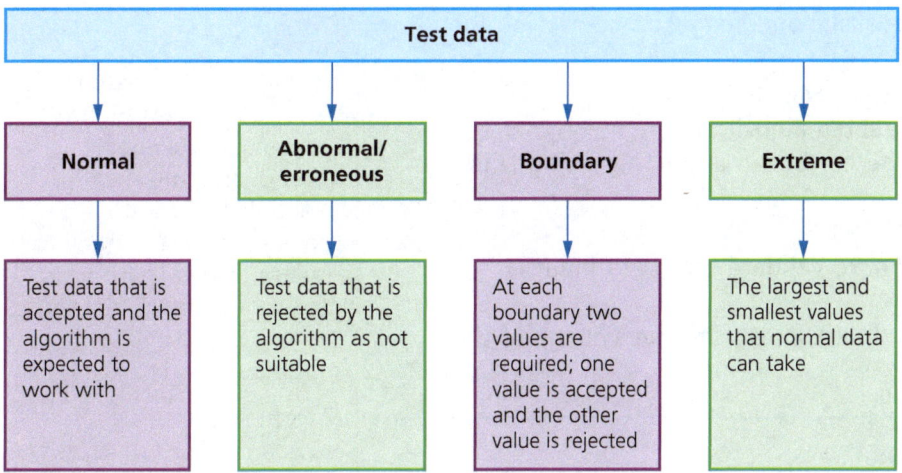

7.7 Trace tables

REVISED

A trace table records the results from each step in an algorithm; it shows the value of each variable every time that it changes. Working through an algorithm step by step is called a dry run. A trace table is set up with a column for each variable and a column for any output. For example:

A	B	C	X	OUTPUT
0	0	100		

Test data is used to dry run the flowchart and record the results in the trace table.

7.8 Identifying errors in algorithms

REVISED

Trace tables and test data can be used to identify errors and correct errors.

Sample questions and answers

REVISED

Look at this algorithm.

```
01 Small ← 0
02 Counter ← 0
03 REPEAT
04     INPUT Num
05     IF Num < Small
06         THEN
07             Small ← Num
08     ENDIF
09     Counter ← Counter + 1
10 UNTIL Counter ← 10
11 INPUT "Smallest number is ", Small
```

Hodder & Stoughton Limited © David Watson and Helen Williams 2022

a) Find the **three** errors in the algorithm and suggest a correction for each error.
b) Write the corrected algorithm as a flowchart.
c) Describe the purpose of the corrected algorithm.
d) Complete the trace table for the corrected algorithm using this input data:
7, 11, 3, 9, 6, 8, 4, 2, −3, 13, −1, −99
e) Extend the pseudocode algorithm to validate that data input is positive.
f) Write an extended pseudocode algorithm to find the average of the data input. [18]

Sample high-level answer

a) 01 should be **Small ← 10000**
   10 should be **UNTIL Counter = 10**
   11 should be **OUTPUT Small**

b)

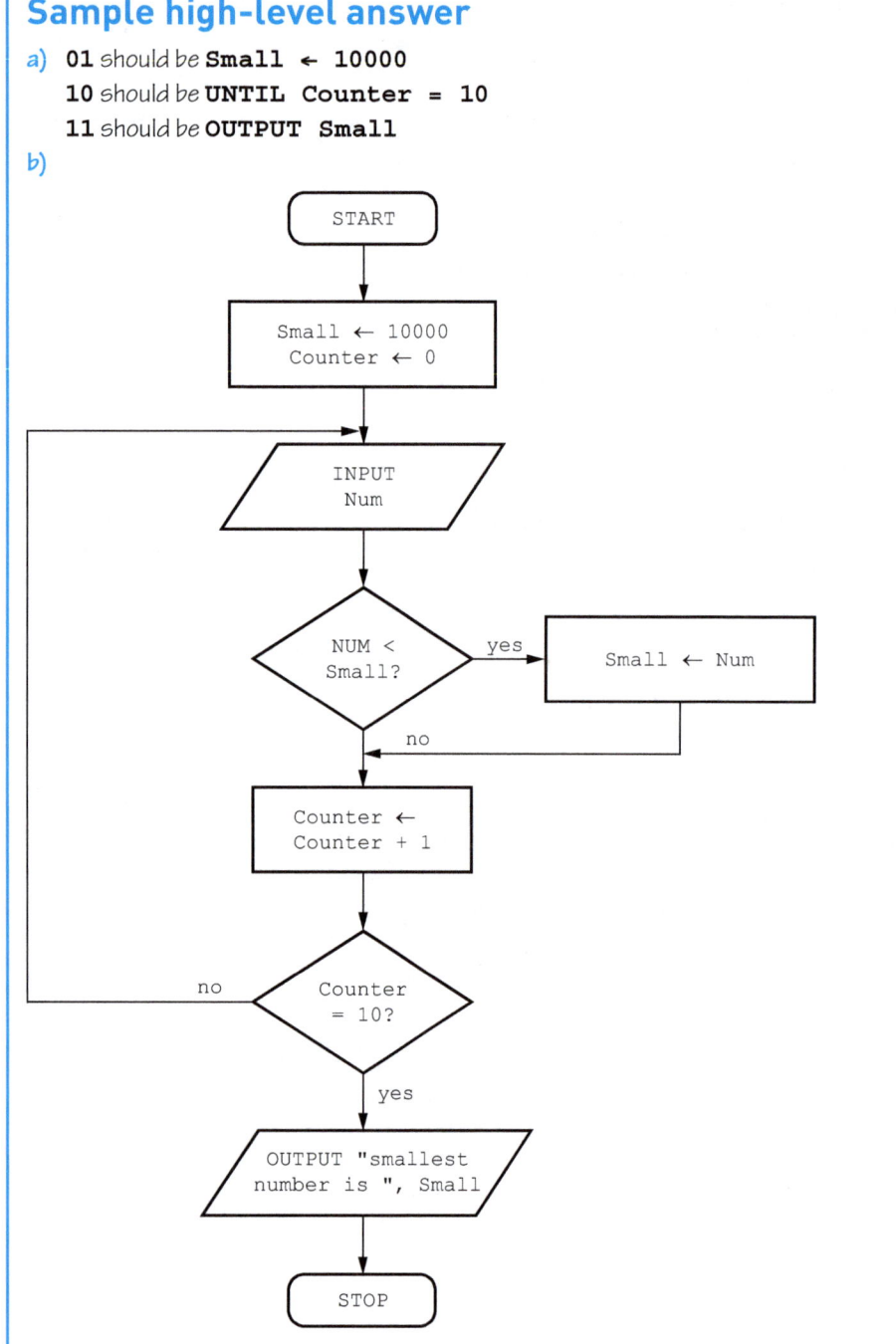

Tips

Part a) of this question asks you to identify the errors and provide a corrections; there will probably be only one mark for this. You need to ensure that each error is clearly identified, quoting the line number if given in the question can help.

Part b) requires a flowchart. For full marks you will need to have the correct structure and the correct content. For the structure, you must use the correct flowchart symbols as given in the syllabus, ensure that each flowline has an arrow and clearly label the flowlines out of a decision.

In part c) for the purpose, you answer must state exactly what the algorithm does.

In part d), the trace table must only contain the data that the algorithm uses; sometimes there can be extra values included that are not needed.

In part e) where validation is required, the algorithm must only allow further actions if data that meets the required rules is entered.

In part f), any pseudocode written should be correctly indented and have meaningful identifier names so the intended logic of the algorithm written can be easily understood by the examiner reading the answer.

c) Input ten numbers, find and output the smallest number input.

d)

Counter	Num	Small	OUTPUT
0		10000	
1	7	7	
2	11		
3	3	3	
4	9		
5	6		
6	8		
7	4		
8	2	2	
9	−3	−3	
10	13		smallest number is −3

e) Replace line 4 with:
```
04  REPEAT
05    INPUT Num
06  UNTIL Num > 0
```

f)
```
01  Small ← 10000
02  Counter ← 0
03  Total ← 0
04  REPEAT
05      REPEAT
06          INPUT Num
07      UNTIL Num > 0
08      IF Num < Small
09        THEN
10            Small ← Num
11      ENDIF
12      Total ← Total + Num
13      Counter ← Counter + 1
14  UNTIL Counter = 10
15  Average ← Total / Counter
16  OUTPUT "Smallest number is ", Small," average is", Average
```

Teacher's comments

The first answer would gain full marks since in part a) all the errors have clearly identified and corrected, quoting the line number of the error. The student has drawn a flowchart showing the corrected algorithm for part b), it has the correct structure and the correct content. Part c) the student states exactly what the algorithm does. Part d) the trace table contains the data that the algorithm uses, and the correct output.

Part e) the input is validated, and the algorithm only allows further actions if data that meets the required rules has been entered. An error message could have been included. Part f) the pseudocode written is accurate and readable; the only improvement could be to add comments to explain the functionality of the pseudocode.

7.8 Identifying errors in algorithms

Sample low-level answer

a) `Small ←` should be `Small ← 1000`
   `← 10` should be `= 10`
   `INPUT` should be `OUTPUT`

b)

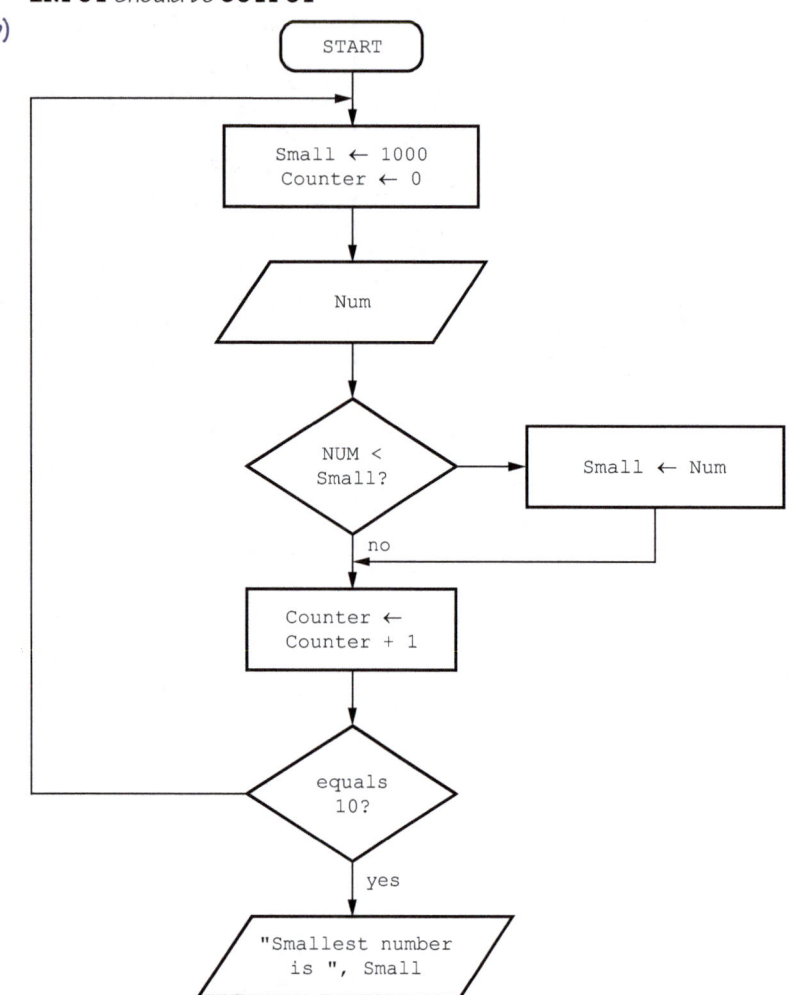

c) Find the smallest number.

d)

Counter	Num	Small	OUTPUT
		1000	
1	7	7	
2	11		
3	3	3	
4	9		
5	6		
6	8		
7	4		
8	2	2	
9	−3	−3	
10	13		
	−1		
	−99	−99	"Smallest number is −99"

e) `04 INPUT Num`
   `05 IF Num < 0 THEN OUTPUT "Not positive"`

Teacher's comments

The second answer would gain one mark for part a) since only one error has been uniquely identified and corrected. The errors in the assignment and input could be in two places as the line number has not been quoted and there is insufficient code quoted to uniquely identify the position. The flowchart for part b) has a STOP missing, not all flowlines are clearly labelled, and it is unclear where the variables are being input or output. There is also an error in the logic as the values are reinitialised every iteration of the loop. Part c) the answer does not state exactly what the algorithm does, the number of values is missing and the need for input is also missing. Part d) the trace table must only contain the data that the algorithm uses; extra values that are not needed have been included for Num, showing that the algorithm has not been traced, and providing an incorrect output. The output incorrectly has quotation marks round it. Part e) the algorithm still allows further actions if the data entered is negative; only a warning message is output. Part f) the pseudocode written is not correctly indented and does not have meaningful identifier names.

f)
```
01 Small ← 0
02 Counter ← 0
04 REPEAT
05 INPUT Num
06 IF Num < 0 THEN OUTPUT "Not positive"
07 IF Num < Small THEN Small ← Num
08 T ← T + Num
09 Counter ← Counter + 1
10 UNTIL Counter = 10
11 OUTPUT Small, T / Counter
```

7.9 Writing and amending algorithms

REVISED

There are a number of stages when producing an algorithm for a problem.
1. Make sure that the problem is clearly specified – the purpose of the algorithm and the tasks to be completed by the algorithm.
2. Break the problem down in to sub-problems. If it is complex, you may want to consider writing an algorithm for each sub-problem. Most problems, even the simplest ones can be divided into:
   - set-up processes
   - input
   - processing of data
   - permanent storage of data (if required)
   - output of results.
3. Decide on how any data is to be obtained and stored, what is going to happen to the data and how any results are going to be displayed.
4. Design the structure of your algorithm using a structure diagram.
5. Decide on how you are going to construct your algorithm, either using a flowchart or pseudocode. If you are told how to construct your algorithm, then follow the guidance.
6. Construct your algorithm, making sure that it can be easily read and understood by someone else. Precision is required when writing algorithms, just as it is when writing program code. This involves setting it out clearly and using meaningful names for any data stores.
7. Use several sets of test data (normal, abnormal and boundary) to dry run your algorithm and show the results in trace tables, to enable you to find any errors.
8. If any errors are found, correct them and repeat the process until you think that your algorithm works perfectly.

Exam-style questions

1. Tick (✓) the appropriate column, in the following table, to indicate whether the description applies to validation, verification or neither.
   You may need to tick more than one column in each row. [5]

Description	Validation	Verification	Neither
Ensuring a number is positive			
Ensuring a password is as intended			
Ensuring a password is correct			
Ensuring a password contains a number			
Ensuring a password contains a special character			

2 In this question you will be given a statement followed by four possible answers. Select which of the four answers you think is correct and tick (✓) the box next to your answer.
   a) This is a conditional statement:
      ☐ `Answer ← Number1 + Number2`
      ☐ `REPEAT … UNTIL Number1 = Number2`
      ☐ `IF Number1 = Number2 THEN …`
      ☐ `WHILE Number1 = Number2 …`
   b) What is meant by the term **decomposition**?
      ☐ Discarding unnecessary details.
      ☐ Breaking a complex problem into smaller parts.
      ☐ Showing how a program should be developed.
      ☐ Writing and testing a program.
   c) What is meant by the term **abstraction**?
      ☐ Identifying data that needs to be stored.
      ☐ Breaking sub-systems down into smaller sub-systems.
      ☐ Keeping the key elements and discarding information not needed.
      ☐ Stage of the program development life cycle. [3]
3 a) Write pseudocode to input 12 numbers and store them in an array.
   b) Change your pseudocode to use a different loop structure.
   c) Identify another loop structure you could have used.
   d) Write pseudocode to find the largest, smallest and the average of the numbers you have stored.
   e) Write pseudocode to sort the numbers you have stored in descending order. [16]
4 Explain the difference between mathematical and comparison operators. Include an example of each type in your answer. [4]
5 Identify **three** types of test data. Include an example of each type in your answer with an explanation of why it is appropriate. [9]
6 Identify **four** errors in this algorithm. [4]

```
01 NumberProducts ← 50 // length of array ProductName[]
02 OUTPUT "Please enter product to find "
03 INPUT Product
04 Found ← FALSE
05 Counter ← 1
06 REPEAT
07    IF Product = ProductName[Counter]
08       THEN
09          Found ← FALSE
10       ELSE
11          Counter ← Counter - 1
12    ENDIF
13 UNTIL Found AND Counter > NumberProducts
14 IF Found
15    THEN
16    OUTPUT Product, " found at position ", Counter, " in the list."
17    ELSE
18    OUTPUT Name, " not found."
19 ENDIF
```

8 Programming

Key objectives

The objectives of this chapter are to revise:
- programming concepts:
  - use of variables, constants and data types
  - input and output
  - sequence
  - selection including nesting
  - iteration
  - totalling and counting
  - string handling
  - operators – arithmetic, logical and Boolean
- procedures and functions including the use of:
  - parameters
  - local and global variables
  - library routines
  - creating a maintainable program
- arrays: including one- and two-dimensional arrays, use of indexes, use of iteration for reading from and writing to arrays
- file handling: including opening, closing, reading from and writing to data and text files

8.1 Programming concepts

REVISED

8.1.1 Variables and constants

Variables and **constants** refer to a data store containing a single value, identified by a meaningful name. Variables may change during the execution of a program, but constants do not change. Constants and variables should be **declared** before they are used in the program.

The diagram below shows examples of how constants and variables are used.

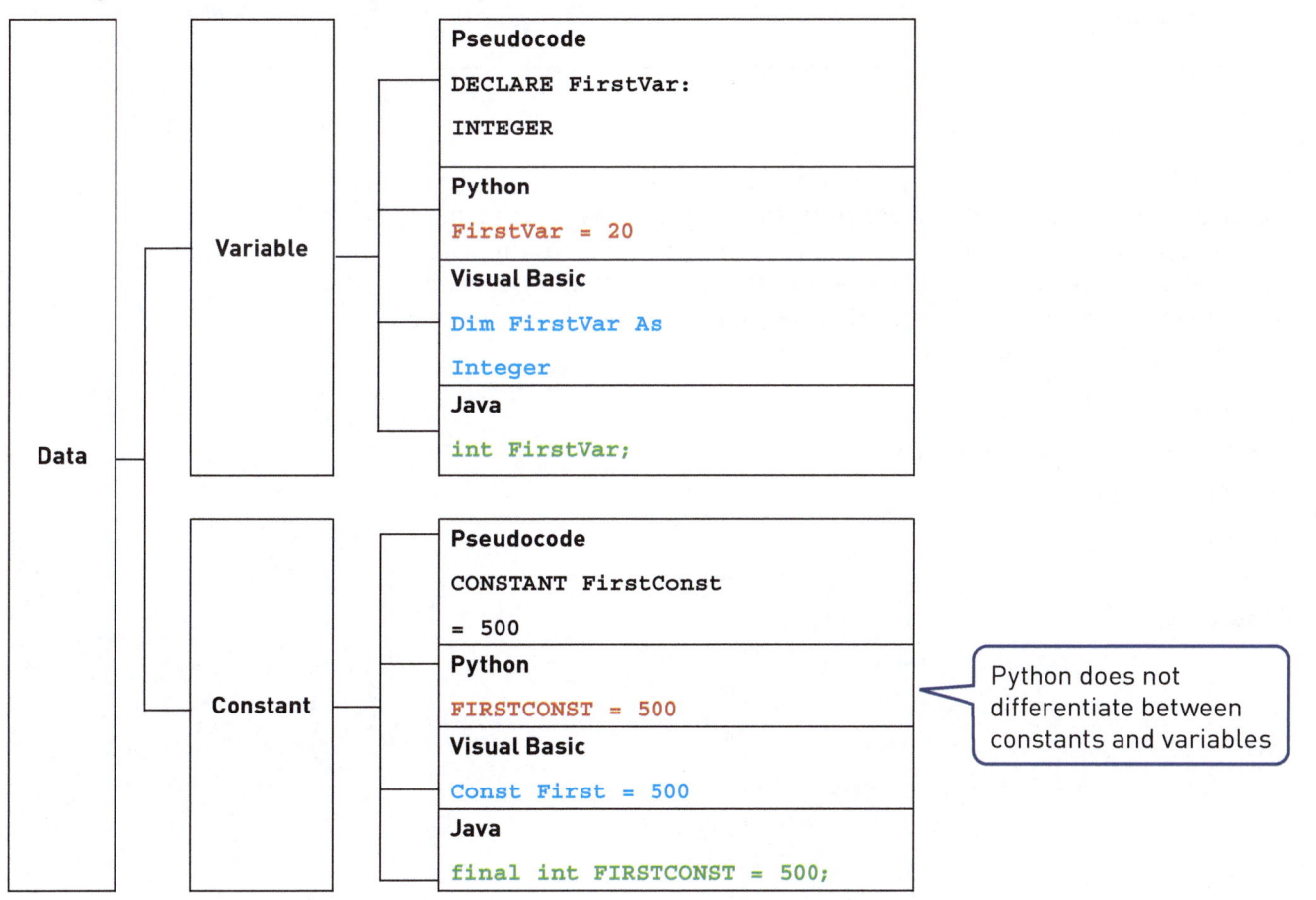

8.1.2 Basic data types

For a computer system to process and store data effectively, different kinds of data are given different types.

- **Integer** – a positive or negative whole number that can be used with mathematical operators.
- **Real** – a positive or negative number with a fractional part; real numbers can be used with mathematical operators.
- **Char** – a variable or constant that is a single character.
- **String** – a variable or constant that is several characters in length.
- **Boolean** – a variable or constant that can have only two values, TRUE or FALSE.

If a number is stored as a string or char then it cannot be used in calculations. The chart below shows examples of data types.

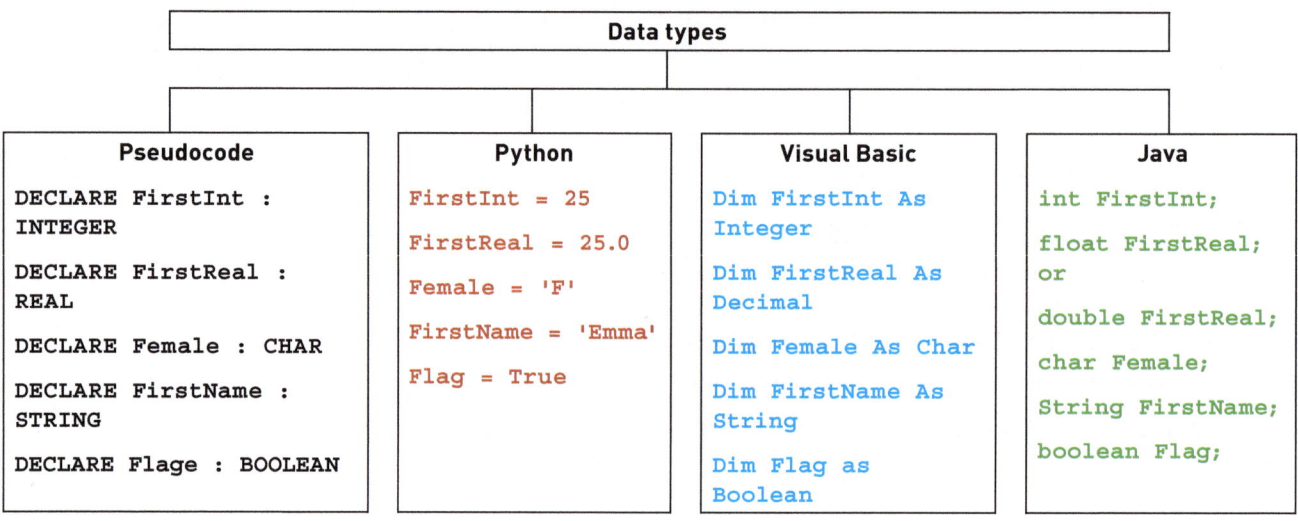

8.1.3 Input and output

To enter data and output results, programs need to use input and output statements. You need to write algorithms and programs that take input from a keyboard and output to a screen. For a program to be useful, the user needs to know what they are expected to input, so each input needs to be accompanied by a **prompt** stating the input required. Here are some examples of input statements with prompts.

Pseudocode
`OUTPUT "Enter a whole number "`
`INPUT FirstInt`
Python
`FirstInt = int(input ("Enter a whole number"))`
Visual Basic
`Console.Write("Enter a whole number ")`
`FirstInt = Integer.Parse (Console.Readline())`
Java
`System.out.println("Enter a whole number ");`
`int FirstInt = myObj.nextInt();`

Here are some examples of outputs that include suitable **messages** as well as values.

Pseudocode
`OUTPUT "Number is " FirstInt`
Python
`Print ("Number is ", FirstInt)`
Visual Basic
`Console.WriteLine("Number is " & FirstInt)`
Java
`System.out.println("Number is " + FirstInt);`

8.1.4 Basic concepts

These are the concepts to be used and understood when writing the steps needed to solve a problem.

Sequence
The ordering of the steps in an algorithm. An incorrect order can lead to incorrect results or unnecessary extra steps. For example, a variable used to store a running total must be set to zero before use otherwise the final total could be incorrect.

Selection
This allows different routes through the steps of a program. Case statements are used when there are multiple choices that can be made.

IF statement examples	Language

`IF Age > 17`
`  THEN`
`    OUTPUT "You are an adult"`
`  ELSE`
`    OUTPUT "You are a child"`
`ENDIF`
	Pseudocode

`if Age > 17:`
`    print "You are an adult"`
`else:`
`    print "You are a child"`
	Python uses `else` with a colon, `:` and indentation:

`If Age > 17 Then`
`    Console.WriteLine("You are an adult")`
`Else`
`    Console.WriteLine("You are a child")`
`End If`
	Visual Basic uses `Else` and `End If`

`If (Age > 17) {`
`    System.out.println ("You are an adult");`
`} else {`
`    System.out.println ("You are a child");`
`}`
	Java uses `else` and curly brackets, `{`, and uses `}` instead of `ENDIF`.

8.1 Programming concepts

Case statement examples	Language
| ```
CASE OF OpValue
  "+" : Answer = Number1 + Number2
  "-" : Answer = Number1 - Number2
  "*" : Answer = Number1 * Number2
  "/" : Answer = Number1 / Number2
  OTHERWISE OUTPUT "invalid operator")
ENDCASE
``` | **Pseudocode** |
| ```
if OpValue == "+":
    Answer = Number1 + Number2
elif OpValue == "-":
    Answer = Number1 - Number2
elif OpValue == "*":
    Answer = Number1 * Number2
elif OpValue == "/":
    Answer = Number1 / Number2
else: print("invalid operator")
``` | **Python** uses `elif` for multiple tests |
| ```
Select Case OpValue
    Case "+"
      Answer = Number1 + Number2
    Case "-"
      Answer = Number1 - Number2
    Case "*"
      Answer = Number1 * Number2
    Case "/"
      Answer = Number1 / Number2
    Case Else
      Console.WriteLine("invalid operator")
End Select
``` | **Visual Basic** uses `Select Case` and `Case Else` instead of `CASE` and `OTHERWISE` |
| ```
switch (OpValue) {
    case "+":
    Answer = Number1 + Number2;
    break;
    case "-":
    Answer = Number1 - Number2;
    break;
    case "*":
    Answer = Number1 * Number2;
    break;
    case "/":
    Answer = Number1 / Number2;
    break;
    default:
    System.out.println("invalid operator");
}
``` | **Java** uses `default` instead of `OTHERWISE` and uses `break` to pass control to the end of the code block when a section is finished. |

Cambridge IGCSE™ and O Level Computer Science Study and Revision Guide Second Edition

Iteration

There are three types of loop structure which perform iterations to repeat programming code.

- count-controlled loops (for a set number of iterations)
- pre-condition loops – may have no iterations
- post-condition loops – always has at least one iteration.

For statement examples	Language

`FOR Counter ← 1 TO 10 STEP 2`
`  OUTPUT Counter`
`NEXT Counter`
	Pseudocode

`for Counter in range (1,10,2):` `    print(Counter)`	**Python** uses the `range` function, a colon to show the start of the for loop and indentation of all statements in the `for` loop.

`For Counter = 1 To 10 Step 2`
`    Console.WriteLine(Counter)`
`Next`
	Visual Basic uses `Step` and `Next`

`for (int Counter = 1; Counter <= 10; Counter = Counter + 2) {`
`    System.out.println(Counter);`
`}`
	Java uses `{}` to show the start and end of the `for` loop.

Pre-condition loop examples	Language

`WHILE TotalWeight < 100`
`TotalWeight = TotalWeight + Weight`
`ENDWHILE`
	Pseudocode

`while TotalWeight < 100:` `    TotalWeight = TotalWeight + Weight`	**Python** uses a colon to show the start of the `while` loop and indentation to show which statements are in the `while` loop.

`While TotalWeight < 100`
`    TotalWeight = TotalWeight + Weight`
`End While`
	Visual Basic uses `While` and `End While`

`while (TotalWeight < 100)`
`{`
`    TotalWeight = TotalWeight + Weight;`
`}`
	Java uses `{}` to show the start and end of the `while` loop.

Post-condition loop examples	Language

`REPEAT`
`   NumberOfItems = NumberOfItems + 1`
`UNTIL NumberOfItems > 19`
	Pseudocode

	Python only uses pre-condition loops.

`Do`
`   NumberOfItems = NumberOfItems + 1`
`Loop Until NumberOfItems > 19`
	Visual Basic uses `Do` and `Loop Until`

`do`
`{`
`   NumberOfItems ++;`
`}`
`while (NumberOfItems <= 20);`
	Java uses `do` and `while` so the condition is the opposite of the `until` condition used in Visual Basic. Look at the code carefully to see the difference. Java uses `{}` to show the start and end of the loop.

8.1 Programming concepts

Totalling and counting
Totalling and **counting** are standard methods.

> See Chapter 7 for more on totalling and counting.

Totalling examples	Counting examples	Language
`TotalWeight = TotalWeight + Weight`	`NumberOfItems = NumberOfItems + 1`	Pseudocode
`TotalWeight = TotalWeight + Weight`	`NumberOfItems = NumberOfItems + 1`	Python
`TotalWeight = TotalWeight + Weight`	`NumberOfItems = NumberOfItems + 1`	Visual Basic
`TotalWeight = TotalWeight + Weight;`	`NumberOfItems ++;`	Java

String handling

Strings store text: every string contains several characters and each character in a string can be found by its position number. The first character of a string in pseudocode is at position 1; the first character of a string is at position zero for Java, Python and Visual Basic.

You need to know these methods:

- **Length** – finding the number of characters in the string. For example, the length of the string `"Computer Science"` is 16 characters as spaces are counted as a character.
- **Substring** – extracting part of a string. For example, the substring `"Science"` could be extracted from `"Computer Science"`.
- **Upper** – converting all the letters in a string to uppercase. For example, the string `"Computer Science"` would become `"COMPUTER SCIENCE"`.
- **Lower** – converting all the letters in a string to lowercase. For example, the string `"Computer Science"` would become `"computer science"`.

Length	Language and notes
`LENGTH("Computer Science")` `LENGTH(MyString)`	**Pseudocode** Text in quotes can be used or a variable with data type string.
`len("Computer Science")` `len(MyString)`	**Python** Text in quotes can be used or a variable with data type string.
`"Computer Science".Length()` `MyString.Length()`	**Visual Basic** Text in quotes can be used or a variable with data type string.
`"Computer Science".Length();` `MyString.length();`	**Java** Text in quotes can be used or a variable with data type string.
Substring – extracts 'Science'	**Language and notes**
`SUBSTRING("Computer Science", 10, 7)` `SUBSTRING(MyString, 10, 7)`	**Pseudocode** Text in quotes can be used or a variable with data type string. First parameter is the string, second parameter is the position of the start character, third parameter is the length of the required substring. Pseudocode strings start at position one.
`"Computer Science"[9:16]` `MyString[9:16]`	**Python** Text in quotes can be used or a variable with data type string. Strings are treated as lists of characters in Python. First index is the start position of the substring, second index is the end position of the substring. Python strings start at position zero.
`"Computer Science".Substring(9, 7)` `MyString.Substring(9, 7)`	**Visual Basic** Text in quotes can be used or a variable with data type string. First parameter is the start position of the substring, second parameter is the length of the substring. Visual Basic strings start at position zero.
`"Computer Science".substring(9,17);`	**Java** Text in quotes can be used or a variable with data type string. First parameter is the start position of the substring, second parameter is the exclusive end position of the substring. Java strings start at position zero.

Cambridge IGCSE™ and O Level Computer Science Study and Revision Guide Second Edition

Upper	Language and notes
`UCASE("Computer Science")` `UCASE(MyString)`	**Pseudocode** Text in quotes can be used or a variable with data type string.
`"Computer Science".upper()` `MyString.upper()`	**Python** Text in quotes can be used or a variable with data type string.
`UCase("Computer Science")` `UCase(MyString)`	**Visual Basic** Text in quotes can be used or a variable with data type string.
`"Computer Science".toUpperCase();` `MyString.toUpperCase();`	**Java** Text in quotes can be used or a variable with data type string.
Lower	Language and notes
`LCASE("Computer Science")` `LCASE(MyString)`	**Pseudocode** Text in quotes can be used or a variable with data type string.
`"Computer Science".lower()` `MyString.lower()`	**Python** Text in quotes can be used or a variable with data type string.
`LCase("Computer Science")` `LCase(MyString)`	**Visual Basic** Text in quotes can be used or a variable with data type string.
`"Computer Science".toLowerCase();` `MyString.tolowerCase();`	**Java** Text in quotes can be used or a variable with data type string.

Arithmetic, logical and Boolean operators

There are three types of operator:

- **arithmetic operators** – for calculations (+, -, *, /, ^, MOD, DIV)
- **logical** – for comparisons
- **Boolean** – to decide whether an expression is true or false.

Arithmetic	Pseudocode	Python	Visual Basic	Java
Add	+	+	+	+
Subtract	-	-	-	-
Multiply	*	*	*	*
Divide	/	/	/	/
Raise to the power of	^	**	^	`import java.lang.Math;` `Math.pow(x, y);`
Group	( )	( )	( )	( )
Remainder division	MOD		*For more on these see section 8.1.7 Library routines.*	
Integer division	DIV			
Logical	**Pseudocode**	**Python**	**Visual Basic**	**Java**
Greater than	>	>	>	>
Less than	<	<	<	<
Equal	=	==	=	==
Greater than or equal	>=	>=	>=	>=
Less than or equal	<=	<=	<=	<=
Not equal	<>	!=	<>	!=
Boolean	**Pseudocode**	**Python**	**Visual Basic**	**Java**
Both True	AND	and	And	&&
Either True	OR	or	Or	||
Not True	NOT	Not	Not	!

8.1 Programming concepts

Sample questions and answers

REVISED

A programmer has been asked to design and write a program to accept inputs about each game player:

- name
- age in years
- nickname
- if the player wants to use their name or their nickname.

The program must include a validation check on the age, ensure the name and the nickname are no more than eight characters long, then output a personalised welcome message for each player.

There can be three, four or five players for each game; the input routine finishes when all the players have entered their details.

a) Give a suitable identifier name and data type for each input. Explain your choice of data type for each input.

b) Write your design for the program in pseudocode. Include the validation checks for input. Your program must include selection and iteration, use comments to show where these have been used and give the reason why thy have been used. [12]

> **Tips**
>
> Part a) of this question asks for the name and the data type of each variable used to store the data input. This means your answer must give a meaningful name for each variable and an appropriate data type from those included in the syllabus. Make sure the names are long enough to be meaningful to someone else and they should begin with a capital letter for example **Age** not **A** or **age**. Also, the data type must clearly belong to that variable, and you need to say why the data type is appropriate.
>
> Part b) requires a complete algorithm written in Pseudocode, not program code, including selection, an IF statement, and iteration, a loop, to provide a design for every step required. This includes declaration and initialisation of the variables required, input, validation and output of a welcome message for every player using their name or nickname as required. Comments must be included for the iteration and selection. To make the algorithm readable suitable indentation must be used.

Sample high-level answer

a)

Identifier	Data type	Reason
Name	String	eight characters or less is required
Age	Integer	a whole number that can be validated with a range check is required
Nickname	String	eight characters or less is required
Choice	Boolean	two choices only required

Teacher's comments

This first answer is clearly set out and readable. The use of a table for part a) ensures that each variable has all the appropriate information.

For part b)
- all the variables used have been declared with meaningful names and initialised if required
- indentation and comments have been used sensibly
- both iteration and selection have been used
- all the inputs have clear prompts
- the validation checks ensure re-entry of data that does not meet a check
- the welcome output only includes the name or the nickname as chosen
- between three and five players can be entered.

b)
```
DECLARE Name : STRING
DECLARE Age : INTEGER
DECLARE Nickname : STRING
DECLARE Choice, Another : BOOLEAN
DECLARE Player : INTEGER
Player ← 0
Another ← TRUE
REPEAT // Iteration to enter at least 3 players
   REPEAT
      OUTPUT "Enter your name, use 8 characters or less "
      INPUT Name
   UNTIL LENGTH(Name) <= 8
   REPEAT
      OUTPUT "Enter your age in years "
      INPUT Age
   UNTIL Age > 5 AND Age < 100
   REPEAT
      OUTPUT "Enter your nickname, use 8 characters or less "
      INPUT Nickname
   UNTIL LENGTH(Nickname) <= 8
   OUTPUT "Use your name (True) or Nickname (FALSE) "
   INPUT Choice
   IF Choice // Selection whether to use the name or the nickname
      THEN
         OUTPUT "Welcome ", Name, " aged ", Age
      ELSE
         OUTPUT "Welcome ", Nickname, " aged ", Age
   ENDIF
   Player ← Player + 1
   IF Player >= 3 AND Player < 6 // selection for another player
      THEN
         OUTPUT "Do you want to add another player TRUE or FALSE? "
         INPUT Another
   ENDIF
UNTIL Player = 6 OR NOT Another
```

8.1 Programming concepts

Sample low-level answer

a) My variables are N1, N2 and A, they are all text because there are no calculations.

b)
```
INPUT N1
IF LENGTH(N1) > 8 THEN OUTPUT "Too long"
INPUT A
INPUT N2
IF LENGTH(N2) > 8 THEN OUTPUT "Too long"
IF Age > 100 THEN OUTPUT "Too old"
OUTPUT "Welcome ", N1, N2 " aged ", A
INPUT N1
IF LENGTH(N1) > 8 THEN OUTPUT "Too long"
INPUT A
INPUT N2
IF LENGTH(N2) > 8 THEN OUTPUT "Too long"
IF Age > 100 THEN OUTPUT "Too old"
OUTPUT "Welcome ", N1, N2 " aged ", A
INPUT N1
IF LENGTH(N1) > 8 THEN OUTPUT "Too long"
INPUT A
INPUT N2
IF LENGTH(N2) > 8 THEN OUTPUT "Too long"
IF Age > 100 THEN OUTPUT "Too old"
OUTPUT "Welcome ", N1, N2 " aged ", A
INPUT N1
IF LENGTH(N1) > 8 THEN OUTPUT "Too long"
INPUT A
INPUT N2
IF LENGTH(N2) > 8 THEN OUTPUT "Too long"
IF Age > 100 THEN OUTPUT "Too old"
OUTPUT "Welcome ", N1, N2 " aged ", A
INPUT N1
IF LENGTH(N1) > 8 THEN OUTPUT "Too long"
INPUT A
INPUT N2
IF LENGTH(N2) > 8 THEN OUTPUT "Too long"
IF Age > 100 THEN OUTPUT "Too old"
OUTPUT "Welcome ", N1, N2 " aged ", A
```

Teacher's comments

This second answer is poorly set out and not easy to understand. Only three variables are identified in part a) and the names are too short to be meaningful to another reader, the single data type is not from the syllabus and the reason is weak.

For part b)
- none the variables used have been declared
- indentation and comments are missing
- only selection has been used; code is repeated instead of using iteration
- inputs have no prompts, one is missing
- the validation checks only give a warning message
- the welcome output includes both the name and the nickname
- only five players can be entered.

8.1.5 Use of nested statements

Selection and iteration statements can be nested one inside another. One type of construct can be nested within another, for example selection can be nested within a condition-controlled loop, or a loop can be nested within a selection statement.

8.1.6 Procedures and functions

There are often similar tasks to perform that make use of the same groups of statements. Many programming languages make use of subroutines, also known as named **procedures** or **functions**, instead of repeating these statements.

- A procedure is a set of programming statements grouped together under a single name that can be called to perform a task at any point in a program.
- A function is a set of programming statements grouped together under a single name that can be called to perform a task at any point in a program. A function returns a value back to the main program.
- **Parameters** are the variables that store the values of the arguments passed to a procedure or function. Some procedures and functions will have parameters.

Procedures and functions are defined once and can be called many times within a program.

Here is an example of a procedure without parameters. Different terminology is used by each programming language for 'procedure' – void functions (Python), subroutines (Visual Basic), methods (Java).

Procedure Stars – definition	Call	Language

`PROCEDURE Stars`
`    OUTPUT "********"`
`ENDPROCEDURE`
	`Stars`	Pseudocode

`def Stars():` `    print("************")`	`Stars()`	Python

`Sub Stars()`
`    Console.WriteLine("************")`
`End Sub`
	`Stars()`	Visual Basic

`static void Stars()`
`{`
`    System.out.println("***********");`
`}`
	`Stars();`	Java

Here is an example of how a procedure with parameters can be defined. For IGCSE Computer Science the number of parameters used is limited to two.

Procedure Stars with parameter – definition	Call	Language
| ```
PROCEDURE Stars (Number:INTEGER)
    DECLARE Counter : INTEGER
    FOR Counter ← 1 TO Number
        OUTPUT "*"
    NEXT
ENDPROCEDURE
``` | Stars(7) | **Pseudocode** Counter is a local variable. |
| ```
def Stars(Number):
    for counter in range (Number):
        print("*", end = '')
``` | Stars(7) | **Python**<br>Note: `end = ''` ensures that the stars are printed on one line without spaces between them. |
| ```
Sub Stars(Number As Integer)
    Dim Counter As Integer
    For Counter = 1 To Number
        Console.Write("*")
    Next
End Sub
``` | Stars(7) | **Visual Basic** Counter is a local variable. |
| ```
static void Stars(int Number)
{
  for (int Counter = 1; Counter <= Number; Counter ++)
  {
    System.out.print("*");
  }
}
``` | Stars(7); | **Java** Counter is a local variable. |

A function is like a procedure, except it always returns a value. Like a procedure, it is defined once and can be called many times within a program, and be defined with or without parameters. Different terminology is used for 'function' by some programming languages: fruitful functions (Python), functions (Visual Basic), methods with returns (Java).

The first statement in a procedure or function is called the **header**. It always contains the name, it may contain the parameters required and it may contain the data type of the return value for a function.

For IGCSE Computer Science the number of parameters used in a function or procedure definition and the **arguments** in the call are limited to two.

There must always be a return statement in a procedure definition to specify the value to be returned.

Here is a function to convert temperature from Fahrenheit to Celsius.

Function with a parameter – temperature conversion example			
Definition		Call	Language

`FUNCTION Celsius(Temperature: REAL) RETURNS REAL`
`    RETURN (Temperature - 32) / 1.8`
`ENDFUNCTION`
		`MyTemp ←`
		`Celsius(MyTemp)`
			Pseudocode

`def Celsius(Temperature):` `        return (Temperature - 32) / 1.8`		`MyTemp =` `Celsius(MyTemp)`	**Python** Data type of function does not need to be defined.

`Function Celsius(ByVal Temperature As Decimal) As Decimal`
`       Return (Temperature - 32) / 1.8`
`End Function`
		`MyTemp =`
		`Celsius(MyTemp)`
			Visual Basic

`static double Celsius(double Temperature)`
`{`
`   return (Temperature - 32) / 1.8;`
`}`
		`MyTemp =`
		`Celsius(MyTemp)`
			Java

Local and global variables

A **global variable** can be used in any part of a program – its **scope** covers the whole program.

A **local variable** can only be used by the part of the program it has been declared in; it is restricted to that part of the program.

8.1.7 Library routines

Library routines are fully tested and ready for use in a program. An IDE includes a standard library of functions and procedures. Examples are:

- `MOD` – returns remainder of a division
- `DIV` – returns the quotient (that is, the whole number part) of a division
- `ROUND` – returns a value rounded to a given number of decimal places
- `RANDOM` – returns a random number.

Here are some examples of these library routines in pseudocode and each programming language.

Examples for MOD, DIV, ROUND and RANDOM	Language

`Value1 ← MOD(10, 3)`
`Value2 ← DIV(10, 3)`
`Value3 ← ROUND(6.97354, 2)`
`Value4 ← RANDOM()`
	Pseudocode

`Value1 = 10%3`
`Value2 = 10//3`
`Value = divmod(10,3)`
`Value3 = round(6.97354, 2)`
`from random import random`
`Value4 = random()`
	Python
	MOD uses the `%` operator and DIV the `//` operator.
	The function `divmod(x,y)` provides both answers where the first answer is DIV and the second answer is MOD.
	RANDOM needs to import the library routine `random`

`Value1 = 10 Mod 3`
`Value2 = 10 \ 3`
`Value3 = Math.Round(6.97354, 2)`
`Value4 = Rnd()`
	Visual Basic
	DIV uses the `\` operator.

Examples for MOD, DIV, ROUND and RANDOM	Language
`import java.lang.Math;`	Java
`Value1 = 10%3;`	MOD uses the `%` operator.
`Value2 = 10/3;`	DIV uses the normal division operator; if the numbers being divided are both integers then interger divison is performed, as shown.
`Value3 = Math.round(6.97354 * 100)/100.0;`	Java imports the library routine `Math`
`import java.util.Random;`	`Math.round` only rounds to whole numbers.
`Random rand = new Random();`	RANDOM needs to import the library routine `Random`
`double Value4 = rand.nextDouble();`	

8.1.8 Creating a maintainable program

A program should be understandable to another programmer. A maintainable program should:

- always use meaningful identifier names for variables, constants, arrays, procedures and functions
- be divided into modules for each task using procedures and functions
- be fully commented using your programming language's commenting feature.

Here are programming languages commenting features.

Example comments	Language
`// pseudocode uses a double slash to start a comment`	Pseudocode
`#Python uses hash to start a comment for every line`	Python
`'Visual Basic uses a single quote to start a comment` `'for every line`	Visual Basic

`// Java uses a double slash to start a single line comment`
`and`
`/* to start multiple line comments`
`and to end them`
`*/`
	Java

8.2 Arrays

REVISED

An **array** is a data structure containing elements of the same data type. The position of each element is identified using the array's **index** and the array name. Arrays are used for storing similar items of data, for example a list names of students in a class or a table of hourly weather station readings for a week.

The first element of an array can have an index of zero or one. Most programming languages automatically set the first index of an array to zero.

8.2.1 One- and two- dimensional arrays

Arrays can be one-dimensional or two-dimensional. A one-dimensional array can be referred to as a list, while a two-dimensional array can be referred to as a table.

Index	myList
[0]	27
[1]	19
[2]	36
[3]	42
[4]	16
[5]	89
[6]	21
[7]	16
[8]	55
[9]	72

A list with 10 elements in it. The first element has an index of zero.

MyTable		
27	31	17
19	67	48
36	98	29
42	22	95
16	35	61
89	46	47
21	71	28
16	23	13
55	11	77
34	76	21

A table with 10 rows and 3 columns. The first element is located at position 0,0

Notes on Python and arrays

Instead of arrays, Python uses another object called a list. The difference between arrays and lists are minimal at IGCSE level but the main differences are:

- a list can contain different data types whereas arrays must all hold the same type of data
- to achieve the same structure as a two-dimensional array, Python embeds one list within another.

8.2.2 Declaring and populating arrays with iteration

The table above can be populated using a nested loop, one for each index:

```
DECLARE MyTable : ARRAY[0:9,0:2] OF INTEGER
OUTPUT "Enter these values in order"
OUTPUT "27, 19, 36, 42, 16, 89, 21, 16, 55, 34"
OUTPUT "31, 67, 98, 22, 35, 46, 71, 23, 11, 76"
OUTPUT "17, 48, 29, 95, 61, 47, 28, 13, 77, 21"
FOR ColumnIndex ← 0 TO 2
    FOR RowIndex ← 0 TO 9
        OUTPUT "Enter next value "
        INPUT MyTable[RowIndex, ColumnIndex]
    NEXT RowIndex
NEXT ColumnIndex
```

Sample questions and answers

REVISED

Extend your program design (from page 120) to store each name and nickname in a two-dimensional array, the age in another array and the choice in another array. The index of the array will identify the player. Use a procedure to output the personalised welcome message for each player when all players have entered their details. This output should be in ascending order of age.
a) Declare and initialise the arrays needed.
b) Write your design for the program in pseudocode. You do not need to include the declarations for the arrays and the validation checks for input.
[12]

8.2 Arrays

> **Tips**
>
> Part a) of this question asks you to declare and initialise each array used to store the data input. This means your answer must write a declaration with a meaningful name for each array and an appropriate data type from those included in the syllabus. Make sure the arrays are large enough to store details for five players. Also, the array for the name and nickname must be a two-dimensional array.
>
> Part b) requires a complete algorithm written in pseudocode, not program code, including a procedure and a sort. Comments should be included to make the algorithm readable, and suitable indentation must be used.

Sample high-level answer

a)
```
DECLARE NameAndNickname : ARRAY[1:5, 1:2] OF STRING
DECLARE Age : ARRAY[1:5] OF INTEGER
DECLARE Choice : ARRAY[1:5] OF BOOLEAN
```

b)
```
// procedure definition for the welcome messages
PROCEDURE Welcome (PlayerNo : INTEGER)
    DECLARE Count, Last, TempAge: INTEGER
    DECLARE Swap, TempChoice : BOOLEAN
    DECLARE TempString : STRING
    Last ← PlayerNo

    REPEAT // bubble sort all arrays on Age in ascending order
      Swap ← FALSE
      FOR COUNT ← 1 TO Last - 1
        IF Age[Count] > Age[Count + 1]
          THEN
            TempAge ← Age[Count]
            Age[Count] ← Age[Count + 1]
            Age[Count + 1] ← TempAge
            TempChoice ← Choice [Count]
            Choice [Count] ← Choice [Count + 1]
            Choice [Count + 1] ← TempChoice
            TempString ← NameAndNickname [Count,1]
            NameAndNickname [Count,1] ← NameAndNickname [Count + 1,1]
```

```
                    NameAndNickname [Count + 1,1] ← TempString
                    TempString ← NameAndNickname [Count,2]
                    NameAndNickname [Count,2] ← NameAndNickname [Count + 1,2]
                    NameAndNickname [Count + 1,2] ← TempString
                    Swap ← TRUE
        NEXT Count
        Last ← Last - 1
    UNTIL (NOT Swap) or Last = 1

    FOR Count ← 1 TO PlayerNo // print welcome messages
        IF Choice[Count]
            THEN
                OUTPUT "Welcome ", NameAndNickname [Count,1], " aged ", Age[Count]
            ELSE
                OUTPUT "Welcome ", NameAndNickname [Count,2], " aged ", Age[Count]
        ENDIF
    NEXT Count
ENDPROCEDURE

DECLARE Player : INTEGER
DECLARE Another : BOOLEAN
Player ← 1
Another ← TRUE
REPEAT  // Iteration to enter at least 3 players
    OUTPUT "Enter your name, use 8 characters or less "
    INPUT NameAndNickname[Player,1]
    OUTPUT "Enter your age in years "
    INPUT Age[Player]
    OUTPUT "Enter your nickname, use 8 characters or less "
    INPUT NameAndNickname[Player,2]
    INPUT Choice[Player]
    Player ← Player + 1
    IF Player > 3 AND Player <= 6 // selection for another player
        THEN
            OUTPUT "Do you want to add another player TRUE or FALSE? "
            INPUT Another
    ENDIF
UNTIL Player = 6 OR NOT Another
Player = Player - 1 // setting Player to the number of players entered
Welcome (Player)// procedure call
```

8.2 Arrays

> **Sample low-level answer**
>
> a) My arrays are N1, N2 and A, they are all text because there are no calculations.
>
> b)
> ```
> INPUT N1[1]
> INPUT A[1]
> INPUT N2[1]
> INPUT N1[2]
> INPUT A[2]
> INPUT N2[2]
> INPUT N1[3]
> INPUT A[3]
> INPUT N2[3]
> INPUT N1[4]
> INPUT A[4]
> INPUT N2[4]
> INPUT N1[5]
> INPUT A[5]
> INPUT N2[5]
> N1.sort()
> A.sort()
> N2.sort()
> OUTPUT "Welcome ", N1, N2 " aged ", A
> ```

Teacher's comments

The first answer is clearly set out and readable. The array declarations for part a) correctly include the two-dimensional array for name and nickname.

For part b)
- local and global variables have been declared with meaningful names and initialised when required
- indentation and comments have been used sensibly
- a procedure has been declared and called
- all the arrays have been sorted on ascending order of age using a bubble sort
- the welcome output only includes the name or the nickname as chosen
- between three and five players can be entered.

The second answer is poorly set out and not easy to understand. Three arrays have been identified but not declared in part a), the names are too short to be meaningful to another reader, and a two-dimensional array for name and nickname has not been used.

For part b)
- none the variables used have been declared
- indentation and comments are missing
- a procedure has not been used
- the three arrays have been sorted independently using a sort library routine
- the welcome output includes both the name and the nickname
- only five players can be entered.

Cambridge IGCSE™ and O Level Computer Science Study and Revision Guide Second Edition

8.3 File handling

REVISED

8.3.1 Purpose of storing data in a file
Computer programs store data that will be required again in a **file**. When data is saved to a file it is stored permanently and can be accessed by the same program at a later date, accessed by another program, or sent to be used on another computer(s).

8.3.2 Using files
Every file is identified by its filename. Files can be created, opened, closed, written to, read from and deleted.

Here is an example of writing a line of text to a file and reading the line of text back from the file. Refer to the *Cambridge IGCSE and O Level Computer Science Second Edition* Student's Book, pages 334 and 335 for examples in other programs.

```
DECLARE TextLine : STRING   // variables are declared as normal
DECLARE MyFile : STRING
MyFile ← "MyText.txt"


// writing the line of text to the file
OPEN MyFile FOR WRITE   // opens file for writing
    OUTPUT "Please enter a line of text"
    INPUT TextLine
    WRITEFILE, TextLine   // writes a line of text to the file
CLOSEFILE(MyFile)    // closes the file


// reading the line of text from the file
OUTPUT "The file contains this line of text:"
OPEN MyFile FOR READ   // opens file for reading
    READFILE, TextLine   // reads a line of text from the file
    OUTPUT TextLine
CLOSEFILE(MyFile)    // closes the file
```

8.3 File handling

Exam-style questions

1 Tick (✓) the appropriate column, in the following table, to indicate whether the statement is assignment, selection or iteration. [3]

Statement	Assignment	Selection	Iteration
`IF Number1 < Number2`			
`Number1 ← Number2`			
`Number1 ← Number2 + 1`			
`FOR Number 1 ← 1 TO 10`			
`CASE OF Number1`			
`WHILE Number1 <> Number2`			
`REPEAT`			

2 In this question you will be given a statement followed by four possible answers.
Select which of the four answers you think is correct and tick (✓) the box next to your answer.
  a) This is a Boolean operator:
     ☐ +
     ☐ DIV
     ☐ >=
     ☐ NOT
  b) What is meant by the term **array**?
     ☐ a list, for example 3, 2.7, TRUE, "Tulip"
     ☐ data structure containing elements of the same data type
     ☐ named data structure
     ☐ data structure containing elements that cannot be changed
  c) Data stored in files ...
     ☐ ... cannot be changed.
     ☐ ... cannot be copied.
     ☐ ... can be transferred to another computer.
     ☐ ... is volatile. [3]

3 a) Explain what is meant by **selection**.
  b) Describe **two** methods of selection. Include examples of each method in your answer. [6]

4 a) Explain what is meant by **iteration**.
  b) Describe **three** methods of iteration. Include examples of each method in your answer. [8]

5 A sentence is to be input and stored in a variable **Sentence**.
  Write pseudocode to:
  – declare the variable **Sentence**
  – input the sentence
  – find the length of the sentence
  – find out how many times the letter 'e' occurs in the sentence. [6]

6 Using a programming language write a program to store the names of 50 people playing a game and their high scores. Output the names and the scores ordered from highest to lowest score and output the average score.
  Your program must include and use meaningful identifier names for
  – variables
  – constants
  – arrays
  – procedures / functions.
  Your program must be fully commented using your programming language's commenting feature. [10]

9 Databases

Key objectives

The objectives of this chapter are to revise:
- the design and use of single-table databases:
  - fields, records, validation
- the use of basic data types:
  - text/alphanumeric, character, Boolean, integer, real, date/time
- the identification, purpose and use of primary keys
- SQL scripts, used to query data stored in a single-table database

9.1 Databases

REVISED

9.1.1 Single-table databases

A **database** is a structured collection of data that allows people to extract information in a way that meets their needs. Data can include text, numbers and pictures. For example, a simple database of items for sale could include a description, the price and a picture of the item.

A **single-table database** contains only one table. A table consists of many **records**. The number of records in a table will vary, as new records can be added and deleted from a table as required. Each record consists of several **fields**. The number of fields in table is fixed so each record contains the same number of fields. An easy way to remember this is:

- each **r**ecord is a **r**ow in the table
- each field is a column in the table.

Data is often validated when input into a field. For more on validation, see Section 7.5.

Table structure

Record 1	Field 1	Field 2	Field 3	Field 4
Record 2	Field 1	Field 2	Field 3	Field 4
Record 3	Field 1	Field 2	Field 3	Field 4
Record 4	Field 1	Field 2	Field 3	Field 4
Record 5	Field 1	Field 2	Field 3	Field 4
Record 6	Field 1	Field 2	Field 3	Field 4

(Column: Field 4 column; Row: Record 2 row)

9.1.2 Basic data types

A **data type** classifies how the data is stored, displayed and the operations that can be performed on the stored value. Each field requires a data type to be selected.

These are the database data types you need to be able to use. They are available to use as *Access* data types, but the names *Access* uses may be different from the terms in the syllabus.

Data type	Description	*Access* data type
Text/alphanumeric	A number of characters	Short text/long text
Character	A single character	Short text with a field size of one
Boolean	One of two values: either True or False, 1 or 0, Yes or No	Yes/No
Integer	Whole number	Number formatted as fixed with zero decimal places
Real	A decimal number	Number formatted as decimal
Date/time	Date and/or time	Date/Time

9.1.3 Primary keys

Each record within a table contains data about a single item, person or event. It is important to be able to uniquely identify each record. The **primary key** is a field that uniquely identifies the record. Each primary key contains a unique value; it must contain data values that are never repeated in the table.

9.1.4 Structured Query Language

Structured Query Language (SQL) is the standard query language for writing scripts to obtain information from a database. An **SQL script** is a list of SQL commands that perform a given task.

Here are some examples of the SQL statements you need to be able to use. Here are some examples of commands.

SQL query statement	Description of statement
`SELECT`	Fetches specified fields (columns) from a table; queries always begin with `SELECT`
`FROM`	Identifies the table to use.
`WHERE`	Includes only records (rows) in a query that match a given condition.
`ORDER BY`	Sorts the results from a query by a given column either alphabetically or numerically.
`SUM`	Returns the sum of all the values in a field (column). Used with `SELECT`
`COUNT`	Counts the number of records (rows) where the field (column) matches a specified condition. Used with `SELECT`

Here are some examples of commands.

`SELECT ItemDescription, Price`
`FROM ItemsForSale`
`WHERE Price > 10.00`
`ORDER BY Price;`
	Displays the description and price of all items for sale with a price of more than 10.00

`SELECT SUM(Price)`
`FROM ItemsForSale`
`WHERE Price > 10.00`
	Displays the total value all items for sale with a price of more than 10.00

`SELECT COUNT(Price)`
`FROM ItemsForSale`
`WHERE Price > 10.00`
	Displays the number of items for sale with a price of more than 10.00

9 Databases

Sample questions and answers

REVISED ☐

A database, **StudentRoom**, was set up to show the room numbers for students living in student accommodation.

Name	Block	RoomNumber
David Smith	A	129
Su Wong	B	124
David Chow	A	129
Amy Tang	A	123
Joe Higgs	B	124
David Smith	B	125
Adel Hoo	A	125
Peter Patel	B	129

a) Explain why none of the fields in the database can be used as a primary key.
b) State, with a reason, a field that could be added as a primary key and give an example of some sample data for that field.
c) ```
SELECT *
FROM StudentRoom
WHERE Block = 'A'
ORDER BY RoomNumber;
```
Show the output from this SQL command.

[6]

> **Tips**
>
> Part a) of this question involves 'explain'. This means your answer needs to give a reason why each field is not suitable to be a unique identifier. In part b), you are asked to identify an item of data that would uniquely identify the record and give the field/column a suitable name. Often if there is no suitable unique fact a short code or number is used. In part c), you are to show the output from the SQL query; make sure you show all the rows and columns required in the appropriate order that satisfy the question.
>
> When practising questions, if you are unsure about what an SQL query would show, build the database and write the query to check your answer.

> **High-level sample answer**
>
> a) All the fields contain duplicate values as there are many students housed in each block, some students share the same room and two of the students have the same name.
> b) A field that gives each student a unique code could be added, for example **StudentID**. This code should be easy to validate and have enough characters to ensure no repeats would be required, for example **ST12345**.
> c)
> | Name | Block | RoomNumber |
> |---|---|---|
> | Amy Tang | A | 123 |
> | Adel Hoo | A | 125 |
> | David Smith | A | 129 |
> | David Chow | A | 129 |
```

9.1 Databases

Low-level sample answer

a) Use the Name.
b) No need for an extra field the Name is good.
c) Block A
Adel Hoo, 125
Amy Tang, 123
David Chow, 129
David Smith, 129

Teacher's comments

The first answer is clearly set out and readable.

For part a), all the fields have been considered and each reason is given in the context of the question. For part b), a new field with a suitable name has been identified, a reason has been given for the choice and some appropriate sample data provided. For part c), the use of a table gives the output a clear structure, only students in Block A have been shown, and they are in room number order. Where two students are sharing the room, the order is the same as in the original table.

The second answer short and some of the questions seem to have been misunderstood. For part a), the question answered is choose a suitable primary key. Not the question set but a common error. For part b), the student now sees no need for a new primary key even though the data in the name has been repeated, indicating that the completed table given was not read carefully enough. For part c), a heading and extra punctuation have been added, the block field has been removed and the ordering is on the name field.

Exam-style questions

1 In this question you will be given a statement followed by four possible answers.
   Select which of the four answers you think is correct and tick (✔) the box next to your answer. You may need to tick more than one box.
   a) What is meant by the term **table**?
      ☐ a collection of fields about the same item
      ☐ it uniquely identifies a record
      ☐ a single piece of data
      ☐ a collection of related records
   b) What is meant by the term **record**?
      ☐ a collection of fields about the same item
      ☐ a column of data
      ☐ a structured collection of data
      ☐ it uniquely identifies a row of data
   c) What is meant by the term **field**?
      ☐ a collection of rows about the same item
      ☐ it uniquely identifies a row of data
      ☐ a column of data
      ☐ a single piece of data   [3]

2 a) Explain what is meant by **Structured Query Language (SQL)**.
   b) Describe **two** SQL commands.
                                                  [6]

3 A company that sells cakes is setting up a single-table database, to store information about cakes that can be ordered. The information includes, name of cake, number of portions, price of cake, main ingredients and decoration available.

   State, with reasons, the structure required, including names of the data items to be stored, the data type and sample data for each item.
                                                  [8]

10 Boolean logic

Key objectives

The objectives of this chapter are to revise:
- the identification and use of the standard logic gates: NOT, AND, OR, NAND, NOR and XOR
- how to use logic gates to create logic circuits from:
  - a given problem
  - a logic expression
  - a truth table
- how to complete truth tables from:
  - a given problem
  - a logic expression
  - a logic circuit
- how to write a logic expression from:
  - a given problem
  - a logic circuit
  - a truth table

10.1 Standard logic gate symbols

REVISED

Electronic circuits in computers, solid-state drives and controlling devices are made up of thousands of **logic gates**. Logic gates are combined to form **logic circuits**. Logic gates take binary inputs and produce binary outputs. A **truth table** lists every binary output for every possible combination of binary inputs.

These are the six logic gates that will be considered:

NOT, AND, OR, NAND, NOR and XOR.

> NOT is the only single input gate. All other gates are limited to two inputs for IGCSE.

10.2 The functions of the six logic gates

REVISED

Gate	Description	Truth table			Notation
NOT A —▷o— X	The output, X, is 1 if: the input, A, is 0	input A		output X	X = NOT A $X = \overline{A}$
		0		1	
		1		0	
AND A —⊓— X B	The output, X, is 1 if: both inputs, A and B, are 1	inputs		output	X = A AND B X = A.B
		A	B	X	
		0	0	0	
		0	1	0	
		1	0	0	
		1	1	1	
OR A —⊃— X B	The output, X, is 1 if: either A or B, or both are 1	inputs		output	X = A OR B X = A + B
		A	B	X	
		0	0	0	
		0	1	1	
		1	0	1	
		1	1	1	

10.3 Logic circuits, logic expressions, truth tables and problem statements

Gate	Description	Truth table			Notation
		inputs		output	
		A	B	X	
NAND (A, B inputs → X output)	The output, X, is 1 if: input A and input B, are both not 1	0	0	1	X = A NAND B $X = \overline{A.B}$
		0	1	1	
		1	0	1	
		1	1	0	
NOR (A, B inputs → X output)	The output, X, is 1 if: neither input A nor input B is 1	inputs		output	X = A NOR B $X = \overline{A + B}$
		A	B	X	
		0	0	1	
		0	1	0	
		1	0	0	
		1	1	0	
XOR (A, B inputs → X output)	The output, X, is 1 if input A is 1 and input B is 0 or The output, X, is 1 if input B is 1 and input A is 0	inputs		output	X = A XOR B $X = (A.\overline{B}) + (\overline{A}.B)$
		A	B	X	
		0	0	0	
		0	1	1	
		1	0	1	
		1	1	0	

Note the use of **Boolean algebra** to represent logic gates. This is optional at IGCSE but you may prefer to use this notation. In the Boolean algebra are three new symbols; these have the following meaning:

- a dot (between letters, such as **A.B**) represents the AND operation
- a plus (between letters, such as **A + B**) represents the OR operation
- a bar (above the letter or letters, such as $\overline{A}$) represents the NOT operation.

10.3 Logic circuits, logic expressions, truth tables and problem statements

REVISED

When logic gates are combined together to carry out a particular function, they form a logic circuit. You need to be able to carry out the following tasks:

- create a logic circuit from a:
  - problem statement
  - logic or Boolean expression
  - truth table
- complete a truth table from a:
  - problem statement
  - logic or Boolean expression
  - logic circuit
- write a logic or Boolean expression from a:
  - problem statement
  - logic circuit
  - truth table.

Given a problem you need to be able to represent it as a logic expression, logic circuit or truth table. You also need to be able to convert between any of the three representations. For more examples of these tasks, see *Cambridge IGCSE and O Level Computer Science Second Edition* Student's Book, pages 360–376.

10 Boolean logic

Worked example

A safety system uses three inputs to a logic circuit. An alarm, X, sounds if input A represents ON and input B represents OFF; or if input B represents ON and input C represents OFF.

Here is a logic expression that uses the inputs and output from the problem. NOT is used if the input is off.

X = 1 if (A = 1 AND B = NOT 1) OR (B = 1 AND C = NOT 1)

Here is a logic circuit that uses the inputs and output from the problem. This must not be simplified.

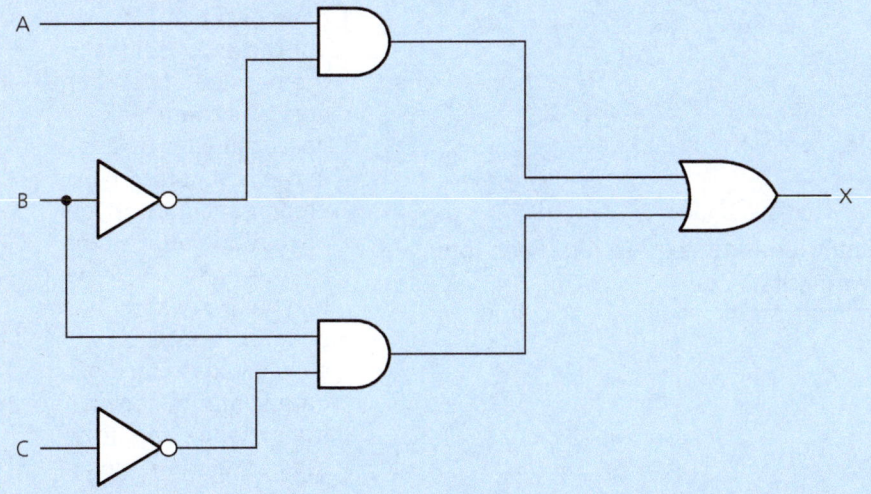

Here is a truth table that uses the inputs and output from the problem. Every set of inputs must have an output.

Inputs			Intermediate values		Output
A	B	C	(A = 1 AND B = NOT 1)	(B = 1 AND C = NOT 1)	X
0	0	0	0	0	0
0	0	1	0	0	0
0	1	0	0	1	1
0	1	1	0	0	0
1	0	0	1	0	1
1	0	1	1	0	1
1	1	0	0	1	1
1	1	1	0	0	0

10.3 Logic circuits, logic expressions, truth tables and problem statements

Sample questions and answers

REVISED

Consider this logic expression.

X = (A AND **B)** OR (NOT **B** AND **C)**

a) Complete the truth table for this logic expression.

Inputs			Working space		Output
A	B	C			X
0	0	0			
0	0	1			
0	1	0			
0	1	1			
1	0	0			
1	0	1			
1	1	0			
1	1	1			

b) Draw a logic circuit for the un-simplified logic expression. Each logic gate must have a maximum of **two** inputs.

[8]

Tips

Part a) of the answer will be marked on the 0s and 1s in the last column; the middle section is for working out. It is good practice to work out the expressions in the brackets first then combine them. Take care that your 0s and 1s in the last column are clear, especially if you have made alterations to your answers. In part b), you are asked to draw a logic circuit. Make sure you use the logic gate symbols shown in the syllabus and draw the connecting lines carefully.

High-level sample answer

a)

Inputs			Working space		Output
A	B	C	A AND B	NOT B AND C	X
0	0	0	0	0	0
0	0	1	0	1	1
0	1	0	0	0	0
0	1	1	0	0	0
1	0	0	0	0	0
1	0	1	0	1	1
1	1	0	1	0	1
1	1	1	1	0	1

b)

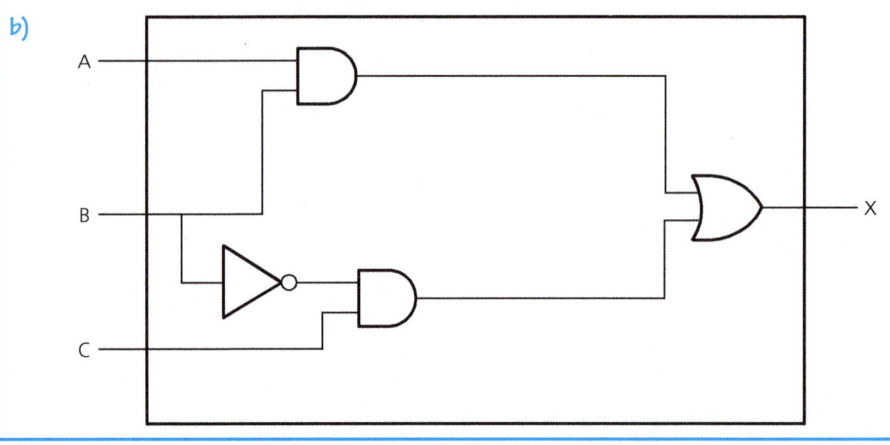

Teacher's comments

The first answer is clearly set out and readable. For part a), the intermediate stages have been included and the final column is clear correct and complete. For part b), the correct symbols have been used, the diagram is clearly set out and all the gates have two inputs or fewer.

Cambridge IGCSE™ and O Level Computer Science Study and Revision Guide Second Edition

10 Boolean logic

Low-level sample answer

a)

Inputs			Working space		Output
A	B	C			X
0	0	0			0
0	0	1			
0	1	0			0
0	1	1			⓪
1	0	0			0
1	0	1			1
1	1	0			0
1	1	1			1

b)
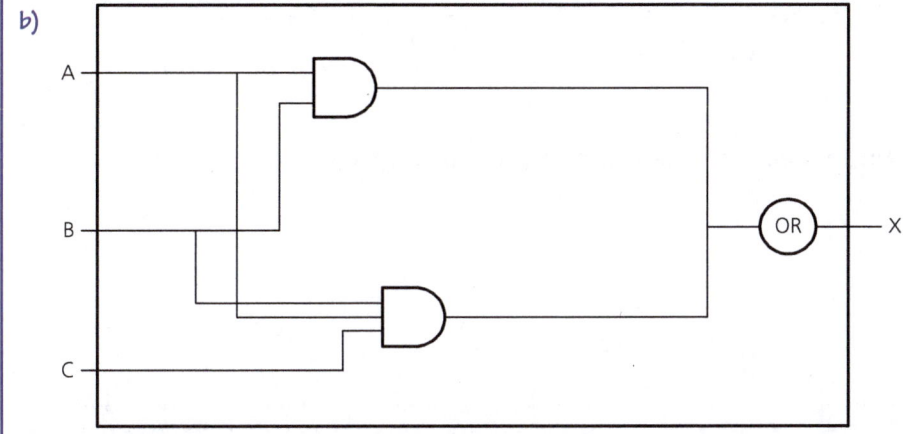

Teacher's comments

The second answer is unclear in places. For part a), the final column is incomplete, and it is unclear if there is a zero or a one on the fourth row. For part b), the lines are confusing, there is a three input AND gate, probably taken from the final row in the table, and the OR symbol is non-standard.

Exam-style questions

1 In this question you will be given a statement followed by four possible answers. Select which of the four answers you think is correct and tick (✔) the box next to your answer. You may need to tick more than one box.

   a) What is the symbol for **AND**?

   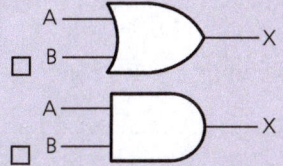   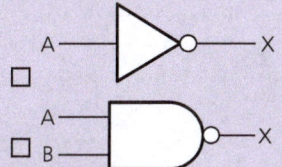

   b) What is meant by the term **logic circuit**?
   ☐ a combination of logic gates with one or more outputs
   ☐ a single gate with on or off
   ☐ a table showing the output from a collection of logic gates
   ☐ a simplified combination of logic gates   [2]

2 a) i) Draw the truth table for an OR gate and an XOR gate.
      ii) State why they are different.
   b) Name these gates and draw the truth tables for them.

         [7]

3 A company offers loans to people who can answer yes to at least two of these three questions:
   – are you over 18? (input A)
   – have you over $1000.00 in the bank? (input B)
   – have you a full-time job? (input J)
   a) Write the logic expression to represent this system.
   b) Write the truth table to represent this system.
   c) Draw the logic circuit to represent this system.   [12]

Hodder & Stoughton Limited © David Watson and Helen Williams 2022

Practice Paper 1A Computer systems

Time allowed: 2 hours and 15 minutes
Maximum number of marks: 100
Answer all questions

1 a Convert the denary number, 112, into an 8-bit binary number.

| | | | | | | | |

[1]

b i) Carry out a logical shift **three places to the right** on your answer to **part a**.

| | | | | | | | |

[1]

ii) Convert the binary number in **part bi)** into denary.

....

....

....

[1]

iii) Comment on your result to part **bii)**.

....

....

....

....

[2]

c i) Write down the two's complement of the binary number in **part bi)**.

| | | | | | | | |

[1]

ii) Convert the binary number in **part ci)** into denary.

....

....

....

[1]

iii) Convert the binary number in part **ci)** into hexadecimal.

....

....

....

2 a i) Describe what is meant by a **USB**.

....

....

....

[1]

ii) Give **three** differences between USB-A and USB-C.

1 ....

....

2 ....

....

3 ....

....

[3]

b The table below shows ticked boxes relating to types of data transmission. The following **five** descriptions have been missed out of the table:
- data sent one bit at a time along a single channel in one direction only
- data sent 8 bits at a time along 8 channels in both directions, but not at the same time
- 16 bits of data sent along 16 channels in both directions at the same time
- 16 bits of data sent one bit at a time along a single channel; the data can be sent in both directions but not at the same time
- data sent 8 bits at a time along 8 channels in one direction only

Write each description in the correct row of the table.

Description	Method used		Data direction		
	Serial	Parallel	Simplex	Half duplex	Full duplex
		✔		✔	
	✔		✔		
		✔	✔		
	✔			✔	
		✔			✔

[5]

3 a i) Describe when a **check digit** would be used as a verification method.

....

....

....

[1]

ii) Give **three** types of error a check digit could identify.

1 ....

....

2 ....

....

3 ....

....

[3]

iii) Name **one** situation where a check digit would not act as an error detection method.

....

....

....

[1]

b ISBN-13 is one way of generating and verifying a check digit. The algorithm to verify if a check digit has been calculated correctly is given below:
- add all the **odd** numbered digits together
- add all the **even** numbered digits together and multiply the result by **3**
- add the results from (1) and (2) together and divide by **10**
- the check digit is correct if the remainder in (3) is zero

Use the above algorithm to find out if the following number has been entered correctly (the check digit is shown as the right-most digit)

9 7 8 1 4 7 1 8 6 8 6 8 4

....

....

....

....

....

....

[4]

4 In Von Neumann architecture, both **buses** and **registers** are used.

a i) Name **two** buses.

1 ....

2 ....

[2]

ii) Name **two** registers.

1 ....

2 ....

[2]

b Explain the purpose of the two buses and the two registers you named in **part a)**.

....
....
....
....
....
....
....
....

[4]

c Explain what is meant by a **quad core processor**.

....
....
....
....

[2]

5 a Describe what is meant by a **QR code**.

....
....
....
....

[2]

b A company advertising its website uses QR codes on the walls of a city metro system. Describe how a passenger using the metro system could use the QR codes to visit the company's website.

....
....
....
....
....
....
....
....

[4]

c Give **one** advantage and **one** disadvantage of using QR codes rather than barcodes.

Advantage:

....

....

....

Disadvantage:

....

....

....

[2]

6 John is taking photographs using a smartphone. The built-in camera uses a detector with a 2048 by 1536 pixel array. The smartphone's camera software uses a bit depth of 24 bits.

  a i) Explain the two terms **pixel array** and **colour depth**.

      Pixel array:

....

....

      Colour depth:

....

....

[2]

  ii) John's smartphone has 64 GiB available memory.
Assuming all the photographs are the same size, calculate how many photographs could be stored on John's smartphone.

....

....

....

....

....

[3]

b The following logo, of a company called CIC, is being designed on a computer. The final design is stored in a file called **logo1**.

Describe how run length encoding (RLE) could be used to reduce the size of file **logo1**. Write down the data you would expect to see in the RLE compressed format file and describe how this would differ from the original file. Include, in your answer, any file reduction you might expect to see.

(You may assume that the colour code for a grey square is 80 and for a white square is 255.)

....

....

....

....

....

....

....

[4]

c Describe the differences between **lossy** and **lossless** file compression.

....

....

....

[2]

Practice Paper 1A Computer systems

7 Data is being sent from a computer to a printer. Interrupts and buffers are used in this process.
   a Explain the role of buffers during the printing process.
   ....
   ....
   ....
   ....
   [2]

   b Explain how interrupts are used in the printing process.
   ....
   ....
   ....
   ....
   ....
   ....
   [3]

8 a Complete the following table by writing an appropriate sensor that could be used in each application being described.
     Each sensor chosen can only be used once. [6]

Description of application	Appropriate sensor
Pick up the noise of breaking glass in an intruder alert system	
Used in mobile phones to switch between portrait and landscape mode when a phone's orientation is changed	
Used in anti-lock braking systems in a vehicle	
Sends data to allow a vehicle's windscreen wipers to turn on automatically when it starts to rain	
Used to detect a leak in the refrigerant in an air conditioning unit	
Monitors the moisture levels in the air in a factory manufacturing microchips	

   b A vending machine dispenses cold cans of soda (at < 4 °C). The vending machine also has an in-built security system to sound an alarm if the machine is tilted by more than 20 degrees.
     The operation and security of the vending machine is controlled by sensors and a microprocessor in an embedded system.
     i) Describe what is meant by an **embedded system**.
     ....
     ....
     ....
     ....
     [2]

ii) Name a sensor that could be used to ensure the soda cans are only dispensed at < 4 °C.

....

....

[1]

iii) Name a sensor that could be used to monitor any attempt at tilting the vending machine by over 20 degrees.

....

....

[1]

iv) Describe how the sensors and microprocessor are used to maintain the temperature below 4 °C and to raise an alarm if it is tilted by more than 20 degrees.

....

....

....

....

....

....

....

....

[4]

9 a i) Explain what is meant by the term **blockchaining**.

....

....

....

....

[2]

ii) Describe how blockchaining is used to prevent data tampering.

....

....

....

....

[2]

b i) Describe what is meant by **social engineering**.

....

....

....

....

[2]

ii) Describe **two** methods used by cybercriminals to target and attack their intended victims.

....

....

....

....

[2]

c i) Explain what is meant by **two-step verification** and why it is used.

....

....

....

....

....

....

[3]

ii) Explain why it is an advantage to allow automatic software upgrades on a computer system.

....

....

....

[2]

10 Seven terms are being described below. Name each term being described.

a A combination of software and hardware designed and programmed to work automatically without the need for human intervention.

....

b Devices that are mechanical and electronic structures designed to automatically carry out a task.

....

c Name for a 'brain' used by a device, such as a robot, that can be programmed to do a specific task.

....

d Robots that have no direct human input and can completely replace any human requirement.

....

e Branch of computer science dealing with the simulation of intelligent human behaviour by a computer.

....

f A form of AI that mimics human knowledge and experience to solve problems difficult enough to require some degree of human expertise.

....

g A subset of AI in which the algorithms are 'trained' and 'learn' from their past experiences and examples.

....

[7]

11 In the following diagram, six descriptions are shown on the left and ten computer terms are shown on the right.
By drawing lines, connect each description to the correct computer term.

[6]

Program that supplies static or moving images on a monitor when a computer has been left idle for a period of time.	Virtual memory
	Descriptor
Software that rearranges blocks of data to remove unused data blocks; it arranges the data into contiguous sectors.	Screensaver
	Bootstrap
USB device drivers contain information such as vendor ID (VI), product ID (PID) and unique serial numbers.	Printer driver
Software that communicates with the operating system and translates data into a format understood by an input/output device.	Disk defragmenter
	Solid-state device
Used by DRAM to recharge capacitors every 15 microseconds to ensure values are retained by the RAM memory.	Disk thrashing
	Refresh
Device that uses floating gate and control gate transistors to allow the rewriting of data.	Cache

Practice Paper 2A Algorithms, programming and logic

Time allowed: 2 hours and 15 minutes

Maximum number of marks: 100

Answer all questions

1 In this question you will be given a statement followed by four possible answers.
   Select which of the four answers you think is correct and tick (✔) the box next to your answer.
   a What is the symbol for NAND?

   ☐ (OR gate)   ☐ (AND gate)

   ☐ (NOT gate)   ☐ (NAND gate)

   b The description of the analysis stage of the program development life cycle.
      ☐ investigating to provide the specification of what a program is required to do
      ☐ testing of the program to make sure that it works under all conditions
      ☐ writing of the program or suite of programs
      ☐ using the program specification to show to how the program should be developed

   c Which statement is used for selection?
      ☐ NEXT
      ☐ PROCEDURE
      ☐ DECLARE
      ☐ CASE

   d The description of a database table
      ☐ a collection of fields about the same item
      ☐ a collection of related records
      ☐ a field that uniquely identifies a record
      ☐ a single piece of data

   [4]

2 a i) Describe what is meant by a standard method of solution.

   ....

   ....

   ....

   ....

   [2]

ii) Counting is a standard method of solution.
Give **three** other examples of standard methods of solution.

1 ....

....

2 ....

....

3 ....

....

[3]

b Describe, using an example, the use of counting as a standard method of solution.

....

....

....

....

....

....

[3]

3 The table below shows ticked (✔) boxes relating to validation and verification checks.
The following five descriptions have been missed out of the table:
- data must be eight characters long
- data must be entered twice and match
- data is displayed on the screen to be confirmed
- data must have a value between 8 and 12
- data must only contain numbers

Write each description in the correct row of the table and name each check.

| Description | Method used | | Name of check |
	Validation	Verification	
		✔	
	✔		
		✔	
	✔		
	✔		

[5]

4 a i) Explain why **test data** is required.

....

....

....

....

[2]

ii) State **three** types of test data.

1 ....

....

2 ....

....

3 ....

....

[3]

b A program accepts values that are whole numbers between 30 and 40 inclusive.
Give examples of test data that are required.
Explain, including the expected outcome, why each piece of test data is needed.

....

....

....

....

....

....

....

....

....

....

....

[6]

5 This algorithm is written in pseudocode.

```
01 REPEAT
02     OUTPUT "Please enter your password"
03     INPUT Password
04     IF Length(Password) < 10
05        THEN
06           OUTPUT "Reject too short"
07        ELSE
08           Symbol ← FALSE
09           PasswordUp ← UCASE(Password)
10            FOR Counter ← 1 TO Length(Password)
11               IF SUBSTRING(PasswordUp, Counter, 1) > 90 OR
                    SUBSTRING(PasswordUp, Counter, 1) < 65
12                  THEN
13                     Symbol ← TRUE
14               ENDIF
15           NEXT Counter
16           IF Symbol
17              THEN
18                 OUTPUT "Accept"
19              ELSE
20                 OUTPUT "Reject no symbol"
21           ENDIF
22     ENDIF
23 UNTIL Symbol AND Length(Password) >= 10
```

a i) State the purpose of the algorithm.

....

....

[1]

ii) Identify the line number(s) for these types of statement.
Assignment

....

Selection

....

Iteration

....

[2]

b i) Complete the trace table for the algorithm using this data **MyPassword!**

Password	PasswordUp	Symbol	Counter	OUTPUT

[4]

ii) Complete the trace table for **MyWord!**

Password	PasswordUp	Symbol	Counter	OUTPUT

[2]

6 a i) Describe the difference between **variables** and **constants** in programming.

....

....

....

....

[2]

ii) Give **three** basic data types that are used in programming.

1 ....

....

2 ....

....

3 ....

....

[3]

b Write pseudocode statements to declare a variable to store the number of children in a class and a constant with the value 30 that is the maximum number of children that could be included in a class.

....

....

....

....

[3]

7 Describe, with the use of examples, the different types of operators that can be used when programming.

....

....

....

....

....

....

....

....

....

[4]

8 In the following diagram, six descriptions are shown on the left and eight library routines are shown on the right.
By drawing lines, connect each description to the correct library routine.

Descriptions	Library routines
Returns the remainder of a division.	DIV
Returns a random number.	LCASE
Returns the number of characters.	LENGTH
Returns a string where all letters are lower case.	MOD
Returns a string where all letters are upper case.	RANDOM
Returns the quotient of a division.	ROUND
	SUBSTRING
	UCASE

[6]

9 a i) Explain what is meant by the term **array**.

....

....

....

....

[2]

ii) Describe, using an example, how a variable is used as an array index.

....

....

....

....

[2]

iii) Describe the difference between **1D** and **2D** arrays.

....

....

....

....

[2]

b Write pseudocode statements to declare and populate a 2D array with 20 rows of four zeros. Use iteration to populate the array.

....

....

....

....

....

....

....

[4]

c Give **one** advantage and **one** disadvantage of using arrays.

Advantage:

....

....

Disadvantage:

....

....

[2]

10 Read this section of pseudocode that inputs fifty (50) negative numbers and then outputs the largest negative number input.

```
01 Large ← 9999
02 Counter ← 50
03 WHILE Counter > 50 DO
04    REPEAT
05       INPUT NegNum
06    UNTIL NegNum > 0
07    IF NegNum < Large THEN Large ←  NegNum
08    Counter = Counter - 1
09 ENDWHILE
10 OUTPUT "Largest number is ", Large
```

There are five errors in this code.
Locate these errors and suggest a corrected piece of code for each error.

1 ....

2 ....

3 ....

4 ....

5 ....

[5]

11 A database of plants for sale, `PlantSale`, is to be set up with the following fields:
- `PlantName` – for example Begonia
- `PlantPrice` – for example $10.00
- `PlantID` – for example PL579
- `Position` – for example, shade or sun
- `PlantHeight` – for example, 1.5
- `StockAvailable` – for example, 25

  a State, with a reason, a suitable data type for these fields:
  `PlantPrice`

  ....

  ....

PlantHeight

....

....

Position

....

....

[3]

b State which field you would choose for the primary key and explain why it is appropriate.

....

....

....

[2]

c Complete this SQL script to display the names, prices and number in stock of all plants taller than 1.8 metres.

SELECT PlantName, Price, ...

FROM ....

WHERE .... **>1.8;**

[3]

12 Consider this logic expression.

X = (A AND **B)** XOR (NOT **B** AND NOT **C)**

a Complete the truth table for this logic expression.

Inputs			Working space		Output
A	B	C			X
0	0	0			
0	0	1			
0	1	0			
0	1	1			
1	0	0			
1	0	1			
1	1	0			
1	1	1			

[4]

b Draw a logic circuit for the un-simplified logic expression. Each logic gate must have a maximum of **two** inputs.

[4]

13 The one-dimensional array **BabyName[]** contains the names of the babies in a nursery. Another one-dimensional array **ParentPhone[]** contains the phone numbers for the parents of the baby.
A final one-dimensional array **BabyAge[]** contains the baby's age in months.
The position of each baby's data in the three arrays is the same; for example, the baby in position 3 in **BabyName[]**, **ParentPhone** and **BabyAge[]** is the same.
Write and test a program that meets the following requirements:
○ uses procedures to display these lists:
 - parent phone numbers and baby names in alphabetic order of baby name
 - baby names for babies aged under three months
○ uses a procedure to display all the details for a baby, with the name used as a parameter
○ uses a procedure to update the details for a baby, with the name used as a parameter.
You must use pseudocode or program code with local and global variables **and** add comments to explain how your code works. All inputs and outputs must contain suitable messages.

[12]

Further space for answering Practice Paper 2A, Question 13.

Answers to exam-style questions

Chapter 1

1. a i) 1100 0000 1101 1110 → C 0 D E
      ii) 2A9F → 0010 1010 1001 1111
   b i) 3FC → (3 x 256) + (15 x 16) + (12 x 1) = 1020
      ii)
16	2816	
16	176	remainder: 0
16	11	remainder: 0
	0	remainder: 11

      Read the remainder from bottom to top to get the hexadecimal number: **B 0 0 (B = 11)**.

2. a i) 95 → 0 1 0 1 1 1 1 1
      ii) 30 → 0 0 0 1 1 1 1 0
      iii) 205 → 1 1 0 0 1 1 0 1
   b i) 0 1 0 1 1 1 1 1 + 0 0 0 1 1 1 1 0 → 0 1 1 1 1 1 0 1
      ii) 0 1 0 1 1 1 1 1 + 1 1 0 0 1 1 0 1 → 1 0 0 1 0 1 1 0 0
          overflow error

3. ○ Any three from:
   Error codes: these refer to memory locations where errors have occurred; these memory locations are shown in hexadecimal.
   ○ MAC address: this identifies a device on a network; MAC address is written as:
   NN – NN – NN – DD – DD – DD (for example, 00–1C–B3–4F–25–FE).
   ○ IP address: this is given to a device when it logs on to a network; there are two types: IPv4 and IPv6 (IPv6 uses hexadecimal).
   ○ HTML codes: colours are made up of combinations of red, green and blue; the amount of each primary colour is represented by a hexadecimal code (for example #B18904 is a tan colour).

4. 75 → 0 1 0 0 1 0 1 1
   75 → 1 0 1 1 0 1 0 1 (either –128 + 53 or invert binary 75 and add 1 to binary).

5. a i)
128	64	32	16	8	4	2	1
116 → 0	1	1	1	0	1	0	0

      ii) Shifting two places to the right gives:

0	0	0	1	1	1	0	1

      iii) Shifting three places to the left gives:

1	0	1	0	0	0	0	0

      1-bits are lost after the shift giving an incorrect answer.

   b i) 3C → 0011 1100 and 44 → 0100 0100
      ii) 00111100 + 01000100 → 1 0 0 0 0 0 0 0
      iii) shifting six places to the right gives:

      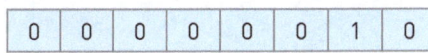

      ($128 \div 2^6 = 2$, which means shift to the right gives correct answer).

6. a Analogue data
   b i) Peak 'A' = 1 0 1 0 and peak 'B' = 1 1 1 0.
      ii) Increase sampling resolution to 32 bits or 64 bits.
   c i) Number of bits used to represent sound amplitude in digital sound recording.
      ii) Number of sound samples taken per second in digital sound recording.
   d i) Using 32 bits increases accuracy of digital sound representation.
      ii) Using 32 bits increases the amount of memory/storage required to store sound samples; it also takes longer to upload/download files or to send sound as email attachments.
      iii) File size = sampling rate x sampling resolution x sample length
      = 20000 x 32 x 30 = 19 200 000 bits
      = 2 400 000 bytes
      = 2.29 MiB

7. a 16 x 16 squares will require 256 bytes.
   b RLE encodes repeated strings of data; it is a lossless file compression method; the image when coded becomes (black = 0 and white = 1):
   20/121/40/31/60/31/20/51/60/10/120/21/20/101/20/21/
   20/61/70/11/60/21/70/11/60/21/60/21/20/21/20/21/20/
   11/20/21/20/21/20/21/20/21/20/21/60/11/70/21/60/11/
   70/61/20/21/20/101/60/51/20/31/60/31/40/121/20

   All of this requires 2 x 65 = 130 bytes of storage; thus RLE gives a potential file reduction of (126/256) x 100 = 49.2%.

8. a MP3 – a lossy file compression method used for music files.
   b JPEG – a lossy file compression method used with image files; it relies on the inability of the human eye to distinguish certain colour changes and hues.
   c 1TiB – this is equivalent to 2^{40} bytes of data; a unit of memory/storage adapted by IEC.
   d Pixel – this stands for 'picture element'; it is the smallest element used to make up an image on a display.

9. a 1 MiB is 1 048 576 (2^{20}) bytes; 1 MB is 1 000 000 (10^6) bytes.
   b Files undergoing lossy compression can't be restored to the original file; the student has actually described lossless file compression.
   c RLE only works where there is a long run of repeated units, otherwise it has little or no file reduction.
   d ASCII code and Unicode are entirely different character sets; however, there is some overlap between ASCII and Unicode (the first 128 characters are the same).

Answers to exam-style questions

e A sound file is stored in digital format on a computer; when the sound file is played back through speakers it needs to be converted into analogue format using DAC.

10 a An image becomes pixelated when a bit-map image is zoomed in. On zooming in, the pixel density becomes smaller and can be diminished to such a degree that the individual pixels can be seen.

b The pixel density gets less as an image is zoomed into; since there are now fewer pixels per square centimetre, the image becomes pixelated.

c i) FF

ii) By varying the value of each colour component, up to 256 x 256 x 256 different colours can be displayed (for example, #FF24A1); each red, green and blue component can take values between 00 to FF.

Chapter 2

1 ○ The software is broken up into data packets; each numbered in sequence and each has the same MAC/IP addresses.

○ Each data packet is sent to its destination via its own route; the route taken is 'decided' by the routers within the network which take various factors into consideration.

○ When the data packets arrive at their destination, they are reassembled into the correct order according to their sequence numbers.

○ A CRC check is carried out on each data packet to ensure no errors occurred during the transmission of the software.

○ Note: mention of hop numbers can also be included in the description and should gain credit.

2 a – IP addresses of sender and recipient.
– Packet sequence number.
– Packet size.

b i) Some indication of the end of the packet.

ii) Number of 1-bits is 44 which is 2C in hexadecimal; the value, 2C, is appended to the data packet and the receiving computer adds up the 1-bits again to make sure it still equals 2C, otherwise a transmission error has occurred.

c i) Data packets keep 'bouncing' around from router to router and never actually reach their destination; this then becomes a lost data packet.

ii) Each data packet is given a hop number; every time a packet leaves a router, the hop number is decreased by 1; if the hop number reaches 0, and it hasn't yet reached its destination, then the data packet is deleted from the system and a request is made for it to be re-sent.

3 a Data skewing: this is data arriving at its destination with the bits no longer synchronised.

b USB – C: a 24-pin symmetrical USB connection; smaller and thinner than older USB connectors and also offers higher power connectivity (so it can support higher charging rates) and faster data transmission.

c Parallel: sending data down several channels several bits at a time simultaneously.

d Half-duplex: data that can be sent in both directions but not at the same time.

4

Statement	Transmission method		Direction of data transmission		
	Serial (✔)	Parallel (✔)	Simplex (✔)	Half-duplex (✔)	Full-duplex (✔)
Data is being sent in both directions, one bit at a time along a single wire, but not at the same time.	✔			✔	
16 bits of data are being sent along 16 individual channels in both directions simultaneously.		✔			✔
Data is being sent 8 bits at a time down 8 wires in one direction only.		✔	✔		
Data is being sent one bit at a time down a single wire; the transmission occurs in both directions simultaneously.	✔				✔

5

Description	Checksum (✔)	Parity check (✔)	ARQ (✔)	CRC (✔)
Makes use of positive and negative acknowledgement.			✔	
An extra bit is sent with each byte of data.		✔		
Uses timeout to determine if data needs to be re-sent.			✔	
If an error is found, a request is made to re-send the data.	✔	✔	✔	
Re-calculation is made on any additional data values sent with the main data block.	✔		✔	✔
A value added to the end of a data item to see if it has been entered correctly.				
Method used to determine which bit in a data block has been altered.		✔		
Additional value sent at the end of a block of data used to check if a data transmission error occurred.	✔		✔	✔
Number of 1-bits are counted before and after a data block has been sent.			✔	✔
Value used as part of a data packet trailer to check if any data corruption has occurred.			✔	✔

6 a i) Byte 8 (five 1-bits), bit 6 (seven 1-bits)

    ii) 1 1 0 0 0 0 1 1

    iii) If two bits have swapped (for example, 1 0 1 1 0 1 1 0 and 1 1 0 1 0 1 1 0) or two or more bits are faulty where the parity of a byte hasn't been changed overall.

b
- ARQ uses positive and negative acknowledgement and timeout.
- The recipient receives an error detection code as part of the data transmission (typically CRC); this is used to detect whether the received data contains any transmission errors.
- If no errors are detected a positive acknowledgement is sent to sending device.
- If an error is detected the receiving device sends a negative acknowledgement to the sending device and requests re-transmission of the data.
- Timeout is used by the sending device by waiting a pre-determined amount of time.
- If no acknowledgement of any type has been received by sending device with the time limit (timeout period), it automatically re-sends the data until a positive acknowledgement is received or until a pre-determined number of re-transmissions has taken place.

7 a
- Daniel uses encryption algorithms to generate matching pairs of keys (private key and public key); they are mathematically linked.
- Daniel sends his public key to Ali.
- Ali uses Daniel's public key to encrypt his document and sends this encrypted document to Daniel.
- Daniel uses his matching private key to unlock Ali's document and decrypt it; this works because the public key used to encrypt the document and the private key used to decrypt it are mathematically paired/linked.

b Daniel can also exchange his public key with any number of people working in the company so he is able to receive encrypted messages and can decrypt them using his matching private key.

8 a Ciphertext is encrypted data that is the result of putting a plaintext message through an encryption algorithm.

b Plaintext is the original message before it is put through an encryption algorithm.

c Encryption is the process of making data meaningless using encryption keys.

d A private key is a type of encryption key that is known only to a single user.

e Encryption algorithms are software that take plaintext and generate ciphertext.

Chapter 3

1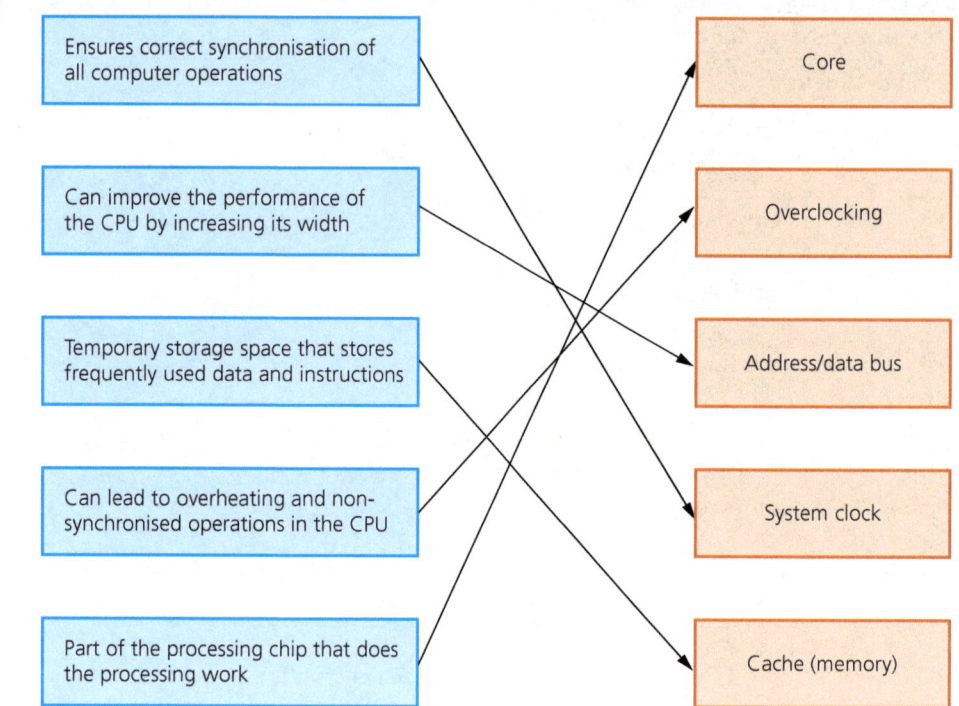

2 Any three from:

Benefits:
- Consume very little power/don't generate much heat.
- Allow devices to be controlled remotely/through an app.
- Devices are more reliable.
- Small size therefore easy to fit into devices.
- Low cost of mass-production manufacturing.
- Dedicated to one task making for simple interfaces and often no requirement for an operating system.

Drawbacks:
- Can be difficult to upgrade devices.
- Interfaces can be complex with some devices.
- Prone to hacking and viruses when communicating remotely.
- Devices often thrown away when they break down rather than fixing them.
- Environmental issues created by a 'throw-away society'.
- Troubleshooting faults in the device is a specialist task.

3 a
- Basic operation of a computer.
- CPU fetches an instruction from memory one at a time and puts them into registers.
- Each instruction is then decoded and finally executed.

b
- Next instruction is fetched from memory address currently stored in MAR and instruction is stored in MDR.
- Contents of MDR are copied to CIR.
- PC is incremented by 1 so it points to the next instruction to be processed.

4 a The barcode is read using a red laser or red LED scanner; the dark and light lines vary in thickness producing a code which is read by the scanner and then interpreted by software. A database could contain a number of records in the following format:

Barcode number	Location of glove	Date glove first installed	'Use by' date on the glove

It is therefore easy to determine where the glove is and therefore its use, when it was first fitted and its useful life – the barcode acts as the key field to the record.

b
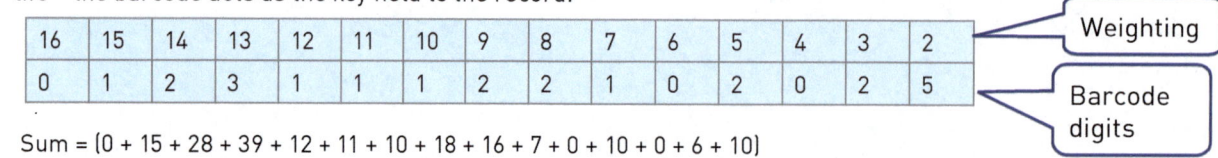

Sum = (0 + 15 + 28 + 39 + 12 + 11 + 10 + 18 + 16 + 7 + 0 + 10 + 0 + 6 + 10)

= 182 ÷ 11 = 16 remainder 6 → check digit = 11 – 6 = 5

Final number is 0 1 2 3 1 1 1 2 2 1 0 2 0 2 5 5

c Any two from:
- System is semi-automatic; it works even if use by label on glove has been lost.
- System can be designed to automatically highlight gloves that need changing, thus improving safety and allows for automatic reordering of new gloves.
- System can automatically produce statistics showing where glove failures occur most often.

d i) QR codes are read by the camera on a smartphone or tablet; barcodes require use of a red laser/LED scanner.

Camera image is interpreted as a binary value by an app on QR system; with barcodes, light and dark lines read by a scanner are used to create binary code.

ii) No need for a database since the QR code could contain all the necessary data within the matrix; a website link could also be part of the QR code matrix that could allow automatic reordering to occur.

iii) More than one QR format exists; this could cause an issue.

Risk of *atagging* where QR codes contain malicious code thus creating a security risk in the company.

5 Capacitive:
- If projective technology is used, multi-touch facility (i.e. pinching and sliding) is allowed.
- Has good clarity in all lighting conditions.
- Durable screens which tolerate scratches.
- Technology can be sensitive to magnetic fields or microwaves.

Infrared:
- Allows multi-touch facility.
- Has good screen durability.
- Not severely affected by scratches or even cracked screens.
- Can be sensitive to moisture on the screen.
- Can be sensitive to light interference.

Resistive:
- Has good resistance to dust and water.
- Low sensitivity and doesn't allow multi-touch facilities.
- Vulnerable to scratches and cracked layers.

6 a 3D printer
b LED/OLED screen
c OLED screen
d LCD projector/DLP
e Laser printer
f Inkjet printer
g Actuator
h Loudspeaker

7 a Monitoring: sensor data is compared to stored data and a warning is given on screen or a sound is used to alert/inform user.

Control: sensor data is compared to stored data and action is taken by the microprocessor if sensor data indicates process parameters are out of range; signals are sent from microprocessor to actuator (via DAC) to change process parameters – this is known as feedback where the output affects future input.

b i) Temperature sensor, humidity sensor

ii)
- Data from the sensors is sent to a microprocessor (passing through ADC first to convert data into a digital format).
- Microprocessor compares sensor data to stored data.
- If temperature > stored data, microprocessor sends signal to actuators to switch on air con system, otherwise air con remains off/switched off.
- If humidity > stored data, microprocessor sends signal to actuators to switch on air con system.
- Otherwise air con remains off/switched off.
- Data from microprocessor passes through DAC before going to actuators.
- Monitoring/control process is continuous.

8

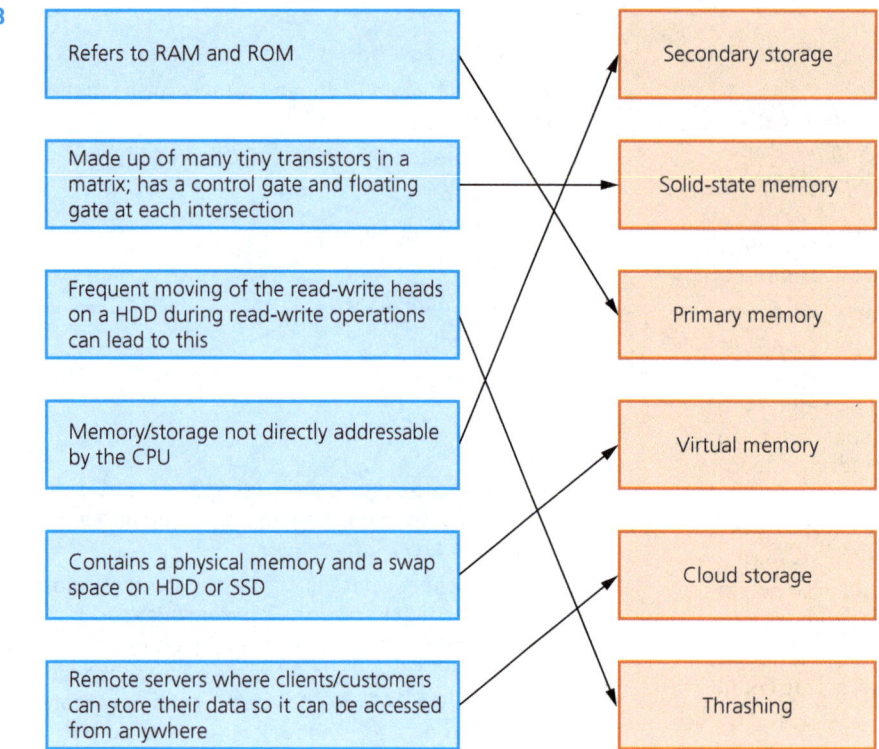

9 a RAM:
- Temporary memory device.
- Volatile memory.
- Can be written to and read from.
- Used to store data, files, programs, part of OS currently in use.
- Can be increased in size to improve operational speed of a computer.

ROM:
- Permanent memory device.
- Non-volatile memory device.
- Data stored cannot be altered.
- Always used to store BIOS and other data needed at start-up.

b The larger the RAM the faster the computer can process data; however, RAM is expensive per unit of memory therefore costs can outweigh any real advantages.

c Mention of any of the data from the following table:

Disk type	Laser colour	Wavelength of laser light	Disk construction	Track pitch (distance between tracks)
DVD (dual-layer)	Red	650 nm	two 0.6 mm polycarbonate layers	0.74 µm
Blu-ray (single layer)	Blue	405 mm	single 1.2 mm polycarbonate layer	0.30 µm
Blu-ray (dual-layer)	Blue	405 nm	two 0.6 mm polycarbonate layers	0.30 µm

10 a Private or hybrid cloud would both work. Since large amounts of data are commercially sensitive, private cloud storage would be needed for some (or all) of the data – however, some data could be in the public domain, so a hybrid cloud option could be taken.

b i) Advantages:
- Customer/client files stored on the cloud can be accessed at any time from any device anywhere in the world provided internet access is available.
- There is no need for a customer/client to carry an external storage device with them, or even use the same computer to store and retrieve information.
- The cloud provides the user with remote back-up of data with obvious benefits to alleviate data loss/disaster recovery.
- If a customer/client has a failure of their hard disk or back-up device, cloud storage will allow recovery of their data.
- The cloud system offers almost unlimited storage capacity.

ii) Disadvantages:
- If the customer/client has a slow or unstable internet connection, they would have many problems accessing or downloading their data/files.
- Costs can be high if large storage capacity is required; it can also be expensive to pay for high download/upload data transfer limits with the customer/client internet service provider (ISP).
- The potential failure of the cloud storage company is always possible – this poses a risk of loss of all back-up data.
- Data security issues – how safely stored and protected is the data from hacking, natural disasters and malware?

c If the internet link is weak/slow, downloading and uploading of drawing would take a long time (and may even crash the computer); large files can be expensive with regards to storage costs.

11 a NIC
b MAC address
c DHCP server
d Router
e IP address

Chapter 4

1

Software	System (✔)	Application (✔)
Screensaver	✔	
Antivirus software	✔	
Printer driver	✔	
Video editing software		✔
Compiler	✔	
QR code reader		✔
On-screen calculator		✔
Operating system software	✔	
Interrupt handling routine	✔	
Photo editing software		✔

2 a A virus is a small program/code that replicates itself and can delete/modify/corrupt important data.
  b
  - Antivirus software looks for known viruses in a database.
  - Many antivirus software products carry out heuristic checking looking for types of behaviour that could indicate software/files have been infected with a new virus.
  - Any files/programs that have been infected are put into quarantine; they are then automatically deleted or action is taken by the user.

3 a Memory management:
   - Manages primary memory (RAM) and allows data to be moved between RAM and HDD/SSD.
   - Keeps track of all the memory locations and contents.
   - Carries out memory protection to ensure competing programs/apps can't use the same memory locations.
  b User account management:
   - Allows more than one user to use a system.
   - User accounts are protected by username and password and monitored by an administrator.
   - Separate folders and files are used to manage users' computer usage.
  c Security management:
   - Carries out operating system updates automatically when they become available.
   - Ensures security of software (for example, virus checkers) by ensuring it is always up to date and also runs software, such as an antivirus, in the background.
   - Communicates with the firewall to check security of internet traffic.
   - Ensures private areas of a computer system are protected by maintaining access rights, for example.
   - Offers data recovery procedures in case of data corruption.

4 a Device drivers are software that communicate with the OS and translate data into a format understood by the hardware device; when a device is plugged into a USB port, the OS looks up the appropriate driver or invites the user to download the appropriate driver.

   All device drivers contain descriptors that allow the OS to recognise newly connected devices; descriptors include: vendor ID (VID), product ID (PID) and a unique serial number.

  b When the camera is plugged in, a buffer is filled with data from the camera's memory; this data is then transferred from the buffer to computer storage; meanwhile the CPU in the computer carries on with other tasks; when the buffer is empty, an interrupt signal is sent from the buffer to the CPU; the CPU suspends its present task and establishes the priority of the interrupt; the CPU stores present register values and then instructs the camera to start filling up the buffer again with data; this process continues until all data has been transferred from camera to computer.

5 Read answers down each column

signal	interrupt	microprocessor
software	priority	streaming
microprocessor	buffer	buffer
attention	temporarily	compensate
microprocessor	microprocessor	download
service	interrupt	

6

Description	Assembler (✔)	Compiler (✔)	Interpreter (✔)
Translates a program written in a LLL	✔		
Translates a program written in a HLL		✔	
Identifies errors	✔	✔	✔
Does not produce an executable file			✔
Allows editing during execution			✔

7 **a** A programming language that is dependent on computer hardware and needs to be translated into binary before it is executed.
  b Finding errors in a computer program by running or tracing the program.
  c A programming language that is independent of computer hardware.

8 **a** An integrated development environment is:
  – A suite of software development tools to aid program writing and development.
  b Any **two** descriptions of features of an IDE.
  – Code editor – to allow editing without using a separate program.
  – Translator – either a compiler, interpreter or both.
  – Runtime environment – to aid debugging.
  – Error diagnostics – to speed up the correction of errors.
  – Auto-completion – to prevent errors in key words and variable names.
  – Auto-correction – to automatically correct errors in key words and variable names.
  – An auto-documenter with prettyprinting – to provide understandable, well set out documentation.

9 An integrated development environment (IDE) is needed to speed up the development of computer software by providing all the development tools required in one application with a Graphical User Interface (GUI).

During development a programmer can edit and test the program in the same environment without having to run another application. The time taken to find and correct errors is reduced as there are on-screen diagnostics during editing for syntax errors and on-screen diagnostics during running the program for runtime errors. The runtime environment provides features such as 'watch windows' to show the values of variables, these help the programmer to find logic errors in the program.

Also, there are fewer errors made when writing the program with the use of auto-completion to prevent some typing errors and auto-correction to correct some errors as well.

Chapter 5

1 **a** frage-eins-beispiel
  b .org
  c example-page
  d https

2

Feature	Internet/WWW
Ability to send and receive emails.	Internet
Makes use of http and https protocols.	WWW
Uses URLs to specify locations of websites and web pages.	WWW
Resources can be accessed by using web browsers.	WWW
Makes use of TCP and IP protocols.	Internet
Allows online chatting (via text, audio and video).	Internet
Collection of multimedia web pages and other information on websites.	WWW
Physical infrastructure that allows networks and devices to connect to each other.	Internet

3 **a** Decentralised database where all transactions are stored; it consists of a number of interconnected computers but not a central server.
  b Any three from:
  – Smart contracts
  – Research (for example, pharmaceuticals)
  – Politics
  – Education

4 **a**

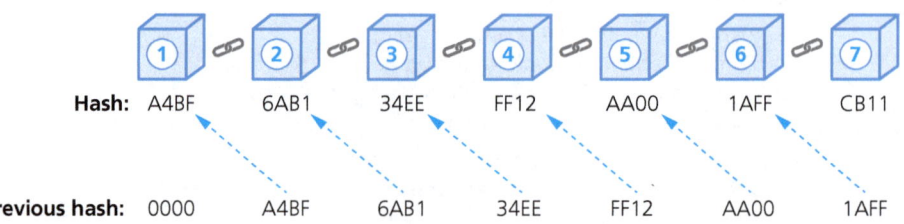

- b The hash value would change and break the chain from blocks 4 onwards; a proof-of-work is also generated that takes ten minutes to complete, thus mitigating the high speed of computers that would otherwise allow all blocks to be altered and therefore maintain the links.

5 a Passwords are used to protect systems from illegal access.
- b Any three from:
  - At least one upper case letter and one lower case letter.
  - At least one numerical value.
  - At least one other keyboard character (for example, &, !, #, %).
  - At least eight characters.
  - Avoid easy to guess passwords, such as name of a pet, birthdays.
- c User clicks on 'forgotten password' and an invitation to change password appears in his email inbox; user clicks on the link in the email and is sent to a website where the password can be changed; a confirmation email is sent to the user including a warning that the password has been changed (it will also include a warning that if it wasn't the user who made the change then they need to go to their account settings and change the password manually).

6 a Authentication
- b Proxy server
- c Privacy settings
- d SSL
- e Firewall
- f Biometrics
- g Social engineering
- h Pharming

7 Brute force:
○ All combinations of letters, numbers and other keyboard characters are tried until possible passwords are eventually found.
○ Relies on the high speed of a computer.
○ Mitigation: use complex passwords that are often changed and kept secret.

Data interception:
○ Tapping into networks to find data.
○ Using a packet sniffer (that examines all data packets on a network and extracts data, or war driving/access point mapping that intercepts wireless signals using a laptop/smartphone, an antenna, GPS device and software to gather data).
○ Mitigation: use Wired Equivalency Privacy encryption protocols and firewalls.

Distributed denial-of-service (DDoS) attacks:
○ An attempt to prevent anyone accessing part of network, for example, a specific server.
○ They can also attack an individual by preventing them accessing their emails or certain websites.
○ DDoS can be achieved by sending out masses of spam which overloads a website or fills up a user's inbox.
○ Mitigation: use up-to-date malware checkers, ensure firewalls are up to date and always running, apply an email filter that can remove spam and so on.

Hacking:
○ Hacking is gaining illegal access to a computer system without the user's permission.
○ It can lead to ID theft, gaining personal data, loss/corruption/stealing of data.
○ Mitigation: use strong passwords that are frequently changed, use an up-to-date firewall and also use anti-hacking software.

Malware:
○ Viruses: programs (or program code) that can replicate/copy themselves with the intention of deleting or corrupting files, or cause the computer to malfunction; they need an active host program on the target computer or an operating system that has already been infected before they can run.
○ Worms: these are types of stand-alone viruses that can replicate themselves with the intention of spreading to other computers; they often use networks to search out computers with weak security that are prone to such attacks.
○ Trojan horses: these are malicious programs often disguised as legitimate software; they replace all or part of the legitimate software with the intent of carrying out some harm to the user's computer system.
○ Spyware: software that gathers information by monitoring, for example, all the activity on a user's computer; the gathered information is then sent back to the person who sent the software (sometimes the software monitors key presses and it is then referred to as key logging software).
○ Adware: software that floods a user's computer with unwanted advertising, usually in the form of pop-ups but can frequently appear in the browser address window redirecting the browser to a fake website which contains the promotional adverts.
○ Ransomware: programs that encrypt the data on a user's computer; a decryption key is sent back to the user once they pay a sum of money (a ransom); they are often sent via a Trojan horse or by social engineering.
○ Mitigation: running antivirus/anti-spyware software and keep them up to date; in the case of ransomware, keep back-up copies of files. Keep vigilant since malware such as a Trojan horses and adware need the user to instigate the malware attack. Malware, such as worms, can avoid antivirus checkers and users need to be vigilant and look for suspicious behaviour (such as spelling errors).

Answers to exam-style questions

Pharming:
○ Malicious code installed on a user's computer or an infected website.
○ Code redirects browser to fake website without the user's knowledge (no action needs to be taken).
○ Creator of pharming attack can gain personal data from the user.
○ If the website is infected, redirection of the user from legitimate to fake website takes place; this is known as DNS poisoning.
○ Mitigation: antivirus can detect unauthorised alterations to website addresses, some browsers can alert the user to pharming attacks, check spelling in websites and also look out for https/ green padlock.

Phishing:
○ Occurs when a cybercriminal sends out legitimate-looking emails.
○ The emails contain links (or attachments containing links), that when clicked on, takes the user's browser to a fake website where personal data can be gathered.
○ Mitigation: train staff to look out for signs of phishing, don't click on links in emails, run anti-phishing toolbars on browsers, look out for https or the green padlock, regularly check online accounts and change passwords regularly and make sure browsers are kept up to date.

8

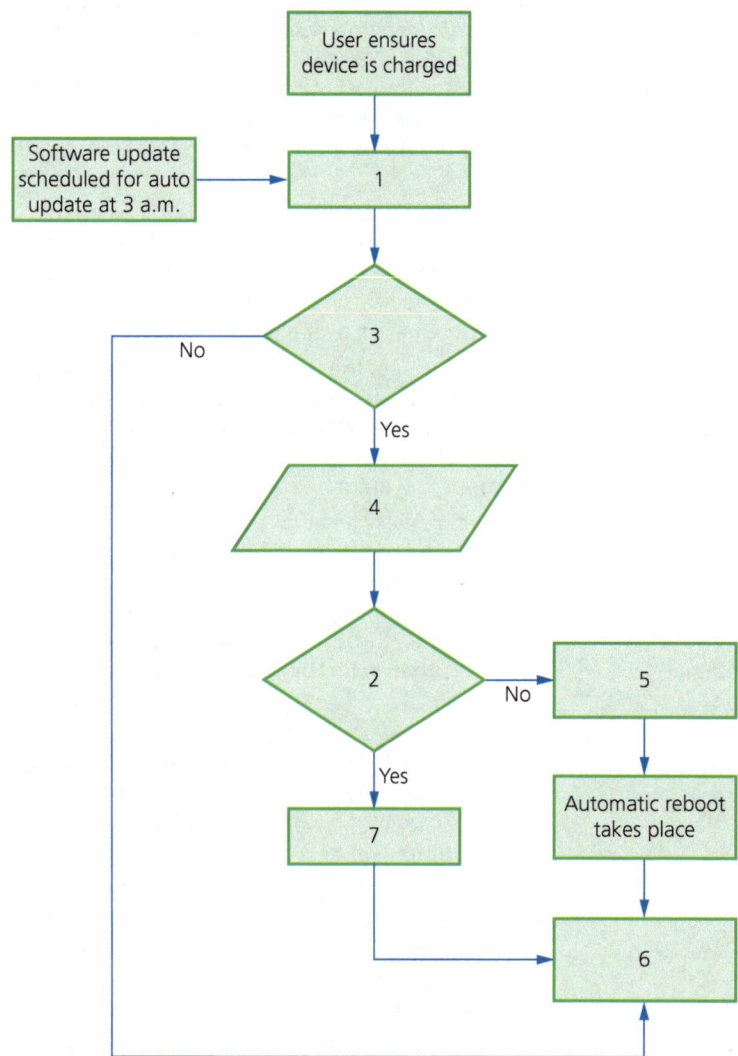

172 *Cambridge IGCSE™ and O Level Computer Science Study and Revision Guide Second Edition*

9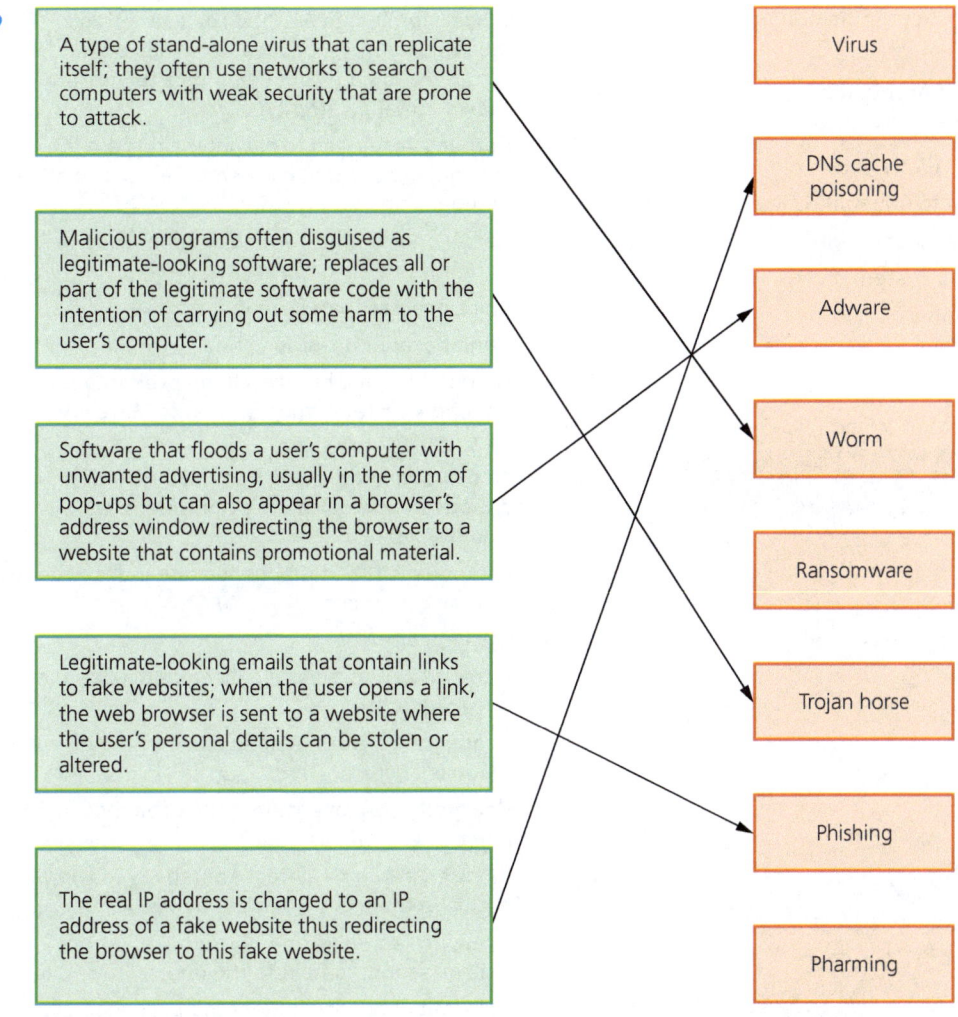

10 Any three from:
- Spellings in the URL (for example, Ammazon).
- Language used (for example, 'Dear <<email address>>').
- Email address itself (for example, xxx.gmail for a big company is unlikely).
- Use the ⓘ next to an email address to find the actual full address.

Chapter 6

1 a
- Level sensors and calorimeter sensors constantly send data to the microprocessor.
- An ADC is used to ensure data reaching microprocessor is digital.
- Microprocessor sends signal to actuator to open tap on burette.
- Once level sensor 2 value matches that stored on microprocessor OR colorimeter value matches stored value, the microprocessor sends signal to actuators to close burette tap.
- DAC used to convert microprocessor signal to analogue current to operate actuators.
- Readings are stored.

b Advantages:
- Automatic process; scientists can do other tasks.
- Since acid involved, it is safer.
- More accurate end point in process, since levels monitored several times a second.
- Leads to more consistent results.

Disadvantages:
- Deskilling is a real risk.
- More expensive to set up initially.
- Risk of viruses and hacking, for example.

2 a i) Flow sensors, temperature sensors
  ii) Light sensors, infrared/motion sensors.
  iii) Infrared/motion sensors, cameras, pressure sensors:
  - Faster response to non-optimum conditions
  - More precise monitoring
  - Greater consistency of product(s)
  - 24/7 monitoring
  - Expensive to set up initially and to maintain
  - May not respond well to unusual conditions
  - Saves money on unnecessary lighting
  - Completely automated system
  - Better control of lighting
  - Much safer
  - Fewer staff needed
  - Still requires human monitoring

Answers to exam-style questions

2 b
- faster response to non-optimum conditions
- more precise monitoring
- greater consistency of product(s)
- 24/7 monitoring
- expensive to set-up initially and to maintain
- may not respond well to unusual conditions
- saves money on unnecessary lighting
- completely automated system
- better control of lighting
- much safer
- fewer staff needed
- still requires human monitoring

3

Statement	True (✓)	False (✓)
Automated systems lead to less consistent results or less consistent products.		✓
Automated systems are more expensive to set up than traditional manual systems.	✓	
Automated systems would be quickly overwhelmed by the amount of data presented to them.		✓
Automated systems are inherently less safe than manual systems.		✓
Automated systems generally require enhanced maintenance when compared to manual systems.	✓	
Automated systems allow processes to run at optimum conditions at all times.	✓	
Software failures, due to unforeseen conditions, are unlikely to impact on an automated system.		✓
Automated systems will react more quickly to unusual process conditions.	✓	

4
- ○ Sensors
- ○ Microprocessor
- ○ Environment
- ○ End-effectors
- ○ Controller
- ○ Programs
- ○ Repetitive
- ○ Adaptive

5 a Sensors can use radar/sonar to detect objects under the sea. Cameras take images which allow objects to be recognised. If a ship is recognised, then the microprocessor sends signals to actuators to operate digital cameras. Actuators are also used to operate electric motors in undersea robots to allow them to move around the shipwreck.

b i) Sensors can be used to recognise samples; data sent to microprocessor after digital conversion (using ADC); if rock samples recognised, microprocessor sends signals to actuators to stop robot's motors to operate 'claws' to take samples of rock.

ii) Cameras are used to recognise terrain, recognise potential rock samples and to allow manoeuvring safely.

c
- Harsh environment which is dangerous to humans.
- More precise than humans.
- Can operate non-stop.
- No need for any humans to be present (useful on long journeys, such as visit to Mars which takes several years).

d Could be used in defusing bombs, clean-up operations in nuclear plants (for example, Chernobyl), etc.

6 a Autonomous is the ability to operate independently without human input.

b Any three from:
- Infrared sensors (active, breaking a beam of infrared light).
- Pressure sensors (transducers that generate electric current).
- Proximity sensors (detect the presence of an object/person).
- Infrared sensors (detect somebody leaving/ entering the train when the doors are open).
- Pressure sensors (measure the existence of a person standing next to the door).
- Proximity sensors (detect the presence of a person).
- Data from sensors used by microprocessor to decide whether it is safe or not safe to open or close the train doors.

c Any three from:

Advantages:
- It is possible to have more frequent service (shorter distance between buses).
- Safer as the human element is removed.
- Reduced running costs (no driver or conductor).

Disadvantages:
- Ever present fear of hacking and viruses.
- High initial capital costs.
- Passenger's reluctance to driverless vehicles.

7 a Subset of AI in which algorithms are 'trained' and learn from past experiences and examples.

b AI:
- Represents simulated intelligence in a machine.
- The aim is to build machines that are capable of thinking like humans.

Machine learning:
- The practice of getting machines to make decisions without being programmed to do so.
- The aim is to make machines that learn through data acquisition so that they can solve new problems.

c – User keys in their search criteria into the search engine; search engine uses search bots (web crawlers) to locate websites matching user's search criteria.
– Search engine classes a 'page 1' listing of relevant websites as a success.
– If 'hits' are not on page 1, this is regarded as a failure and the search engine learns from this and becomes more sophisticated and accurate.

8 a i) Stop words: words removed during the cleaning process (for example: the, and, a, etc.)
   ii) Collaborative filtering: process of comparing customers who have similar shopping habits to those of a new customer.
   iii) Web crawlers: these roam the internet scanning websites and categorising them so that they can be identified by a search engine.
   iv) Web scraping: method used to obtain data from websites.
   b First of all, emails are cleaned (to remove stop words); the cleaned email contains key words and phrases that can now be used to determine if the email is spam; a machine learning model is built and a 'training data set' is used to train the model and make it learn from past email content known to be classified as spam.

9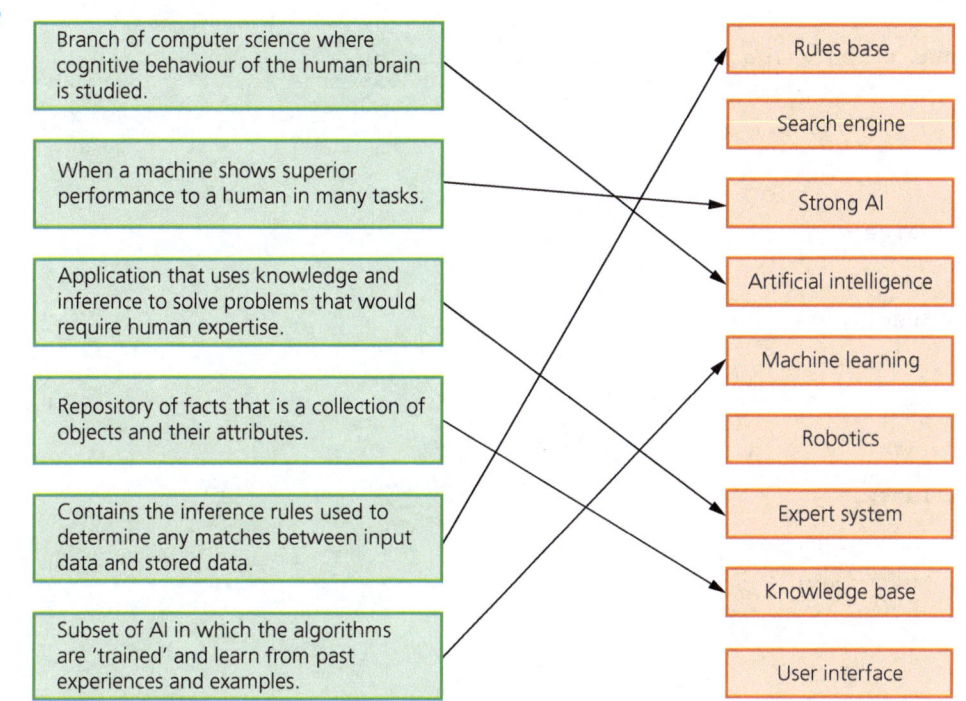

10 a 1 = user interface; 2 = inference engine; 3 = rules base; 4 = knowledge base.
   b – Gather information from human experts and written resources.
      – Populate knowledge base with gathered facts.
      – Create rules base, which is made up of inference rules to enable inference engine to draw conclusions.
      – Set up the inference engine.
      – Develop a user interface to allow effective communications.
      – Once set up, the system needs to be fully tested by running the expert system with known outcomes; results are compared and the expert system is modified if necessary.

Chapter 7

1

Description	Validation (✔)	Verification (✔)	Neither (✔)
Ensuring a number is positive	✔		
Ensuring a password is as intended		✔	
Ensuring a password is correct			✔
Ensuring a password contains a number	✔		
Ensuring a password contains a special character	✔		

Answers to exam-style questions

2 a `IF Number1 = Number2 THEN …`
   b Breaking a complex problem into smaller parts.
   c Keeping the key elements and discarding information not needed.

3 a
```
FOR Index ← 1 TO 12
    INPUT Value[Index]
NEXT INDEX
```
   b
```
Index ← 1
REPEAT
   INPUT Value[Index]
   Index ← Index + 1
UNTIL Index > 12
```
   c `WHILE … DO … ENDWHILE`
   d
```
Index ← 2
Large ← Value[1]  //use first value in list for initialisation
Small ← Value[1]
Total ← Value[1]
REPEAT
   IF Value[Index] > Large
     THEN
        Large ← Value[Index]
   ENDIF
   IF Value[Index] < Small
     THEN
        Small ← Value[Index]
   ENDIF
   Total ← Total + Value[Index]
   Index ← Index + 1
UNTIL Index > 12
Average ← Total / 12
OUTPUT Large, Small, Average
```
   e
```
First ← 1
Last ← 12
REPEAT
   Swap ← FALSE
   FOR Index ← First TO Last - 1
      IF Value[Index] < Value [Index + 1]
         THEN
             Temp ← Value [Index]
             Value [Index] ← Value [Index + 1]
             Value [Index + 1] ← Temp
             Swap ← TRUE
      ENDIF
   NEXT Index
   Last ← Last - 1
UNTIL (NOT Swap) OR Last = 1
```

Answers to exam-style questions

4 A mathematical operator performs a calculation, for example the multiplication operator * used in the expression B * C gives a result of the value identified by B multiplied by the value identified by C. A comparison operator compares two values and the result is true if the comparison is correct and false otherwise, for example the comparison operator > used in the expression B > C.

5 A suitable context and any **three** types of test data from:

   For a value input that must be a positive whole number between 0 and 100 inclusive:
   - **Normal data** that must be accepted by the program could be 75.
   - **Abnormal data** that must be rejected by the program could be an out of range number for example –12 or 106 or data of the incorrect type for example the words twenty-four.
   - **Extreme data** is the largest or smallest value that would be accepted, these are 100 and 0.
   - **Boundary data** one value that will be accepted as either the largest or smallest value and the closest value to it that would be rejected, for example 0 and –1 or 100 and 101.

6
```
01   NumberProducts ← 50 // length of array ProductName[]
02   OUTPUT "Please enter product to find "
03   INPUT Product
04   Found ← FALSE
05   Counter ← 1
06   REPEAT
07       IF Product = ProductName[Counter]
08       THEN
09           Found ← FALSE   Found ← TRUE
10       ELSE
11           Counter ← Counter - 1   Counter ← Counter + 1
12       ENDIF
13   UNTIL Found AND Counter > NumberProducts   OR Counter > NumberProducts
14   IF Found
15     THEN
16       OUTPUT Product, " found at position ", Counter, " in the list."
17     ELSE
18       OUTPUT Name, " not found."   OUTPUT Product, " not found."
19   ENDIF
```

Chapter 8

1

Statement	Assignment (✔)	Selection (✔)	Iteration (✔)
IF Number1 < Number2		✔	
Number1 ← Number2	✔		
Number1 ← Number2 + 1	✔		
FOR Number 1 ← 1 TO 10			✔
CASE OF Number1		✔	
WHILE Number1 <> Number2			✔
REPEAT			✔

2 a NOT
   b Static data structure containing elements of the same data type.
   c Can be transferred to another computer.
3 a Selection allows the selection of different paths through the steps of a program depending whether the condition tested is evaluated as true or false.

Answers to exam-style questions

  b Method 1 for choosing an alternative route on the basis of a single question, for example:

```
IF Number > 0
   THEN
      PositiveTotal ← PositiveTotal + Number
   ELSE
      NegativeTotal ← NegativeTotal + Number
ENDIF
```

Method 2, for choosing a variety of routes depending upon a value, for example:

```
CASE OF Operator
   "+" : Value ← Value + Number
   "-" : Value ← Value - Number
   "*" : Value ← Value * Number
   "/" : Value ← Value / Number
   OTHERWISE Value ← Value
ENDCASE
```

4 a Iteration allows a section of programming code to be repeated under certain conditions.

  b Method 1 is used for a fixed number of iterations, for example:

```
FOR Number ← 1 TO 10
   PositiveTotal ← PositiveTotal + Number
NEXT Number
```

Method 2, the number of iterations depends on a condition that is tested at the end of the loop so the code inside the loop is always executed, for example:

```
REPEAT
   Value ← Value + Number
UNTIL Value > 100
```

Method 3, the number of iterations depends on a condition that is tested at the beginning of the loop so the code inside the loop may not executed, for example:

```
WHILE Value <= 100
   Value ← Value + Number
ENDWHILE
```

5
```
DECLARE Sentence : STRING
OUTPUT "Please enter a sentence"
INPUT Sentence
Long ← LENGTH(Sentence)
Times ← 0
FOR Counter ← 1 to Long
   IF SUBSTRING(Sentence, Counter, 1) = 'e'
      THEN
         Times ← Times + 1
   ENDIF
NEXT Counter
```

6 Python:
```
def FindAverage(): # function to find the average
 Total = 0
 for Counter in range(50):
```

```
    Total = Total + GamerHighScore[Counter]
  return Total / 50

def SortGamers():# function to sort names and scores in descending order
  Swap = True
  First = 0
  Last = 50
  while Swap and Last > 0:
    Swap = False
    for Counter in range(Last - 1):
      if GamerHighScore[Counter] < GamerHighScore[Counter + 1]:
        TempHighScore = GamerHighScore[Counter]
        GamerHighScore[Counter] = GamerHighScore[Counter + 1]
        GamerHighScore[Counter + 1] = TempHighScore
        TempName = GamerName[Counter]
        GamerName[Counter] = GamerName[Counter + 1]
        GamerName[Counter + 1] = TempName
        Swap = True
    Last = Last - 1

# input routine
GamerName=[]
GamerHighScore=[]
for Counter in range(50):
  GamerName.append (input("Enter next gamer's name "))
  GamerHighScore.append (int(input("Enter next gamer's high score ")))
print (GamerName, GamerHighScore)
print ("Average is ", FindAverage())
SortGamers()
print (GamerName, GamerHighScore)
```

Notes: no need to declare array (list) or size, append is used; whole list is printed out in one command; final value for range is not used.

Visual Basic:

```
Module Module1
    Dim GamerHighScore(4), Counter As Integer
    Dim GamerName(4) As String

    'input routine
    Sub Main()
        For Counter = 0 To 49
            Console.Write("Enter next gamer's name  ")
            GamerName(Counter) = Console.ReadLine()
            Console.Write("Enter next gamer's high score  ")
            GamerHighScore(Counter) = Integer.Parse(Console.ReadLine())
        Next
```

Answers to exam-style questions

```
        For Counter = 0 To 49
            Console.WriteLine(GamerName(Counter) & " " &
                GamerHighScore(Counter))
        Next
        Console.WriteLine("Average is " & FindAverage())
        SortGamers()
        For Counter = 0 To 49
            Console.WriteLine(GamerName(Counter) & " " &
                GamerHighScore(Counter))
        Next
        Console.ReadKey()
    End Sub

    ' function to find average
    Function FindAverage() As Decimal
        Dim Total As Integer
        Total = 0
        For Counter = 0 To 49
            Total = Total + GamerHighScore(Counter)
        Next
        Return Total / 50
    End Function
    ' procedure to sort names and scores in descending order
    Sub SortGamers()
        Dim Swap As Boolean
        Dim TempHighScore, First, Last As Integer
        Dim TempName As String
        First = 0
        Last = 49
        Do
            Swap = False
            For Counter = 0 To Last - 1
                If GamerHighScore(Counter) < GamerHighScore(Counter + 1) Then
                    TempHighScore = GamerHighScore(Counter)
                    GamerHighScore(Counter) = GamerHighScore(Counter + 1)
                    GamerHighScore(Counter + 1) = TempHighScore
                    TempName = GamerName(Counter)
                    GamerName(Counter) = GamerName(Counter + 1)
                    GamerName(Counter + 1) = TempName
                    Swap = True
                End If
            Next
            Last = Last - 1
        Loop Until Not Swap Or Last = 1
    End Sub
```

End Module

Notes: global declarations at start of program; subroutine and function declarations at end of program.

Java:

```java
import java.util.Scanner;
class Ch8Q6Java {
    static int GamerHighScore [] = new int[5];
    static String GamerName [] = new String[5];

    static double FindAverage(){
        int Counter, Total;
        Total = 0;
        for ( Counter = 0; Counter <= 4; Counter ++) {
            Total = Total + GamerHighScore[Counter];
        }
        return Total / 5;
    }

    static void SortGamers(){
        int TempHighScore, First, Last, Counter;
        First = 0;
        Last = 4;
        boolean Swap;
        String TempName;
        do{
            Swap = false;
            for (Counter = 0; Counter<= Last - 1; Counter ++){
                if (GamerHighScore[Counter] < GamerHighScore[Counter + 1])
                {
                    TempHighScore = GamerHighScore[Counter];
                    GamerHighScore[Counter] = GamerHighScore[Counter + 1];
                    GamerHighScore[Counter + 1] = TempHighScore;
                    TempName = GamerName[Counter];
                    GamerName[Counter] = GamerName[Counter + 1];
                    GamerName[Counter + 1] = TempName;
                    Swap = true;
                }
            }
            Last = Last - 1;
        } while (!Swap || Last > 1);
    }
    public static void main(String args[]){
        Scanner myObj = new Scanner(System.in);
        int Counter;
        for (Counter = 0; Counter <= 4; Counter ++) {
```

```
            System.out.print("Enter next gamer's name ");
            GamerName[Counter] = myObj.next();
            System.out.print("Enter next gamer's high score ");
            GamerHighScore[Counter] = myObj.nextInt();
        }
        for (Counter = 0; Counter <= 4; Counter ++) {
         System.out.println(GamerName[Counter] + " " + GamerHighScore[Counter]);
        }
          System.out.println("Average is " + FindAverage());
          SortGamers();
          for (Counter = 0; Counter <= 4; Counter ++) {
         System.out.println(GamerName[Counter] + " " + GamerHighScore[Counter]);
            }
      }
    }
```
Note: global declarations at start of program need to be static.

Chapter 9

1   **a**   A collection of related records.
    b   A collection of fields about the same item.
    c   A column of data OR a single piece of data.

2   **a**   Structured Query Language (SQL) is the standard query language for writing scripts to obtain useful information from a relational database.
    b   Any two from:

SELECT	A select statement fetches specified fields (columns) from a table; queries always begin with **SELECT**
FROM	A from statement identifies the table to use.
WHERE	A where statement includes only records (rows) in a query that match a given condition.
ORDER BY	An order by statement sorts the results from a query by a given column either alphabetically or numerically.
SUM	A sum statement returns the sum of all the values in a field (column). Used with **SELECT**
COUNT	A count statement counts the number of records (rows) where the field (column) matches a specified condition. Used with **SELECT**

3   A single-table database, CAKE, with records containing these fields:
    - Name: name of cake; data type – text as it will be a single word or short phrase, example rich fruit.
    - Portion: number of portions in cake; data type – number as could be used for calculations, example 12.
    - Price: price of cake; data type – currency as should be displayed with the appropriate currency sign, example $45.99.
    - Ingredients: main ingredients of cake; data type – text as this field will contain a list of ingredients, example sultanas, cherries, raisins and currants.
    - Decoration: decoration required for cake; data type – Boolean as cakes come with or without decoration, example Yes.

Chapter 10

1 a

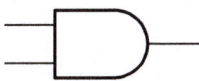

b A combination of logic gates with one or more outputs

2 a i) OR:

Inputs		Output
A	B	X
0	0	0
0	1	1
1	0	1
1	1	1

XOR:

Inputs		Output
A	B	X
0	0	0
0	1	1
1	0	1
1	1	0

ii) An OR gate includes an output when both inputs are one whereas an XOR gate does not.

b

NAND

Inputs		Output
A	B	X
0	0	1
0	1	1
1	0	1
1	1	0

NOR

Inputs		Output
A	B	X
0	0	1
0	1	0
1	0	0
1	1	0

Answers to exam-style questions

3 a L = (A AND B) OR (B AND J) OR (A AND J)

b

Inputs			Working space			Output
A	B	J	A AND B	B AND J	A AND J	L
0	0	0	0	0	0	0
0	0	1	0	0	0	0
0	1	0	0	0	0	0
0	1	1	0	1	0	1
1	0	0	0	0	0	0
1	0	1	0	0	1	1
1	1	0	1	0	0	1
1	1	1	1	1	1	1

c

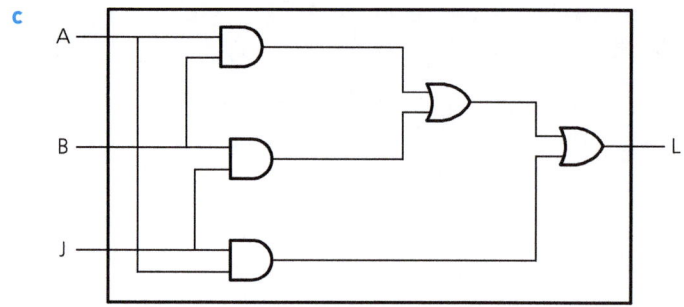

Answers to Practice Paper 1A

1 a

0	1	1	1	0	0	0	0

b i)

0	0	0	0	1	1	1	0

ii) 14

iii) $112 \div 2^3 = 14 \rightarrow$ result from shifting is correct.

c i)

128	64	32	16	8	4	2	1
1	1	1	1	0	0	1	0

ii) −14

iii) F 2

2 a i) Universal serial bus; standard connection used to connect devices to a computer.

ii) Any three from:
- USB-C is a 24-pin symmetrical connection.
- USB-C is much thinner cable than USB-A.
- USB-C offers 100W power connectivity (allowing full-sized devices to be charged).
- USB-C has better connectivity (up to 10Gbps) and can support 4K video.

b

Description	Method used		Data direction		
	Serial	Parallel	Simplex	Half duplex	Full duplex
Data sent 8 bits at a time along 8 channels in both directions, but not at the same time		✔		✔	
Data sent 1 bit at a time along a single channel in one direction only	✔		✔		
Data sent 8 bits at a time along 8 channels in one direction only		✔	✔		
16 bits of data sent 1 bit at a time along a single channel; the data can be sent in both directions but not at the same time	✔			✔	
16 bits of data sent along 16 channels in both directions at the same time		✔			✔

3 a i) When entering numerical data into a computer, thus ensuring no errors following entry.

ii) Any three from:
- incorrect digit entered (for example, 5327 instead of 5307)
- transposition error where two digits have changed place (for example, 5037 instead of 5307)
- omitted or extra digits (for example, 537 or 53107 instead of 5307)
- phonetic errors (for example 13 (thirteen) instead of 30 (thirty))

iii) When the error didn't change the check digit value then no error would be flagged.

b Stage 1: $9 + 8 + 4 + 1 + 6 + 6 = 34$
Stage 2: $(7 + 1 + 7 + 8 + 8 + 8) \times 3 = 117$
Stage 3: $34 + 117 = 151 \div 10 = 15$ remainder 1

4 a i) Two from: address bus, data bus, control bus

ii) Two from:
- Current instruction register (CIR)
- Accumulator (ACC)
- Memory address register (MAR)
- Memory data register (MDR)
- Program counter (PC)

b Buses:
- System buses are parallel transmission channels.
- Each channel transmits one bit at a time.
- Address bus carries addresses throughout computer system.
- Data bus carries data between CPU, memory and I/O devices.
- Control bus carries signals from control unit to all other components.

Registers:
- Registers are used by the CPU to store data values needed during processing (for example, the next instruction to be executed).
- CIR stores current instruction being decoded and executed.
- ACC used when carrying out ALU calculations; stores data temporarily during calculations.
- MAR stores address of memory location currently being read from or written to.

- MDR stores data that has just been read from memory or data that is about to be written to memory.
- PC stores the address where the next instruction to be read can be found.

c Cores are made up of ALU, control unit and registers; quad core processors are made up of four cores and each core communicates with the other three cores using 6 channels:

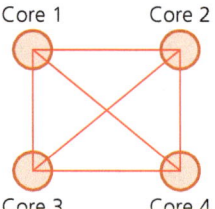

(6 channels)

5 a QR codes are a type of barcode which use a matrix of dark squares on a light background, rather than dark and light lines of varying thickness. There are three large squares at the corners – these are used to align the QR code when being read by a camera.

b
- Passenger points camera on a phone/tablet at the QR code.
- The image of the QR code is stored on the phone/tablet.
- A QR app will now process the camera image converting dark squares into binary data.
- Browser software on the phone/tablet automatically reads the data generated by the app and also decodes any web addresses contained within the QR code.
- The user will be sent to any websites automatically or information will show on phone/tablet screen.

c Any one from
Advantages:
- Possible to hold large amounts of information.
- Fewer errors since QR codes contain built-in error detection methods.
- Easier to read than barcodes (doesn't need expensive laser/led scanners).
- QR code can be encrypted which gives greater security protection.

Disadvantages:
- More than one QR code format exists.
- Anyone can generate QR codes (software readily/freely available).
- QR code can contain malicious codes and/or fake website addresses (called attagging).

6 a i) Pixel array is a matrix of tiny sensors which make up a CCD; colour depth is the number of bits used to represent the colour of each pixel.

ii) No. of pixels = 2048 x 1536 = 3 145 728 bits
x colour depth = 24 x 3 145 728 = 75 497 472 bits
÷ 8 to get no. of bytes = 75 497 472/8 = 9 437 184 bytes
÷ (1024 x 1024 x 1024) = 0.00878906 GiBytes
Maximum no. of photos = 64/0.00878906 = 7281 photos

b Using RLE (lossless compression) the logo code becomes:

12 80	1 255	4 80	1 255	2 80	1 255	1 80	2 255	2 80	2 255	1 80	2 255	1 80	2 255	2 80	2 255
1 80	1 255	2 80	1 255	4 80	1 255	12 80									

The original 10 x 6 logo would need 60 bytes of storage; using RLE this reduces to 46 bytes – a reduction of about 23%.

c Lossy: the original file cannot be reformed once the compression algorithm has been performed.
Lossless: it is possible to get the original file back again after compression has taken place.

7 a Buffers are used to hold data temporarily; they allow the CPU to carry on with other tasks while printing is taking place; once a buffer is empty it needs to be refilled – this process continues until all data has been printed out.

b When the buffer is empty, the printer sends an interrupt to the CPU requesting more data; the CPU suspends its present task (and stores the data) and checks the interrupt priority before servicing the interrupt; this procedure occurs each time the buffer is emptied until no more data remains to be printed.

8 a

Description of application	Appropriate sensor
Pick up the noise of breaking glass in an intruder alert system	Acoustic, microphone
Used in mobile phones to switch between portrait and landscape mode when phone changes its orientation	Accelerometer
Used in anti-lock braking systems in a vehicle	Magnetic field
Sends data to allow a vehicle's windscreen wipers to turn on automatically when it starts to rain	Infrared (active)
Used to detect a leak in the refrigerant in an air conditioning unit	Gas, level
Monitors the moisture levels in the air in a factory manufacturing microchips	Humidity

b i) Embedded systems are a combination of hardware and software designed to carry out a specific function; the hardware is electronic, electrical or electro-mechanical.

ii) Temperature sensor

iii) Accelerometer/tilt sensor (e.g. mercury switch)

iv)
- Temperature sensor and tilt sensor constantly send data to a microprocessor.
- Data goes through an ADC to ensure it is digital before being sent to the microprocessor; the microprocessor checks the temperature.
- If temperature >= 4, then a signal is sent to an actuator to start the air con compressor.
- If temperature < 4, then a signal is sent to an actuator to stop the air con compressor.
- Microprocessor checks data from accelerometer/tilt sensor.
- If tilt value > 20 then the microprocessor sends a signal to operate an alarm.
- Process continues indefinitely.

9 a i) Decentralised database where all transactions are stored; it consists of a number of interconnected computers but no central server.

ii) Each block has a unique hash value; if the data in a block is tampered with, then the hash value will also change; its links with the other blocks will then be broken thus preventing any transaction taking place.

b i) Manipulating people into breaking their normal security procedures (such as giving away a password) in order to gain illegal access to their computer system or to place malware on their computer.

ii) Two from: instant messaging containing malicious links, scareware (for example, fake virus checkers), phishing scams, memory sticks left lying around infected with viruses and other malware or bogus phone calls claiming a user's mobile phone has been compromised.

c i)
- A type of authentication that requires two methods of verification to prove the identity of a user.
- User logs onto website and enters their username and password.
- An 8-digit PIN is then sent to user's mobile phone (number) or user's email address.
- The mobile phone number or email address have already been registered with the website being used.
- The user now enters the 8-digit code (OTP) into the website giving them authorised access.

ii) They allow for patches that update software security, patches that improve software performance/features.

10 a Automated system
b Robot
c Controller
d Autonomous
e Artificial intelligence
f Expert system
g Machine learning

11

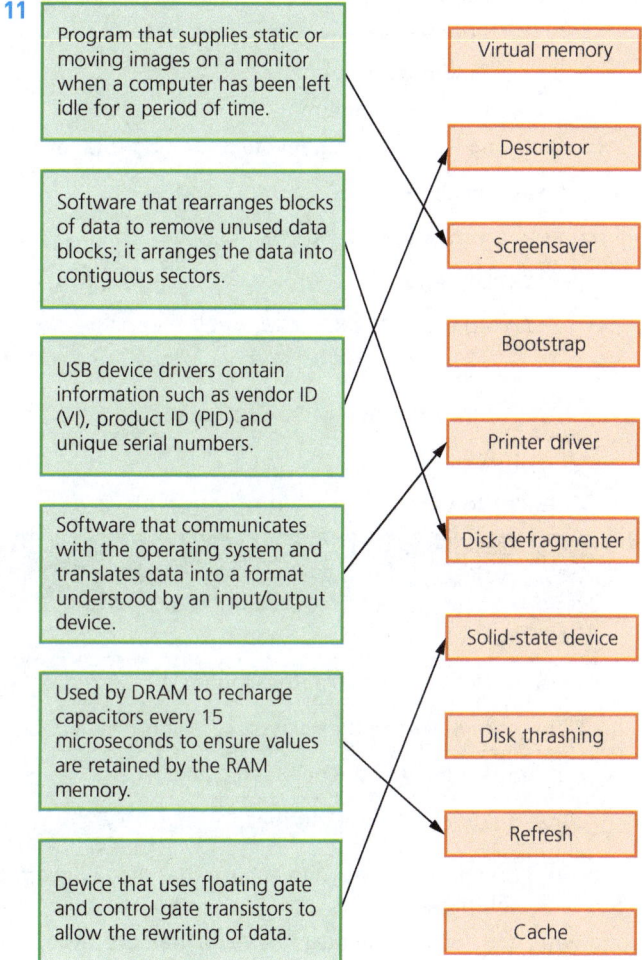

Answers to Practice Paper 2A

1. **a**
   b Investigating to provide the specification of what a program is required to do.
   c CASE
   d A collection of related records.

2. **a** **i)** A standard method of solution is one that is needed on a regular basis and can be used a part of many different algorithms.
   ii) Any three from:
   - Totalling
   - Linear search
   - Bubble sort
   - Finding average
   - Finding maximum
   - Finding minimum

   b Counting is used to add one to a running total every time an event occurs, for example:

   ```
   TeenCount ← 0
   FOR Counter ← 1 TO 50
      INPUT Age
      IF Age > 12 AND AGE < 20
         THEN
            TeenCount ← TeenCount + 1
      ENDIF
   NEXT Counter
   ```

3.

Description	Method used		Name of check
	Validation	Verification	
Data must be entered twice and match		✔	Double entry
Data must be eight characters long	✔		Length
Data is displayed on the screen to be confirmed		✔	Visual
Data must have a value between 8 and 12	✔		Range
Data must only contain numbers	✔		Type

4. **a** **i)** Test data is needed to ensure that the program completes all parts of the solution without error and that the solution is robust.
   ii) Any three from: normal; abnormal; extreme; boundary.

   b) Sample answer:
   Normal data for, example 37, to ensure that the program accepts this value and provides an acceptable solution.
   Boundary data, for example 29 and 30, to ensure that 29 is rejected as out of the required range and 30 is accepted as just in the required range.
   Abnormal data, for example 67 or 35, to ensure that these values are rejected.

5. **a** **i)** To check if a password is 10 characters or more and contains at least one symbol.
   ii) Assignment: 08
   Selection: 04
   Iteration: 01 to 22

Answers to Practice Paper 2A

b i)

Password	PasswordUp	Symbol	Counter	Output
MyPassword!	MYPASSWORD!	FALSE		Please enter your password
			1	
			2	
			3	
			4	
			5	
			6	
			7	
			8	
			9	
			10	
		True	11	Accept

ii)

Password	PasswordUp	Symbol	Counter	Output
MyWord!				Please enter your password
				Reject too short

6 a i) A variable is a value that can be changed during the execution of a program whereas a constant does not change its value during the execution of a program.

  ii) Any three from: integer; real; char; string; Boolean.

  b `DECLARE ClassSize : INTEGER`

  `MaxClassSize = 30`

7 Mathematical for calculations, for example:

`Num3 ← Num1 + Num2`

Logical for selection of different paths through a program when a condition is true or false, for example:

`IF Num3 > Num1`

  `THEN`

  `Num2 ← Num3`

`ENDIF`

Boolean to combine (AND OR) or reverse (NOT) conditions, for example:

`IF Num1 > Num2 AND Num1 > Num3`

Answers to Practice Paper 2A

8
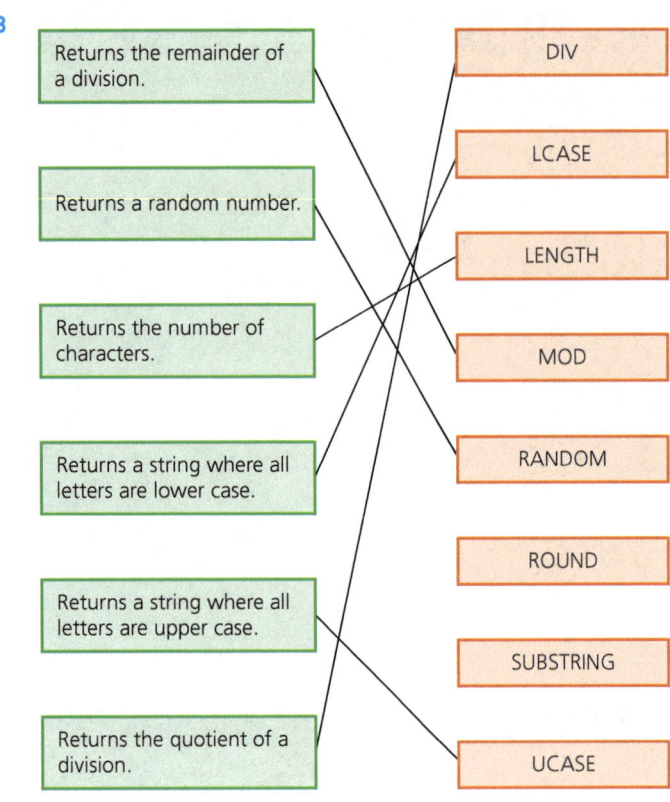

9 a i) An array is a data structure containing several elements of the same data type; these elements can be accessed using the same identifier name.

  ii) An integer variable is used as an array with an index as it can be increased or decreased according to the position of the data in the array, for example to set all the elements of an array to blank:

```
FOR Index ← 1 TO 10
  MyName[Index] ← ""
NEXT Index
```

  iii) A 1D array is a list with a single column and a 2D is a table with rows and columns.

  b
```
FOR RowIndex ← 1 TO 20
  FOR ColumnIndex 1 TO 4
    MyArray[RowIndex, ColumnIndex] ← 0
  NEXT ColumnIndex
NEXT RowIndex
```

  c Advantage: arrays can be populated or searched using repetition as only the value of the index will change to access each element.

  Disadvantage: as arrays have a fixed size, space may be wasted if there are unused elements.

10 1 01 `Large ← 9999`

        `Large ← -9999`

    2 02 `Counter ← 50`

        `Counter ← 00`

    3 03 `WHILE Counter > 50 DO`

        `WHILE Counter < 50 DO`

    4 06 `UNTIL NegNum > 0`

        `UNTIL NegNum < 0`

5 08 Counter = Counter - 1

    Counter = Counter + 1

11 a PlantPrice – currency as it needs to be shown in dollars.

   PlantHeight – real as it may be used for calculations or comparisons.

   Position – Boolean as there are only two possible values.

b PlantID as it would uniquely identify the plant.

c SELECT PlantName, Price, StockAvailable

   FROM PlantSale

   WHERE PlantHeight > 1.8;

12 a

Inputs			Working space		Output
A	B	C			X
0	0	0	0	1	1
0	0	1	0	0	0
0	1	0	0	0	0
0	1	1	0	0	0
1	0	0	0	1	1
1	0	1	0	0	0
1	1	0	1	0	1
1	1	1	1	0	1

b

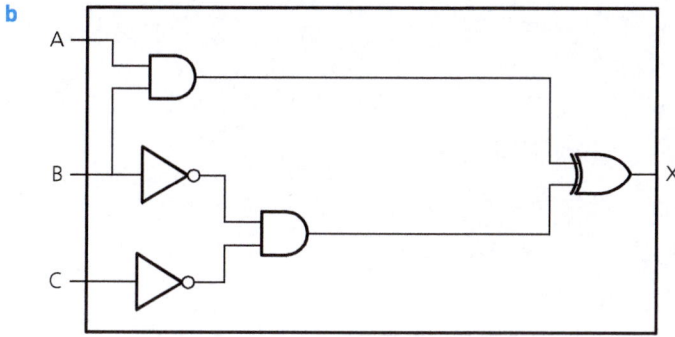

13 Python:

```
def YoungBabies(): # procedure to find babies under 3 months
    print("Names of babies under 3 months")
    for Counter in range(Length):
        if BabyAge[Counter] < 3:
            print (BabyName[Counter])

def FindBaby(Baby): # procedure to find a baby
    print("Baby's details")
    for Counter in range(Length):
        if BabyName[Counter] == Baby:
            print (BabyName[Counter], BabyAge[Counter], ParentPhone[Counter])
```

```python
    def UpdateBaby(Baby): # procedure to update a baby's details
        print("Baby's details")
        for Counter in range(Length):
            if BabyName[Counter] == Baby:
                BabyAge[Counter] = int(input("Enter baby's age in months "))
                ParentPhone[Counter] = input("Enter parents' phone number ")

    def SortBabys(): # procedure to sort babies in ascending order of age
        Swap = True
        First = 0
        Last = 5
        while Swap and Last > 0:
            Swap = False
            for Counter in range(Last - 1):
                if BabyName[Counter] > BabyName[Counter + 1]:
                    TempBabyName = BabyName[Counter]
                    BabyName[Counter] = BabyName[Counter + 1]
                    BabyName[Counter + 1] = TempBabyName
                    TempAge = BabyAge[Counter]
                    BabyAge[Counter] = BabyAge[Counter + 1]
                    BabyAge[Counter + 1] = TempAge
                    TempPhone = ParentPhone[Counter]
                    ParentPhone[Counter] = ParentPhone[Counter + 1]
                    ParentPhone[Counter + 1] = TempPhone
                    Swap = True
            Last = Last - 1

YoungBabies()

FindBaby(input("Enter baby's name "))

UpdateBaby(input("Enter baby's name "))

SortBabys()
print (BabyName, BabyAge, ParentPhone)
```

Visual Basic:

```vb
Module Module1
    Dim GamerHighScore(4), Counter As Integer
    Dim GamerName(4) As String

    'input routine
    Sub Main()
        For Counter = 0 To 49
            Console.Write("Enter next gamer's name   ")
            GamerName(Counter) = Console.ReadLine()
```

```vb
            Console.Write("Enter next gamer's high score  ")
            GamerHighScore(Counter) = Integer.Parse(Console.ReadLine())
    Next
    For Counter = 0 To 49
        Console.WriteLine(GamerName(Counter) & " " &
            GamerHighScore(Counter))
    Next
    Console.WriteLine("Average is " & FindAverage())
    SortGamers()
    For Counter = 0 To 49
        Console.WriteLine(GamerName(Counter) & " " &
            GamerHighScore(Counter))
    Next
    Console.ReadKey()
End Sub

' function to find average
Function FindAverage() As Decimal
    Dim Total As Integer
    Total = 0
    For Counter = 0 To 49
        Total = Total + GamerHighScore(Counter)
    Next
    Return Total / 50
End Function
' procedure to sort names and scores in descending order
Sub SortGamers()
    Dim Swap As Boolean
    Dim TempHighScore, First, Last As Integer
    Dim TempName As String
    First = 0
    Last = 49
    Do
        Swap = False
        For Counter = 0 To Last - 1
            If GamerHighScore(Counter) < GamerHighScore(Counter + 1) Then
                TempHighScore = GamerHighScore(Counter)
                GamerHighScore(Counter) = GamerHighScore(Counter + 1)
                GamerHighScore(Counter + 1) = TempHighScore
                TempName = GamerName(Counter)
                GamerName(Counter) = GamerName(Counter + 1)
                GamerName(Counter + 1) = TempName
                Swap = True
            End If
```

```
            Next
            Last = Last - 1
        Loop Until Not Swap Or Last = 1
    End Sub
End Module
```

Notes: global declarations at start of program subroutine and function declarations at end of program

Java:

```java
import java.util.Scanner;
class Ch8Q6Java {
    static int GamerHighScore [] = new int[5];
    static String GamerName [] = new String[5];

    static double FindAverage(){
        int Counter, Total;
        Total = 0;
        for ( Counter = 0; Counter <= 4; Counter ++) {
            Total = Total + GamerHighScore[Counter];
        }
        return Total / 5;
    }

    static void SortGamers(){
        int TempHighScore, First, Last, Counter;
        First = 0;
        Last = 4;
        boolean Swap;
        String TempName;
        do{
            Swap = false;
            for (Counter = 0; Counter<= Last - 1; Counter ++){
                if (GamerHighScore[Counter] < GamerHighScore[Counter + 1])
                {
                    TempHighScore = GamerHighScore[Counter];
                    GamerHighScore[Counter] = GamerHighScore[Counter + 1];
                    GamerHighScore[Counter + 1] = TempHighScore;
                    TempName = GamerName[Counter];
                    GamerName[Counter] = GamerName[Counter + 1];
                    GamerName[Counter + 1] = TempName;
                    Swap = true;
                }
            }
            Last = Last - 1;
        } while (!Swap || Last > 1);
    }
```

```java
public static void main(String args[]){
    Scanner myObj = new Scanner(System.in);
    int Counter;
    for (Counter = 0; Counter <= 4; Counter ++) {
    System.out.print("Enter next gamer's name ");
    GamerName[Counter] = myObj.next();
    System.out.print("Enter next gamer's high score ");
    GamerHighScore[Counter] = myObj.nextInt();
    }
    for (Counter = 0; Counter <= 4; Counter ++) {
    System.out.println(GamerName[Counter] + " " + GamerHighScore[Counter]);
    }
     System.out.println("Average is " + FindAverage());
     SortGamers();
     for (Counter = 0; Counter <= 4; Counter ++) {
    System.out.println(GamerName[Counter] + " " + GamerHighScore[Counter]);
        }
}
```

Index

3D printers 36

A
accelerometers 38
access levels 55, 72
access point mapping (war driving) 69
acknowledgements 21
actuators 34, 90
adaptive cruise control 81
address bus 26
administrators 54
adware 70
agriculture, use of robots 88
algorithms 100
   error identification 106–7
   purpose of 104
   sample question and answers 107–11
   sequence 115
   standard methods used 104–6
   writing and amending 111
analogue to digital converters (ADCs) 37
AND 137
anti-spyware software 73
antivirus software 73
application software 49, 50
apps 50
arguments 124
arithmetic and logic unit (ALU) 26
arithmetic operators 119
arrays 126–7
   sample question and answers 127–30
artificial intelligence (AI) 92
   AI systems 93–4
   characteristics of 92–3
   machine learning 94–5
   sample question and answers 95–6
ASCII code 9, 32
assemblers 59
assembly languages 58, 59
assignment 101
asymmetric encryption 23
attagging 32
authentication 73–4
automated systems 80
   advantages and disadvantages 83, 84
   examples 80–3
   sample question and answers 83–4
automatic repeat requests (ARQ) 21
autonomous vehicles 88
averages, algorithm for 105

B
back-up software 52
barcodes 31
Basic Input Output System (BIOS) 55
binary number system 1
   addition of numbers 3–4
   converting to and from denary 1–2
   converting to and from hexadecimal 2
   logical shifts 4–5
   sample question and answers 6–8
   two's complement 5–6
biometrics 73–4
bitmap images 10
bits 1, 10
blockchaining 67, 68
Blu-ray discs 43–4
Boolean algebra 137–8
Boolean data 114, 134
Boolean operators 119
booting up 55
browsers (web browsers) 62, 63
brute force attacks 69
bubble sort 106, 128–9
buffers 56
buses 26, 29
bytes 10

C
cache memory 27, 41
cache poisoning 71
cameras 32
capacitive touchscreens 34
case/CASE OF statements 116
CDs 43, 44
central processing unit (CPU) 25
   components of 26
   performance 27, 29, 41
character sets 9
char data type 114
charge couple devices (CCDs) 32
chatbots 87
check digits 21
checksum 20
ciphertext 23
clock cycle 27
clock speed 27
cloud storage 44–5
cognitive functions 92
collaborative filtering 95
colour codes 3
colour depth 10
command line interfaces (CLIs) 53
command words viii

comparison operators 102
compilers 51, 59–60
complementary metal oxide semiconductor (CMOS) chip 55
compression 11–12, 52
   sample question and answers 12–13
computer-aided design (CAD) 33
computer architecture 25–9
   sample question and answers 29–30
computer systems 99
   sample question and answers 102–3
conditional statements 101
constants 113
control and measuring software 50
control bus 26, 27
controllers 87, 90
control unit 26
cookies 64–5
   sample question and answers 65–6
cores 27
counting algorithm 104, 118
cryptocurrency 67–8
cyber security 72–6
   sample question and answers 77
   threats to 69–72
cyclic redundancy check (CRC) 15

D
data arrays 126–7
databases 50, 133–4
   sample question and answers 135–6
data bus 26
data interception 69
data packets 15
data redundancy 32, 44
data storage 41–5
   bits and bytes 10
   compression 11–12, 52
   file size calculation 10
   sample question and answers 45
   secondary storage 42–5
data transmission 17–18
data types 114, 120, 133–4
data validation and verification 106
decomposition 99
defragmenters 52
denary number system 1
   converting to and from binary 1
   converting to and from hexadecimal 2–3
denial-of-service (DoS) attacks 69
device drivers 51, 52, 54

Index

digital currencies 67–8
digital to analogue converters (DACs) 37
disk repair software 52
disk thrashing 44
distributed control systems (DCSs) 81
distributed denial-of-service (DDoS) attacks 69–70
DIV 125
domain name servers (DNSs) 63–4
　DNS cache poisoning 72
domestic robots 89
drones 86
DVDs 43, 44
dynamic RAM (DRAM) 42

E
echo check 20
electronically erasable programmable ROM (EEPROM) 55
emails
　security precautions 74–5
　spam identification 95
embedded systems 28–9
encryption 23–4
　sample question and answers 24
end-effectors 87
error codes 3
error detection 19–21
　sample question and answers 21–2
ethical hacking 70
exam tips vi–viii, 6
expert systems 93–4

F
face recognition 74
Fetch–Decode–Execute cycle 26–7
fields 133
file handling 131
file management 54
file sizes 10
fingerprint scans 74
firewalls 75
firmware 55
flash drives 43
flowcharts 100
flow rate sensors 38
fragmentation 42, 52
full-duplex data transmission 17
functions 123, 124–5

G
gaming systems 82
gas sensors 38
global variables 125
graphical user interfaces (GUIs) 53
graphics manipulation software 50

H
hacking 70
half-duplex data transmission 17
hard disk drives (HDDs) 42
hardware management 54
headers 124
hexadecimal number system 2
　converting to and from binary 2
　converting to and from denary 2–3
　uses of 3
high-level languages 58, 59
hop numbers 15
human computer interfaces (HCIs) 53
　sample question and answers 56–7
humidity sensors 37
hyperlinks 63
hypertext mark-up language (HTML) 62, 63, 64
　colour codes 3
hypertext transfer protocol (http) 63

I
IF statements 115–16, 121, 128–9
image files 10
　run length encoding 12
image resolution 10
index of an array 126
industry
　automated systems 81
　use of robots 88, 90
infrared sensors 38
infrared touchscreens 34
inkjet printers 35
input devices 31–4
　sensors 37–8
inputs 101, 114
instruction sets 27
integers 114, 134
integrated circuits 25
integrated development environments (IDEs) 60
internet
　browsers 63
　cookies 64–5
　difference from World Wide Web 62
　hypertext transfer protocol (http) 63
　retrieval and location of webpages 63–4
　uniform resource locators 62–3
Internet Protocol (IP) addresses 3, 47, 63, 64
　sample question and answers 48
interpreters 59–60
interrupts 55–6

interrupt service routines (ISRs) 56
irrigation systems 83–4
iteration 101, 117, 121, 129
　populating arrays 127

J
JPEG 11

K
keyboards 32
keys
　databases 134, 135
　encryption 23–4

L
laser printers 36
latency 42
length of a string 118
level sensors 38
library routines 125–6
light-emitting diode (LED) screens 36
lighting systems 82
light sensors 37
linear search 105
linkers (link editors) 51
liquid crystal (LCD) screens 36
lists (Python) 127
local variables 125
logical binary shifts 4–5
logical operators 119
logic circuits 138–9
　sample question and answers 140–1
logic gates 137–8
loops (iteration) 101, 117
lossless file compression 11–12
lossy file compression 11
loudspeakers 37
lowercase, conversion to 118, 119
low-level languages 58, 59

M
machine code 58, 59
machine learning 94–5
magnetic field sensors 38
magnetic storage 42
maintainable programs 126
malware 70
manufacturing
　automated systems 81
　use of robots 88, 90
mathematical operators 100
maximum values, algorithm for 105
Media Access Control (MAC) addresses 3, 46–7
　sample question and answers 48
medicine, use of robots 89
memory 26

Index

caches 27
  primary 41–2
  virtual 44
  see also data storage
memory management 54
memory sticks 43
mice 33
microphones 33
microprocessors 25
  use in robotics 90
miners 67
minimum values, algorithm for 105
MOD 125
moisture sensors 37
most significant bit 4
MP3, MP4 11
multitasking 54

N

NAND 138
negative numbers, two's complement notation 5–6
nested statements 101–2, 123
  populating arrays 127
network interface cards (NICs) 46
NOR 138
NOT 137
nuclear power stations 81
number systems 1–6
  sample question and answers 6–8

O

one-time passcodes (OTPs) 77
opcodes 27
operands 27
operating systems (OSs) 51, 52
  functions 53–4
  sample question and answers 56–7
operators 119
optical character recognition (OCR) 33
optical mouse 33
optical storage devices 43–4
OR 137
organic light emitting diode (OLED) screens 36
output devices 34–7
outputs 101, 115
overclocking 27
overflow errors 4, 7

P

packet headers 15
packets 15
packet sniffers 69
packet switching 15
  sample question and answers 16
packet trailer 15
parallel data transmission 17
parameters 123, 124

parity bit 19
parity blocks 19
parity checks 19–20
passwords 73
patches 74
payloads 15
persistent cookies 65
pH sensors 38
pharming 71
phishing 71
photo editing software 50
pixels 10
plaintext 23
pointing devices 33
post-WIMP interfaces 53
pressure sensors 38
primary keys 134, 135
primary memory 41–2
printers 35–6
privacy settings 76
private keys 23–4
procedures 123–4
program development life cycle 98–9
programming concepts 115–19
  data types 114
  input and output 114–15
  library routines 125–6
  maintainable programs 126
  nested statements 101–2, 123
  procedures and functions 123–5
  sample question and answers 120–2, 127–30
  variables and constants 113
programming languages 58–9
  sample question and answers 60–1
projectors 34–5
prompts 114
proof-of-work 67
proximity sensors 38
proxy servers 75–6
pseudocode 100–2, 103
public keys 23–4

Q

quad core processors 27
quick response (QR) codes 31–2

R

RANDOM 125
random access memory (RAM) 26, 41–2
  dynamic and static 42
ransomware 70
read-only memory (ROM) 26, 41–2
  EEPROM 55
real data type 114, 134
reasoning 92–3
records 133
registers 26, 29
repetitive strain injury (RSI) 32
resistive touchscreens 34

resolution
  images 10
  sound sampling 10
retina scans 74
robotics 86
  advantages and disadvantages 88–9
  applications 88–90
  characteristics of 87
  sample question and answers 90–1, 95–6
ROUND 125
routers (nodes) 15, 48
run length encoding (RLE) 11–12

S

sampling rate 9
sampling resolution 9
scanners 33–4
screens 36
  touchscreens 34, 53
screensavers 52
  sample question and answers 56–7
SD cards 43
search algorithms 105
search engines 95
secondary storage 41, 42–5
secure sockets layer (SSL) 76
  SSL certificates 76
security management 52, 54
security threats see cyber security threats
selection 115–16, 121
self-parking cars 81–2
sensors 37–8
  sample question and answers 38–9
  use in robotics 90
sequence of algorithms 115
serial data transmission 17
session cookies 65
simplex data transmission 17
simulators 82
single-table databases 133
social engineering 71–2
software 49
  application 50
  system 52–4
software robots 87, 91
software updates 74
solid-state drives (SSDs) 43
sort algorithms 106
sound sensors 38
sound storage 9
speakers 37
spear phishing 71
spreadsheets 50
spyware 70, 73
static RAM (SRAM) 42
string data 114
string handling 118–19
structure diagrams 100

structured query language (SQL) 134
substring extraction 118
surgery, robotic 89
symmetric encryption 23
system clock 25, 26, 27
system software 49, 51–3
    operating systems 52–4
    utility programmes 52

T
temperature sensors 37
test data 106–7
text files 9
    run length encoding 11
thrash point 44
timeout 21
tomography 33–4
top-down design 99
totalling algorithm 104, 118
touchscreens 34, 53
trace tables 107
translators 59–60
transport
    automated systems 81–2
    use of robots 88, 90

Trojan horses 70
truth tables 137–8, 139
two's complement 5–6
two-step verification 74
typo squatting 75

U
Unicode 9
uniform resource locators (URLs) 62–3
universal serial bus (USB) 17–18
uppercase, conversion to 118, 119
user accounts 54
    access levels 55, 72
utility programmes 51, 52
    translators 59–60

V
validation 106
variables 113
    local and global 125
verification 106
video editing software 50
virtual memory 44
virus checkers 52

viruses 70
voice recognition 74
von Neumann architecture 25

W
war driving (access point mapping) 69
weather stations 82
web crawlers 87, 95
web scraping 95
windows, icons, menu and pointing (WIMP) interfaces 53
wired equivalence privacy (WEP) encryption protocol 69
word processors 50
World Wide Web (WWW) 62
worms 70

X
XOR 138